VALUES AND ORGANIZATIONS:

A Study of
Fraternities
and Sororities

VALUES AND ORGANIZATIONS

**A STUDY OF FRATERNITIES
AND SORORITIES**

WILLIAM A. SCOTT

University of Colorado

with the collaboration of

RUTH SCOTT

RAND M^CNALLY & COMPANY • CHICAGO

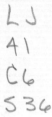

LJ
41
C6
S 36

RAND M^cNALLY SOCIOLOGY SERIES

EDGAR F. BORGATTA, *Advisory Editor*

Alford, *Party and Society*

Christensen, ed., *Handbook of Marriage and the Family*

Demerath, *Social Class in American Protestantism*

Faris, ed., *Handbook of Modern Sociology*

March, ed., *Handbook of Organizations*

Nye and Hoffman, *The Employed Mother in America*

Scott, *Values and Organizations*

Warren, *The Community in America*

To Theodore Mead Newcomb:

Pioneer in the systematic study of organizations

PREFACE

This book is primarily a report of research conducted in ten fraternities and sororities at the University of Colorado. It was a longitudinal investigation, over a one-year period, aimed at discovering how personal values enter into various organizational processes.

The study is set within two different problem contexts. One concerns the nature and function of "morality" — a topic that has interested a few psychologists for many years, and is currently attracting wider attention in the literature on child development. My own interest in values was stimulated most directly by the research that Daniel Katz and Helen Peak were conducting at the University of Michigan when I was a graduate student there.

The other context of the study is organizational sociology, specifically as it describes how an individual comes to take part in a pre-established group. This context became necessarily relevant as a result of my decision to study values in a natural interpersonal setting. It is a truism that in order to understand natural settings we must eventually study them directly. Whether the direct study is preceded by a period of artificially controlled laboratory investigations or not is a matter of optional strategy; I believe that as much progress can be made toward formulating "general laws" of behavior by studying the complex conditions to which they will be applied, as by creating unusual conditions to simplify the relationships. Hence this study began directly "in the field."

In many ways it bears closest kinship to Theodore Newcomb's pioneering work, *Culture and Personality Change*. That was essentially a long-term study of adolescent socialization at Bennington College, and of the relation between personality characteristics and susceptibility to group influence. The dedication of this book expresses my intellectual indebtedness to Newcomb. More recently, in *The Acquaintance Process*, he has studied the development of friendship patterns in a natural group setting over a period of several months. This was another ground-breaking investigation in that it brought forth systematic data on a real-life phenomenon that is widely experienced but little scrutinized.

My immodest hope was to improve on such classic studies in certain specific ways. First, there seemed to be some advantage in studying not just one organizational process at a time, but several of them together. If we take our systemic theories of social organization seriously, we should be prepared to find interactions among processes of selection, influence, friendship development, etc., which would be missed if only one of these were studied alone. It is my impression from the social psychological literature that processes of influence have been better studied than processes of selection. (Perhaps this reflects the contemporary penchant for experimentation rather than ethology.) It was hoped that the present study could add some needed systematic data in the latter area.

The second improvement I aimed to incorporate was an enlarged sample of groups. In most sociological investigations the unit of analysis is an aggregate of persons. Even though data may be collected from individuals, the typical generalization refers to a population of groups; therefore one needs a sample of groups as a basis for inference. Though the present sample size still left much to be desired, it permitted us to detect relationships that were common to all organizations, and also some relationships that varied from one organization to another.

Finally, we have introduced more analytical rigor than was common in earlier investigations. Descriptive statistics were chosen so as to represent obtained relationships as precisely as possible. Instead of relying on case histories or on the reader's intuitive interpretation of differences and trends, we have always tried to find some significance test against a null hypothesis that was to be rejected. Whenever feasible, the critical results were compared with those obtained from a control group or from a control variable measured on the same subjects.

It is for the reader, and for future researchers, to decide whether these intended improvements have yielded substantial benefits in this instance, and whether the analysis procedures employed here will be useful in other organizational studies.

Most of the research was conducted under grant M-1597 from the National Institute of Mental Health. The University of Colorado's Council on Research and Creative Work provided funds for additional analyses, and free computer time was made available by the Western Data Processing Center. I am grateful to all these sources of financial support, as well as to James Byrum and Fred Malone, whose consultation greatly facilitated the IBM analyses.

The following research assistants participated in one or more phases of the study: Brenda Dickey, Jacob Hautaluoma, Robert Kassebaum, Shirley Otterson, Basil Sherlock, and Nancy Ulehla. In addition, the report includes ancillary data collected by Karilyn Frampton, Basilio Manago, Daphne Monroe, Leon Rappoport, Teresa Smith, Greg Tolson, and Lois Wolf. The prefinal draft and final copy were typed by Bonnie Ammons, Irene Blauers, Mary Carter, Virginia Cunningham, Patricia Frost, Maxine Harding, and Donna Tibbals.

Lyle Bourne, Donald Campbell, James Doi, Seymour Feshbach, Clyde Johnson, and Anselm Strauss have carefully read one or more chapters of the manuscript. It has benefited substantially from their comments.

My greatest debts are to the members of the ten anonymous organizations who participated so graciously and to my wife and collaborator, who contributed to all phases of the study and bore the major burden of planning and supervising the analyses.

Boulder, Colorado
November 1964

W.A.S.

TABLE OF CONTENTS

CHAPTER 1

VALUES AND MORALITY

Ethical concepts have played a central role in the development of human civilization. Conceptions of "right" and "wrong" lie at the core of great religions, distinguish saints from sinners, provide the postulates of social ideologies and utopias, determine standards of conduct for institutionalized roles and casual interpersonal encounters. Together with language facility and historical perspective, moral processes would appear to be distinctive and characteristic features of man as we know him. He recognizes concepts of "absolute" good and bad, subjectively independent of his own dispositions, and uses these in framing social institutions, striving toward self-perfection, praising and censuring the actions of others.

It has been said that values — the bases of moral judgments — cannot be studied empirically. The reasoning behind this assertion is that empirical inquiry is limited to existential propositions concerning means-end relationships; the ends themselves cannot be chosen on empirical grounds, and therefore cannot be the object of scientific inquiry. While agreeing that ultimate values themselves are, in principle, not subject to evaluation, one may nevertheless believe that the human *process* of evaluation and moral judgment, of arriving at ultimate values against which means are assessed, *is* a matter amenable to empirical inquiry, since the aim of the study is not to choose among ends, but to investigate the psychological process of choosing — how it develops, and its consequences for human behavior.

The main barrier against inquiry into moral processes is not so much the obscurity of the processes themselves (though this is certainly to be acknowledged); rather it is the moralistic habits of the investigator and his culture. An officially sanctioned orthodox morality is bound to be threatened by objective inquiry, because the objectification of a phenomenon for study deprives it, to some degree, of its absolute and necessary character. One is inevitably led to question, "Why this morality and not some other?" "Why any morality at all?" There are cultures in which an objective inquiry concerning certain values could not proceed, for the final answers would have already been prescribed in the orthodox ideology. To some extent, the inquiring empiricist is limited by the moral orthodoxies of his culture (or of that part of the sub-culture which he has internalized most thoroughly). He must believe in the moral prerogative of empirical inquiry, at least for himself; and he can easily extol this to an absolute virtue against which to appraise all other bases for value judgment. To remain dispassionately objective even when assessing one's own values is a feat of which few mortals are capable.

A morality may be either inhibitive or prescriptive. It may deal with universal, commonly threatening, domains of human experience — such as sex, death, aggression, human relations — or with "secular" domains treated as "sacred" by a relevant interest group. What is a moral matter for one person is not necessarily so for another. A researcher may espouse absolute standards of scholarship, a music critic absolute standards of aesthetics, a soldier absolute standards of bravery. Among students at the University of Colorado, and among the townspeople of Boulder, were found wide differences in the kinds of personal qualities regarded as "inherently good." What is essential to the moral attitude in any of these values is the individual's view of the standard: he regards it as right, proper, good (or the reverse), independently of his own personal judgment. He regards himself as merely recognizing an objectively real standard, which is available for any other qualified and right-thinking person to see as well.

THE MEANING OF VALUE AND MORALITY

The concept "value" provides a focus of study for a variety of disciplines, from theology to economics. It is currently employed, loosely or systematically, in every one of the behavioral sciences, though with such diverse meanings as to render discussion across fields chaotic. Dukes' (1955) review implicitly acknowledged the difficulty of translation across disciplines by restricting the scope of his survey to "psychological studies of values." It is nevertheless apparent that even the studies designated by him as "psychological" use the concept with quite different meanings. Though the definition to be employed here will be defended on both theoretical and empirical grounds, the principal reason for offering it is to clarify the presentation and justify the research procedures used in the present studies, rather than to proscribe alternative meanings.

A *value*, or *moral ideal*, is here defined as *an individual's concept of an ideal relationship (or state of affairs), which he uses to assess the "goodness" or "badness," the "rightness" or "wrongness," of actual relationships that he observes or contemplates.* The present studies were focused on *personal values* — concepts of ideal relations among people, or of ideal personal traits (as expressed in interpersonal relations). This definition is intended to be very close to that of Clyde Kluckhohn (1951), and the theoretical formulation leans heavily on his, with only an occasional exception or elaboration. In the form stated, this constitutes a "pure type" definition, phrased categorically for the sake of simplicity; later it will be appropriate to introduce certain dimensions, or variable qualities, of values which transform the "pure type" into a continuously differentiated definition.

A value is a hypothetical construct assigned to that class of hypothetical constructs known as the individual's phenomenology — the way one views the world and himself in relation to it. Thus, a value (as the term is used here) is "conscious" and verbalizable by the person who holds it; though insufficient thought and intellectual limitation may make his spontaneous verbalization less than adequate, he is at least capable of assenting to the statement of a value he espouses. In this restriction to explicit, "conscious" values, the present usage departs from Kluckhohn's, principally for theoretical and empirical clarity. Too often, it is felt, an external observer — especially a psychologist — is inclined to attribute "unconscious" motivation to an act when he really means nothing more than that the person acts in a way that is not predictable from his own self-concept or from his own stated goals. The failure of correspondence between a person's behavior and his phenomenology certainly calls for the postulation of additional constructs to explain his action, but it needlessly confuses terminology to classify such constructs in the same system as the phenomenological concepts that the actor uses to describe himself and the world as he sees it. The meaning of "value" is conceptually clearer and empirically more accessible when it is defined as a state that its host can at least approximately express.

A value provides more than a concrete goal of action; it provides a criterion by which goals are chosen (Williams, 1951). It does not simply represent something that is preferred, but something the person feels *ought to be preferred*. This is because, from his point of view, the value of the preferred state inheres in the state itself, and does not depend on any characteristic of himself, such as desire or ability to perceive it (Catton, 1959).

Ultimate values are probably not attainable in practice, and many individuals would never regard them as completely attainable, for any action is generally relevant to multiple values, not all of which can be realized by a given concrete choice. The more an institution's policy pursues the goal of democratic equalitarianism, for example, the more it may threaten the value of recognition for individual excellence of achievement. These two potentially conflicting values may be held simultaneously, as absolutes, by the same individual; more commonly, they may be emphasized by different segments of the institutional community. In any case, the individual's view of either value is likely to be something like: "It would be good if we could all be democratic (or all rewarded for merit), but we can't because it isn't possible." It isn't possible because of conflicting values or because of non-value considerations which determine concrete actions. The individual's choice may be motivated by self-interest and irrational considerations (to some extent he recognizes this); the institution's choice is influenced by pragmatic considerations and the need for compromise. In spite of the inevitable disparity between action and ideal, people still try to maintain their concepts of the essential and absolute goodness of values.

As with any other common event about which people communicate, it is inevitable that culturally shared understandings play a role in defining what is valued. Though some concepts of desirable things could conceivably arise in a completely isolated individual simply through his need to adapt to a relatively constant environment, most of the values that are important in human affairs would seem to be products of human interaction. Without this, it is doubtful that they would be conceived, for most people's notions of the desirable are transmitted to them through instructions from others, or through socially arranged experiences in which the value is implicitly taught. Parsons (1951, p. 12) goes so far as to define a value as "an element of a shared symbolic system," emphasizing that an individual's conception of the desirable is acquired through social interaction.

Conceiving a valued state of affairs as universally and absolutely good, the individual is almost certain to assume that his conception is shared, or potentially sharable, by all other human beings — unless they be morally defective. Just as the typical naive realist assumes that his sense impressions are shared by others, so the typical moralist assumes that his conceptions of the desirable are available for others to recognize as well. Piaget (1932) has termed this stance "moral realism," asserting that, with social and intellectual development, it may ultimately give way to a more relativistic "moral reciprocity." The results of the present studies among college students indicate that, though the contents of values *(what* is valued) may change with increasing maturity, the "moral attitude" itself (one's belief in the inherent, absolute goodness of the valued state — whatever it is) may survive. In this respect, values are phenomenologically different from motives, attitudes, tastes, and beliefs; with those concepts the individual is prepared to expect (and perhaps even respect) individual differences in reactions to objects. But moral values are regarded as absolutes; there seems to be something wrong with the person who fails to recognize them, just as there is something wrong with one who fails to distinguish red from green.

There is, of course, no a priori reason for all people's holding morals in the sense described here. The value-less person is hypothetically conceivable. In Chapter 2 we shall consider certain psychological and social functions that are filled by values and morality; this will lead to a speculation about alternate modes of fulfilling the functions in the absence of morality.

Different Meanings of "Value"

The meaning intended here may be clarified by contrast with other usages of the term "value" that are current in the behavioral sciences. Adler's (1956) classification of different meanings provides a useful frame of reference. He sees the concept applied variously to (1) absolute qualities inherent in events or in contemplated states of affairs, (2) characteristics of objects as apprehended by people, (3) characteristics of the people who do the evaluating, and (4) the actual behaviors of people toward objects. The first meaning (absolute quality inherent in an object) would appear to be empirically comprehensible only if there were consensus among people — either all people or a select, qualified elite — as to the inherent value; hence this may be subsumed under (2). The essential ingredient of the second meaning is consensus about the value of a thing either among all people or at least among those who are appropriately disposed toward it. It is doubtful if complete consensus concerning the value of anything can be demonstrated, and if the judged value depends on who is doing the judging, then it is difficult to attribute "value" solely to the object itself.

When students at the University of Colorado (Scott, 1963) were asked to indicate how desirable various personal traits were, their judgments were found to correlate substantially with their own self-ratings on these traits. Among another sample of college students, Fillenbaum (1961) found that judgments about the desirability of various human heights and weights depended considerably on the height and weight of the judge.

One might even carry this point to the extreme of applying it to all judged properties of things, such as color, for example. Since color depends in part on the nature of the organism's receptors and on the light in which an object is viewed, one could say that an object has no color of its own. We don't go this far, but are instead willing to attribute color to an object, because one can define standard light conditions, and can disqualify as judges persons whose receptors are defective. (The "color-blind" person generally learns to disqualify himself.)

If a community of persons could agree upon a qualified group of value-judges — such as ministers, politicians, or scientists, for example — and if this elite group itself were in agreement concerning the value of an object, then it would be appropriate to speak of value as belonging to the object, as far as this particular community was concerned. But it is doubtful if these two stages of consensus — designating the judges and getting them to agree among themselves — could be achieved. Thus it is hard to maintain that the value of a thing resides in the thing itself.

Adler's class (3) — values as characteristics of the evaluating persons — includes the definition that is used in the present research. A value is here regarded as a frame of reference applied by a person to assess the goodness of an object. Though he may typically believe that its value inheres in the object itself or in the imagined state of affairs with which the object is compared, this is only the person's view of things, rather than a statement that would be made by an external observer who knew about the diverse values of many persons. Adler objects to this formulation of "value" as an intrapersonal construct, since, he says, it is thereby made inaccessible to empirical study. If "inaccessible" means that values cannot be observed directly, this is certainly true, just as it is true for any other hypothetical construct attributed to the personality system — a motive, a belief, or an attitude, for example. As a hypothetical construct, a value "exists," not in the biological organism, but in the theoretical system that defines

7

the construct. Its conceptual usefulness is not to be gauged by its empirical visibility, but by its fruitfulness in guiding the study of empirically observable phenomena — chiefly the overt and verbal responses of human subjects.

Adler's fourth category of meanings (which he prefers) defines a value as synonymous with action, overt or verbal. Two objections may be made to such a definition. First, by equating value with behavior, it requires a proliferation of terminology, such that each different response to an object requires the designation of a different value. A major gain from employing hypothetical constructs in the scientific explanation of behavior is that they lend economy to the conceptualization of what is, in the raw, an exceedingly complex set of events, virtually incomprehensible to the most superior intellect. Second, even if for operational purposes one chooses to equate the concept "value" with observable actions, it is at least necessary to delimit the class of defining behaviors. This Adler does not do, but instead merely states that "value equals action." What kind of action? Does all action imply value? Or only certain kinds of behavior, such as choosing between two objects desired by a person, or verbally stating the basis for his choice?

Ultimately, the difficulty that a psychologist encounters in attempting to equate a theoretical construct with a particular set of behaviors arises from the fact that any behavior is, by postulate in most psychological theories, multiply determined, and hence cannot be treated as a pure manifestation of any single determining tendency. All responses of the organism must necessarily depend on both organismic and environmental determinants, and probably on several variables within each of these classes. The problem in designating appropriate operational definitions of psychological constructs is to find some set of behaviors which, a priori and on the basis of whatever empirical evidence can be collected, seem to depend most closely on the intended construct, and as little as possible on other dispositions or situational influences. Though no conceivable operation for representing values will meet this aim fully, the theoretical definition of the construct directs attention to certain kinds of behaviors that appear to provide more appropriate operations than others. Given the definition proposed here — an individual's concept of an ideal state of affairs — verbal responses professing an absolute standard of excellence would appear to provide appropriate operationalizations of values. Given any other useful theoretical definition, it should be possible to delimit the domain of defining behaviors to some sub-set within the totality of all action.

Although a person's overt action may be influenced by his values to varying degrees, it also depends on a number of other characteristics of the individual and of the situation in which he behaves. An individual, "knowing" what is "right," may nevertheless act without thinking, act for selfish motives, act in order to please others, or because the situation impels some particular action. Only to a degree will the average person's behavior in any situation reflect his conception of what constitutes ideal behavior. The proportion of value-directed determination will vary from one person to another and from one situation to another. Even if value considerations are paramount in a given action choice, the alternatives available may be relevant to several different values, some of which must be ignored or compromised in favor of others.

Therefore, we distinguish values from behavior in general, and take as the best indicators of values the person's verbal profession of ideal standards of conduct. This definition clearly implies a distinction between two kinds of research questions concerning morality: "To what extent does an individual profess a certain moral standard?" and "To what extent does he usually abide by the standard in his own behavior?" Answers to the two questions may be quite different for a given person. The relation between professed values and overt behavior has been studied by Hartshorne and May (1928) and by Scott (1963), among others. In general, it has been concluded that the degree of correspondence is not great for the average person. But this may reflect difficulties in defining "moral behavior," as well as failure of the person to act morally by his own standards. When the researcher defines a particular action situation in which the presence or absence of moral behavior is to be assessed, he is necessarily imposing his own interpretation on the act. But behaving "honestly" or "religiously" or "creatively" may mean different things to his subjects than to himself; what is value-congruent for them may appear less so to the researcher.

Though the interpretation of verbal questions poses similar problems of consensual meaning, we may hope to lessen the ambiguity by dividing the problem of morality into two separate questions: "To what extent does the person profess a particular moral code?" and "To what extent does the person's professed morality permit prediction of particular overt action specified by the researcher?" A value is thus regarded as a hypothetical construct, inferred from verbal behavior, that is conceived as potentially influencing overt action, along with numerous other influences, both consonant and dissonant with the value.

Utility of the Value Concept

In order to avoid needless proliferation of terminology, it is appropriate to examine each construct included in the description of personality to see if it contributes anything new to the understanding of behavior beyond what is provided by other concepts already in general use. This can be attempted at two levels, theoretical and empirical. First, one should inquire whether or not "value" is intended to convey anything different from certain closely related concepts, such as "motive" and "attitude." Motives and attitudes are proposed for comparison because they have gained wide theoretical currency and they appear to convey meanings similar to that proposed for value. Second, one should determine whether the operations used to assess values are empirically distinguishable from those for assessing the related concepts. Finally, one should see whether or not the measures of values lead to conclusions about behavior that are in any way different from conclusions arrived at through the assessment of motives and attitudes. Here we shall consider only the theoretical distinctions between values and the two closely related psychological constructs. The question of empirical distinctiveness must rest on accumulating research evidence.

To anticipate the ensuing discussion somewhat, values may

be treated as a sub-class of "attitude" and of "motive," theoretically distinguishable from other sub-classes in the following ways:

1. A motive refers to a phenomenologically optional goal and has the subjective counterpart: "I want to act this way." A value refers to a phenomenologically absolute goal and has the subjective counterpart: "I ought to act this way."

2. A value refers to an end-state deemed desirable for its own sake; attitude refers to an object that is liked or disliked because of its perceived instrumentality to a desirable end. (At least it can be rationalized in this fashion.)

3. A person with a value wants other people to share in the goal-oriented activity; a person with a non-value motive (e.g., for food or power) does not necessarily feel a desire for such co-orientation; he may even wish that others *not* share his goal.

4. A person will blame others for failure to strive toward a valued state, but will not blame them for failure to strive toward the object of a motive.

5. One will feel moral righteousness as a consequence of value attainment (or striving), and pleasure as a consequence of motive satisfaction.

6. One will feel guilt (or self-abasement) for failing to strive toward a value, and frustration for failing to attain other motive-goals.

7. A value will be publicly appealed to as justification for one's action; an attitude or motive will usually not command such legitimacy.

One class of definitions that has been explicitly rejected in the present formulation treats values as general dispositions to approach or avoid certain kinds of objects. Vernon and Allport (1931) provide no explicit definition of the attribute measured by their well-known test (see Allport, Vernon & Lindzey, 1951), but the content of the test is consistent with Spranger's (1928) reference to "enduring dispositions to experiences and acts." Similarly, Lundberg (1950) says, "It is possible to infer values of groups from the way in which they habitually spend their time, money, and energy" (p. 103). And Hull: "That may be said to be valued which is striven for and, other things being equal, the maximum amount of work which an organism will execute to attain a given reinforcing state of affairs may be taken as an indication of the valuation of that state of affairs by the organism" (1945, p. 80). Such definitions are not clearly distinguishable from those commonly offered for motives and attitudes, or their counterparts in the phenomenal world, incentives and valences.

Though values have goal-directing and goal-setting properties and, hence, may be considered as a sub-class of motivational constructs, they may be theoretically distinguished from other types of motives on the basis of the person's own view of them. He regards a value as inherently desirable; not only does he feel positively toward it, but he believes that other people should feel similarly, because valuableness inheres in the state of affairs envisaged. Thus, the distinction between a motive and a value corresponds to the distinction between that which is desired, or needed, and that which is deemed desirable — the latter being a sub-class of the former.

Though psychological theorists are by no means agreed on the matter, it may be useful to consider attitudes also as a special class of motivational constructs, which represent the way an organism feels about an object — whether he desires to decrease or increase his psychological distance from it. Attitudes are motivating, but so are other non-phenomenological states of the person such as tissue needs, identifications, and defense mechanisms. Values are distinguishable from other attitudes (1) by the host's view of them as absolute and inherent in the object and (2) by the host's treating them as referring to ultimate ends, rather than as the appraisal of means to these ends. (Many attitudes may, of course, be held without an explicit means-end relationship in mind; but most of them can at least be rationalized by their host on the basis of presumed relevance of the focal object for his values; the values themselves are not further justified, but simply regarded as good for their own sakes.)

Dimensions of Values

Up to this point, a value has been defined in categorical fashion as an individual's conception of the desirable, implying an absolutely good end-state which other people ought to aim at and share. But these implicit properties may be found to varying degrees in many attitudes and motives (also, perhaps, in perceptions and beliefs as well). So it is nearer to empirical fact to conceptualize continua of absoluteness, of means-end contingencies, and of moral *oughtness*, which may apply to a variety of psychological constructs; and then to consider any particular concept a value to the extent that it embodies each of these defining properties.

The distinction between means and ends is a fluctuating one, varying within a single person over time, as well as over different people. Clearly, an object of value for one person may simply represent the object of another's attitude. Capitalism may be valued as an end in itself, or as a means toward the more ultimate end of individual liberty or toward the end of personal wealth. The means-end distinction must depend on a particular individual's view of things; it makes no sense, within the present framework, to designate any given state of affairs as a universal value for all people.

Even within a particular person, what is a means at one time may become an end at another. The process of value acquisition may be analogous to the acquisition of secondary reward value in motive development. If the attainment of one valued end-state is seen by the person as depending essentially on a particular means, that means may acquire value-potential for him. Especially under threat or under other conditions that restrict one's view of alternative means, the favored means may become absolutized to the point that one's attitude toward it is indistinguishable from his attitude toward the ultimate value it was supposed to bring about. This process may also be reversed: if a person is induced to think about the consequences of an initially valued state of affairs, he may come to regard it more as a means than as an end. Thus the value of supreme power for one's nation, acquired as patriotic catechism, may, on reflection, be transformed subjectively into a means for promoting individual liberty, for example.

This potential for shifting between mediate and ultimate

status implies that at any given time varying degrees of ultimacy may be accorded attitudinal objects. The more they are conceived as final, sufficient ends, the more would they be expected to behave as values, in the above pure-type definition.

Likewise, the absolute character of a value may be a matter of degree. This would seem to present a contradiction in terms, but after all, the very notion "absolute" is a human conception which need not function psychologically in the way one defines it logically. With sufficient imagination one could conceive circumstances in which almost any value would be over-ridden by conflicting considerations. The fact that such circumstances are hypothetical rather than actually expected by the individual justifies the label "absolute," but again a gradation is suggested: the fewer the circumstances that (subjectively) would suspend it, the more absolute is the value.

Finally, the subjective universality of a value may be limited in varying degrees. One may not expect ideal behavior of certain classes of people — infants, feeble-minded, savages, the morally unenlightened. Even for these exceptional classes, the *potential* applicability of the value is often asserted, and education is seen as a means of making the unenlightened aware of the value, hence capable of participating in its realization. More permanent exclusions are defined in some societies on the basis of role distinctions: different sets of values may be prescribed for men and women, for high caste and low caste, for master and servant. To the extent that such distinctions are based on ascribed, rather than achieved, status, the value fails of potential universal applicability, and hence departs from the ideal type defined above.

Gradations of these three dimensions — ultimacy, absoluteness, and universality — may be expected to covary within and across individuals. To a considerable degree, all of these may covary with the strength of the value, or its importance to the individual. The measures of individual differences in values employed in the present studies were conceived as measures of value strength, and there is some evidence that this dimension adequately represents the other three within the population studied. There may be some people for whom this is not true, in which case the degrees of ultimacy, absoluteness, and universality would have to be assessed separately.

Other distinctions among values have been proposed — for instance, the common classification into moral, aesthetic, and utilitarian types, or Kluckhohn's (1951, p. 414) designation of categorical, preferential, and utopian values. Though it is not explicit in their definitions, these terms seem to refer to assumed characteristics of the desirable end-state, rather than to the individual's own phenomenology. Beauty and elegance would be called aesthetic values, truth and justice moral values. Within Western society, human life might be a categorical value, scholarly achievement a preferential value, and humility a utopian value. Such a basis for designating value types is akin to the definition of value as inhering in the object, rather than in the person who judges. It fails to recognize that one person's aesthetic value may be another's moral value, that preferential for one may be categorical for another. Within the present framework, it is the person's own view of the valued state of affairs that provides the essence of the concept, so a universal or even culture-wide classification of value-types would be of little use. A particular individual may, of course, *learn* to classify his own values in these ways, but it is assumed that such distinctions are not fundamental or widespread in the population of college students studied here. Likewise, Sumner's (1906) well-known distinction between "folkways" and "mores" is probably better conceived as continuously graded, and varying from one individual to another, along the dimensions of ultimacy, absoluteness, and universality.

With these considerations in mind, a revised definition of the construct "value" may be proposed: *A person may be said to entertain a value to the extent that he conceives a particular state of affairs as an ultimate end, an absolute good under all circumstances, and a universal "ought" toward which all people should strive.* A value is a phenomenological construct, which refers to a person's own conceptual scheme; it need not correspond with someone else's conception, and it is subject to changes as the person's view of the world changes, for whatever reason, rational or otherwise.

ASSESSMENT OF PERSONAL VALUES

The measures of values that have been developed for the present study reflected these considerations, as applied specifically to the domain of interpersonal relations: A personal value is seen as a concept that an individual entertains of an ideal personal trait, an ideal way of relating to others. What is aimed at in operationalizing the construct is to determine the notions of ideal traits (if any) that a particular subject holds. Though a subject's description of his own preferences and usual patterns of behaviors, such as is assessed by the Allport-Vernon-Lindzey (1951) *Study of Values,* may bear some relation to his moral ideals, this is hardly a direct measure of the construct; hence this widely used technique for assessing "values" was deemed inappropriate to the present definition. Also, the Allport-Vernon test is limited to six "values," most of which do not appear centrally relevant to fraternity and sorority life; quite different content areas were required in this investigation.

Open-question Assessment

One preliminary way of assessing personal values is simply to ask people what traits they admire in others. This was done in a study of three communities (Scott, 1959a) in order to investigate the utility of such an open-question technique. After some "warm-up" questions, designed to focus attention on evaluated attributes, respondents were asked, "What is it about any person that makes him especially good?" and "What is it about any person that makes him especially bad?" For each trait mentioned, the interviewer probed, "Why is that good (or bad)?", until the respondent could offer no further justification than, "It just is, that's all." The free answers given to this broad-band stimulus were coded into a large number of categories representing positively valued traits. "Bad" traits were coded by inferring their opposites. It was found that subjects tended to mention these same attributes when discussing good and bad things about their acquaintances or about themselves, and when describing their aims in child-rearing. Hence, it may be inferred that values, in the intended sense, were actually tapped by the open-question procedure.

Evidence concerning the absolutistic nature of values assessed in this way was obtained from two samples of college students — 45 at the University of Hawaii and 85 at the University of Colorado. The following questions were read to them, and they were required to answer each one in turn in their own words (except for Questions 3 and 6, which provided fixed alternatives).

1. Think about the various people you admire, and try to reflect on what it is about them that is admirable. Now consider the general question: What is it about any person that makes him good? What personal traits would you say are particularly admirable?

2. Please look at the traits you have mentioned on the preceding question. Regardless of your own personal feelings about them, which ones do you think are inherently good, and should properly be regarded as good by all people?

3. To what extent do you live up to the ideal traits listed above? a. I follow them nearly always; b. I follow them most of the time; c. Sometimes I follow them, sometimes I don't; d. I don't follow them very often; e. I almost never follow them.

4. When you *have* lived up to these ideal traits, how do you feel?

5. When you *have not* lived up to these ideal traits, how do you feel?

6. To what extent do you think that other people admire these traits also? a. Everyone admires them; b. Most people admire them; c. Some people do, some people don't; d. Few people admire them; e. Almost no one admires them.

7. Suppose that, as a result of this test, you discovered that nobody else in the class regarded these traits as worthwhile. What would be your reaction?

8. Suppose that, in discussing this matter with your close friends, you found that they did not admire these traits. Would you still regard them as worthwhile, or not? Why?

9. Can you conceive of any circumstances under which these traits might not be good, or would they always be admirable regardless of the circumstances? a. They would always be admirable qualities; b. They would not be admirable under the following circumstances: _____

The first question is a slightly modified form of the one that had been used in private interviews (see Scott, 1959a) to assess personal values without suggesting specific traits to subjects. Responses were coded into some 50 categories, the most frequent of which were the following: interpersonal kindness (considerateness, human warmth); intelligence; honesty; sincerity; happiness (vitality, optimism); ambition (purposefulness); social skills (ability to get along with others); sense of humor; friendliness ("pleasant personality"); intellectualism (appreciation of "cultural refinements").

Questions 4 and 5 were intended to ascertain the subject's reactions to his own adherence and violation, as a check on the evaluative significance of these admired traits with reference to his behavior. Of the 129 subjects, 83% reported feeling "good" or self-satisfied upon adherence, and 72% said they felt "bad" or guilty upon violation, with only 8% reporting "no feelings in particular."

Questions 2, 7, 8, and 9 were intended to tap feelings of absolutism or relativism, under various kinds of prompting. In every case more absolutistic than relativistic replies appeared, though the proportions of uncodable answers were high in Questions 7 and 8, where the dimension was not explicitly suggested. In Question 2, 38% of the subjects regarded all of the traits they had mentioned as universals; another third of them regarded most (but not all) of their ideal traits in this way. Only 8% said that none of their admired traits was inherently good.

About half the replies to both Questions 7 and 8 manifested an absolutistic attitude: They either rejected the premises ("I wouldn't believe this possible") or indicated that they would lower their opinions of the dissenting people. Less than one-fourth of the replies to these two questions were relativistic (indicating acceptance of divergent values in others). The remaining responses generally indicated that the subject would retain his own values, but did not explicitly indicate either acceptance or rejection of others and their values.

In Question 9, 44% of the subjects said that their values would be admirable under all circumstances, and another 13%

stated exceptional circumstances that were themselves morally reprehensible to them (e.g., "among criminals" or "during war-time"). Two-fifths of the replies indicated that the traits would not be admirable if carried to the extreme, or if they conflicted with some other (legitimate) value, or that they might not be considered admirable by certain other people whom the subjects regarded as reasonable and acceptable.

It seems that values tapped by this open-question procedure were conceived by a majority of these college students as absolutely and universally "good" qualities that other people ought to recognize as good also; however, a sizable minority of subjects claimed a "moral relativist" position — at least under the hypothetical circumstances posed in this inquiry.

Three sets of contrasting replies are offered for illustration in the accompanying boxes (pp. 20–22).

The chief defect of such an open-question technique is that it yields an imprecise measure of any specific value. Only the presence or absence of each value can be scored, yielding just a two-point scale. Moreover, a respondent's answers are likely to be unduly affected by momentary, transient concerns, and there is a good chance that his meanings will be misrepresented in coding his reply into the value categories.

Multiple-item Scales

In order to develop more precise measures of specific values, a multiple-question instrument was constructed which invites a subject to accept or reject each of several trait descriptions, all intended to tap the same value. The number accepted is taken as an index of the strength of that value for him. By assessing several values at the same time and mixing up the order of statements in a single questionnaire, it is possible to control, to some extent, a respondent's tendency to appear spuriously consistent by replying similarly to all related statements.

The particular values measured by this multiple-question method were determined in part by a priori considerations of what would be relevant in Greek student organizations, in part by a preliminary open-question survey of student values in this university. Up to a dozen statements were written for each of twelve selected value areas and these were administered to try-out samples of students with the instructions, "Please read over the following statements, and for each one indicate (by a check in the appropriate space) whether it is something you *always admire* in other people, something you *always dislike*, or something that *depends on the situation* whether you admire it or not." The term "admire" was chosen to represent a positive evaluation because it seemed to convey an appropriate meaning to subjects. It was initially suspected that the terms "right" and "wrong," or "good" and "bad," would elicit rejections, or excessive use of the "depends" category, among confirmed relativists who entertained no moral absolutes. Subsequent analyses allayed this suspicion, and indicated that it would have been quite satisfactory to replace "admire" with either "right" or "good."

In any event, the values instruments reported here provided the "always admire," "always dislike," and "depends on the situation" categories of response to each statement. A subject's total score for any given value was determined by the number of times he checked the "admire" category for a statement in that set. Since a "depends" response would imply that the trait was not regarded as universally virtuous, it was coded along with "dislike" as indicating absence of the value.[1] Preliminary total scores for each value scale were computed, using all the statements designated, a priori, as relevant to it. This total score was tabulated against each statement separately, and those which did not discriminate among subjects, or did not correlate well with

[1] This scoring procedure would yield exclusively positive-scored statements in all value areas. In fact, the final instrument (see Appendix A) included only three reverse-scored statements, in which the "depends" and "dislike" responses were scored positive for a particular value. Though seemingly appropriate to the proposed concept of a value as something positively admired, this method of scoring has the disadvantage of contaminating the value score with a possible response set either to "admire" or not to admire all statements. (Actually, the "dislike" category was infrequently used, so most of the negatively scored responses fell in the "depends" category.) Though the effect of such a response set is probably small (see Scott, 1963, pp. 582-83), it seemed prudent to control for it in many of the analyses by making differential predictions concerning which values would and would not appear as significant correlates. Such a differential analysis is logically akin to Campbell and Fiske's (1959) multitrait-multimethod paradigm.

A Moral Absolutist Replies to the Questions on Page 17

1. (Values) "He is sensitive to other people: their ideas, needs, emotions. He tries to understand them, and help them achieve their needs when possible. He is intelligent and *uses* this intelligence to the maximum."

2. (Inherently good) "Sensitivity, understanding, behaving intelligently."

3. "b" [I follow them most of the time.]

4. "When I actually sit down and think of this achievement, [living up to ideals], I feel as though I have really accomplished something fine."

5. "I feel *stupid* when I have not lived up to them."

6. "a [Everyone admires them] — of course, unless one is a hermit!"

7. (If class didn't agree on values) "I know the test results would be faked! I have faith in my own judgment of admirable traits! In any case, I would stick to my opinions on the same."

8. (If friends didn't agree on values) "No, I would not regard them as worthwhile. If they did not appreciate these traits, they could not successfully deal with other human beings, let alone keep a true friendship with me. Without sensitivity and understanding, they would alienate other people. If they didn't behave intelligently, they would be impossible to get along with, needless to say!"

9. "These traits would *always* be admirable under any circumstances!"

A Moral Relativist Replies

1. (Values) "Generous, kind, aware of others' needs, emotional control but with human warmth, dependable, cheerful, open-mindedness, sincerity."

2. (Inherently good) "Human warmth, dependable, sincerity."

3. "b" [I follow them most of the time.]

4. (When live up to ideal traits) "I feel that I have done a good turn to others and myself."

5. (When don't live up to them) "I feel like a dog, and don't particularly like myself."

6. "c" [Some people do; some people don't admire same traits.]

7. (If class didn't agree on values) "I would be in a dilemma as to how to act toward them, because it would be hard to change my concepts just to please them — right away, at least. A compromise may be accomplished later.

8. (If friends didn't agree on values) "I would be very surprised and perhaps have a lower regard for them. But I would still regard them as worthwhile. This rather contradictory attitude is perhaps explainable if you wonder how you came to regard them as close friends in the first place. I would also take a second look at my own values and check to see whether I have been deviating from my professed values."

9. "b [They would not be admirable under the following circumstances:] Generosity when you deprive yourself or family; cheerfulness when at a funeral or someone needs consolation or empathy."

A Mixture, Predominantly Absolutist

1. "Adaptive personality; able to get along in most social situations; able to speak his own opinion and does not conform to group attitudes very rigidly; able to handle most situations without too much frustration and conflict; is not dependent upon others for decisions; learns from past experience and modifies personality accordingly; neatness in work and most situations."

2. "Able to get along in most situations; able to handle most situations without too much frustration and conflict."

3. "b" [I follow them most of the time.]

4. "I feel that I have done no one harm and have a feeling of accomplishment."

5. "I feel that I have not done my part in being an individual in society. My self-concept is low because of the undone behavior."

6. "c" [Some people do; some people don't admire them.]

7. "I would like to find out why [the class doesn't admire these traits], but not change many of them to suit group attitudes, because they have been satisfactory to me in the past."

8. "I would not have these friends in the first place, but I would alter them [traits] in minor ways to be accepted by my friends."

9. "b [not admirable] in a circumstance where I would have to live in a prejudiced society where anything I did could be used against me, unless I conformed to the social behaviors of the group."

the total, were eliminated. This left between four and six items in each value scale, selected so as to provide maximally homogeneous instruments of relatively short length.

The final value scales appear in Appendex A (p. 245). A brief summary of their contents follows:

1. *Intellectualism:* Having strong intellectual and cultural interests; trying to learn a great deal about things, even though the knowledge may not be useful.

2. *Kindness:* Being mostly concerned about other people; doing good for them, and trying to make them happy, even if it is against one's own interests.

3. *Social skills:* Being charming, popular, well mannered, and getting along with all kinds of people.

4. *Loyalty:* Being a loyal, devoted member of the group, never criticizing it to outsiders, and working hard to get it ahead of other groups.

5. *Academic achievement:* Studying a great deal and working hard to get good grades.

6. *Physical development:* Being a well-developed outdoors type who enjoys physical activity.

7. *Status:* Having strong leadership qualities, being respected by others, and gaining recognition for one's achievements.

8. *Honesty:* Always telling the truth and being completely honest; never cheating or lying, even though these might make for an easier relationship with others.

9. *Religiousness:* Being a religious person, both in belief and practice; attending church regularly; and abiding by the Bible's teachings.

10. *Self-control:* Always being patient and self-controlled; never losing one's temper, no matter what the provocation.

11. *Creativity:* Being inventive, creative, and always thinking of different ways of doing things.

12. *Independence:* Being independent, outspoken, free-thinking, and unhampered by the bounds of tradition or social restraint.

Scale homogeneities, computed from a new sample of subjects, are reported in Table 1. From the size of the average inter-item correlations (Col. 1), it seems that the value domains may be reasonably well identified from the common item contents; these correlations — ranging from .20 to .43 — are considerably higher than those that would be found for most psychological instruments, such as the *F* scale or an intelligence

TABLE 1

HOMOGENEITIES OF VALUE SCALES, CORRELATIONS WITH OPEN-QUESTION MEASURES AND COEFFICIENTS OF STABILITY

Value	*Measures of Homogeneity*		*Correlations with Open Question*		*Coefficients of Stability*	
	(1) H.R.[a]	(2) r_{tt}[b]	(3) r_{pb}[c]	(4) P.B.R.[d]	(5) Scale	(6) Open
Intellectualism	.28	.68	.15	.20	.64	.35
Kindness	.33	.66	.27	.32	.68	.39
Social skills	.29	.70	.19	.23	.74	.13
Loyalty	.25	.71	.01	.02	.58	.38
Academic achievement	.37	.69	.11	.12	.68	.49
Physical development	.40	.77	.16	.39	.74	.37
Status (leadership)	.27	.65	.17	.35	.70	.27
Honesty	.28	.61	.15	.20	.74	.51
Religiousness	.43	.78	.23	.47	.77	.49
Self-control	.31	.68	.10	.18	.72	.27
Creativity	.24	.64	.05	.12	.66	.46
Independence	.20	.55	.15	.39	.73	.26
Mean	.30	.67	.16	.25	.70	.36

[a]Homogeneity Ratio (Scott, 1960), which equals the mean of all inter-item correlations, each weighted by the geometric mean of the item variances.
[b]Cronbach's (1951) Coefficient *alpha* for estimating scale reliability.
[c]Point-biserial correlation coefficient.
[d]Point-biserial Ratio (Scott, 1960), a ratio between the obtained r_{pb} and the maximum value possible, given the marginals.

test. However, the reliability estimates (Col. 2) — ranging between .55 and .78 — are generally not high enough to permit accurate measurement of individual subjects. This is primarily because of the short length of the scales (4 to 6 items each), which was required by the over-all research strategy of assessing many values at one time, together with a number of other relevant variables, without undue subject fatigue. As measures for distinguishing between large groups, the present scales may be deemed adequate; but more precise individual assessment would require the addition of equally homogeneous items to each scale. This has since been attempted, and the resulting lengthened scales appear in Appendix A (p. 249).

Also reported in Table 1 is the correlation of each scale with the open-question measure of values mentioned above.[2] The generally small magnitude of these correlations indicates that it would be quite inappropriate to translate from one measure to the other. The traits that people mention spontaneously when asked what they admire in others are not necessarily the same as the traits they assent to when asked specifically about each one separately. This poor correspondence is due partly to limitations of the open-question method: Subjects do not mention spontaneously all the admirable qualities that might come to mind if they were given unlimited time and sufficient probing. It is also due to a distortion of certain value contents in constructing the scales. The "loyalty" value, for example, was coded from free responses whenever a subject said that he admired loyalty to friends or family (the most common responses coded in this category). But since the present research was aimed at assessing values relevant to fraternities and sororities, nearly all the loyalty items in the scale referred specifically to group affiliations, which were rarely mentioned spontaneously. Similarly,

[2] The point-biserial correlation coefficient has a maximum less than 1.00 in all practical cases (i.e., where one variable is continuous). The P.B.R., or point-biserial ratio (Scott, 1960a), reported in the fourth column of Table 1, is the ratio between the obtained point-biserial correlation and the maximum size possible given the obtained marginals.

the scale of achievement referred exclusively to academic situations and striving for grades, whereas achievement-related responses coded from the open questions referred to striving for excellence in various areas of endeavor, with grades rarely mentioned as a specific goal.

Finally, the stability coefficients for each of the value scales and for the open-question measures are presented in Table 1. These were obtained in a General Psychology class at the University of Colorado, with a two-week interval between test and retest. The instructions for the retest were, "Please fill out this questionnaire to indicate how you feel now, without trying to be either consistent or inconsistent with what you said before." It will be noted that the stability coefficients for the scales are considerably higher than those for the open question, and occasionally exceed the reliabilities estimated from internal consistency. This probably results from some subjects' "memories" for specific item responses, which exceeded the degree of inter-item similarity within a single scale.

The twelve value scales certainly provide more reliable measures than the open-question procedure, but it cannot be said for certain that they are more valid. A comparative validity study would incorporate both methods of value assessment, combined with a number of other variables deemed theoretically relevant to the concept. Such a study has yet to be undertaken; in the meantime, while we tentatively accept the more reliable scales as the more appropriate measures of values, we recognize that they often do not correspond closely with what people profess to admire when they are simply asked without specific probing.

Intercorrelations Among Scales

Nothing in the definition of these values requires that they be factorially independent. Orthogonal factors may be developed empirically from an intercorrelation matrix in which a large number of haphazardly selected items are related to each other.

TABLE 2
INTERCORRELATIONS AMONG VALUE SCALES
(n = 218)

	Indep.	Intell.	Creat.	Acad.	Hon.	Relig.	Self-cont.	Kind.	Loy.	Soc. sk.	Status	Phys.
Independence	(.51)											
Intellectualism	.22	(.69)										
Creativity	.21	.51	(.54)									
Academic achievement	.07	.34	.31	(.63)								
Honesty	.04	.09	.00	.23	(.30)							
Religiousness	-.22	.18	.13	.15	.17	(.76)						
Self-control	-.18	.15	.08	.08	.06	.31	(.61)					
Kindness	-.10	.23	.19	.11	.15	.43	.51	(.57)				
Loyalty	-.07	.06	.13	.18	-.10	.36	.31	.26	(.62)			
Social skills	-.27	.01	.07	.18	-.09	.26	.33	.20	.36	(.62)		
Status	-.10	.13	.12	.28	-.01	.14	.12	.07	.35	.42	(.47)	
Physical development	-.12	.04	.15	.30	-.06	.25	.11	.11	.41	.25	.41	(.71)

The factor scales emerging from such an analysis might turn out to have psychological meaning, but chances are they would not, since most psychological concepts have not been developed with a view toward empirical independence of their referents. Though orthogonal factors may provide an efficient set of reference axes for locating variables in multidimensional space, the positions of these axes are in large part arbitrary and should not be expected to be theoretically interpretable, unless the theory and measures were designed with this end in mind.

The present effort at scale development did not start as an empirical search for orthogonal factors. It started rather from explicit conceptions of the values to be measured, and items were constructed to fit these conceptions. In fact, certain of these conceptually defined scales turned out to be substantially inter-correlated. The relevant test of independence within this strategy consists of determining whether or not the several items within a scale are more highly correlated with each other than they are with items from different scales; or, more efficiently, determining whether or not the scale reliabilities (internal consistencies) are higher than the correlations among different scales. Table 2, based on a random cross-section of the university student body, shows that this condition obtains for each scale in relation to every other scale — that is, no correlation between scales exceeds the separate reliabilities of the two scales (in parentheses along the diagonal). This means that the scales are measuring distinct, though correlated, values.

Table 2 is arranged so as to show two broad clusters of values, which might be identified, after Riesman (1950), as "inner-directed" and "other-directed." The former group consists of the values of independence, intellectualism, and creativity, while the latter group includes loyalty, social skills, kindness, status, physical development, self-control, and religiousness. The average intercorrelation within the inner-directed cluster is .33, while that within the other-directed cluster is .29; the average correlation between the two clusters is .03. Thus, to the extent that this population of college students can be classified by these value scales into the two broad orientations, inner-directedness and other-directedness tend to be independent, rather than mutually exclusive dispositions.[3] The value of honesty does not fit particularly well in either cluster, while academic achievement correlates substantially with both.

Construct Validity

If this instrument measures values in the sense intended, the scales should relate sensibly to certain other subject characteristics that are conceptualized as concomitants of values. Certain correlates relevant to the construct validity of the instrument have been investigated, and the results justify some confidence in the appropriateness of the scales. The presentation of them here should help convey more clearly the intended meaning of the concept "value." For example, values measured in terms of what a subject personally admires in other people should correlate substantially with his notions of what traits are "objectively" right, independent of his own feelings in the matter. To test this assumption, the same 60 items were administered to a new sample of General Psychology students under the instructions, "Now, for each of the traits mentioned in Part I, regardless of whether or not you personally admire the trait, would you please indicate if you think it is the *right* thing to do, or if you think it is the *wrong* thing to do, or if it is *neither* right nor wrong."

A few subjects objected to filling out this form, for they regarded it and their answers to the previously administered "admire" set as redundant. As one student put it, "Well, naturally, if I admire anything, I would think it is the right thing for everybody to do." In fact, most of the subjects tended to answer the items administered in this way very much as they

---

[3] The average intercorrelation between clusters might have been somewhat negative, had it not been for the contaminating acquiescence set built into most of the scales (see footnote 1, p. 20).

had answered the items administered in the usual form. Any subject who simply omitted the right/wrong set, replying "same as previously," was excluded from the analysis, in order to avoid spurious inflation of the predicted correlations. As Table 3 shows, the correlations between paired scales were about as high as their reliabilities, since the *r*s corrected for attenuation average .97.

TABLE 3

CORRELATIONS BETWEEN PERSONAL VALUES
AND (1) CONCEPTIONS OF "RIGHT" AND "WRONG"
AND (2) PRESCRIBED VALUES FOR OTHERS
($n = 208$)

Value	"Right" and "Wrong"		Prescribed for Others	
	r	r_{oor}[a]	r	r_{oor}[a]
Intellectualism	.63	.95	.44	.67
Kindness	.72	1.00	.61	.95
Social skills	.74	1.00	.54	.90
Loyalty	.69	.96	.46	.75
Academic achievement	.52	.74	.48	.72
Physical development	.69	.88	.63	.88
Status	.64	1.00	.54	.93
Honesty	.69	1.00	.57	1.00
Religiousness	.78	.98	.53	.67
Self-control	.69	.96	.58	.83
Creativity	.57	.86	.47	.77
Independence	.74	1.00	.56	1.00
Median	.69	.97	.54	.86

[a] *r*s corrected for attenuation (see Gulliksen, 1950, p. 101); when computed values exceed 1.00, they are reported as 1.00.

The same items were administered under a third set, "Now, for each of the traits mentioned in Part I, regardless of your own opinion about it, we would like to know how you think *other people should feel* about the matter. Please check in the appropriate space below whether you think *other people should admire the trait*, whether *other people should disapprove* of it, or whether other people might legitimately *differ* in their opinions on the matter."

31

This time the correlations with the usual value scales were somewhat lower, but still averaged .54 and, corrected for attenuation, .86. Taken together, these results indicate that values, as measured by the present instrument, are indeed concepts that these subjects tend to regard as absolutes and universals. Though it might have been expected that relatively sophisticated college students, amply exposed to doctrines of cultural relativism, would disclaim any professions of universal "oughts," such relativist tendencies did not appear in any substantial proportion of these samples. Whenever a subject claimed to admire a personal trait himself, he was very likely to regard it as "right" and to think that other people should admire it also.

Another theoretical property of a value is its capacity for inducing feelings of guilt when it has been violated. An appropriate test of an instrument's adequacy with respect to this property would require an actual forced violation of people's values to see if the expected guilt ensued. This is a problem for major study in itself; a rather less satisfactory substitute consists in having subjects estimate their own degree of guilt under hypothetical circumstances which may, a priori, be expected to violate the valued state of affairs. A random sample of students at the university responded to a questionnaire which posed a series of hypothetical situations that might thwart the several values — for instance, "to be unable to read any books or magazines for several weeks" as a violation of the intellectualism value. (See Appendix B, p. 261, for the complete set of hypothetical circumstances.) For each situation, the respondent was to indicate how bad he would feel by checking in one of the four spaces:

Would not bother me at all.
Would bother me a bit, but I would soon forget it.
I would try to forget it, but it would bother me whenever
   I thought about it.
Would bother me a lot.

If subjects' estimates of how much each of these circumstances would "bother" them can be taken as indications of anticipated guilt over value transgression, then the expected relationship appears—namely, the stronger a particular value, the greater is the anticipated guilt over transgression. Table 4 reports the relevant

TABLE 4

CORRELATIONS BETWEEN VALUE STRENGTH AND
ANTICIPATED GUILT OVER TRANSGRESSION
($n = 218$)

Value	r
Intellectualism	.23**
Kindness	.15*
Social skills	.20**
Loyalty	−.04
Academic achievement	.31**
Physical development	.31**
Status	.06
Honesty	.26**
Religiousness	.57**
Self-control	.26**
Creativity	.11
Independence	.27**
Mean (via z transformation)	.23**

* $\alpha < .05$.
** $\alpha < .01$.

correlation for each of the value areas. Nine of the twelve are significantly different from zero ($\alpha < .05$) and the mean r is .23. The fact that they aren't larger may be due in part to inappropriately designated circumstances for violating any given value.

GROUP DIFFERENCES IN VALUES

The scales used in this research should be regarded as preliminary measures of the twelve values. Each of them would require considerable expansion of the kind proposed in Appendix A (p. 249) before it could be used in further research aimed at precise individual assessment. Nevertheless, we may note some tentative evidence of their validity in detecting differences among groups that would be expected from a priori considerations. Not all of the scales have been subjected to this "known groups" validation procedure — indeed, it is difficult to designate appropriately contrasting groups for some of them — but the results thus far tend to conform to expectations.[4]

Religiousness

The entire set of twelve scales was administered to a sample of 81 Jesuit seminarians at Loyola University. Their mean scores on the religiousness value were significantly higher than the mean scores of a representative sample of 113 male students at the University of Colorado. Since some of the other scales also showed significant differences between these two groups, it is important to show that the difference is greater in religiousness than it is for the remaining scales. The magnitude of difference between groups, in relation to total score variability, may be represented by the point-biserial correlation coefficient. This was $+.51$ for the religiousness value, $-.43$ for the independence value, $+.36$ for the kindness value. (A $+$ means that the Jesuit seminarians scored higher than the college males.) None of the other scales showed significant differences between the two groups.

Independence

Nineteen members of the Players Club at the University of Colorado were compared with a representative (random) university cross-section. The Players Club was selected to validate the independence scale, because it has a reputation as a "professionally deviant" group on campus which enjoys its nonconformity to the wider cultural norms. Its mean was significantly higher than the average for the campus on the independence value (point-biserial $r = +.35$). On all the remaining values

[4] I am indebted to the following persons for administering the tests to the groups reported here: Basilio Magnago, Lois Wolf, Basil Sherlock, Teresa Smith, Daphne Monroe, Karilyn Frampton, and Greg Tolson.

34

it showed lower mean scores; the significant differences were: kindness ($r = -.29$), social skills ($r = -.25$), status ($r = -.26$) honesty ($r = -.27$), religiousness ($r = -.24$), and self-control ($r = -.28$).

Physical Development

The Women's Physical Education Club ($n = 27$) was compared with the cross-sectional sample of female students ($n = 59$). The former group showed a significantly higher mean score on the physical development scale ($r = +.34$). It also tended to score differently on some of the other scales, but the magnitudes of difference were relatively less; self-control ($r = +.33$). religiousness ($r = +.32$), honesty ($r = +.29$), loyalty ($r = +.25$), independence ($r = -.25$), status ($r = +.24$).

Creativity

Twenty art majors (male and female) at the University of California were compared with the representative sample of Colorado students. The only value for which their means were significantly different was creativity ($r = +.28$).

Academic Achievement

A random sample of 23 male and female undergraduates at the University of California who had obtained grade-point averages over 3.5 (on a 4-point scale) during the preceding semester was compared with an equal number of students who had obtained grade-point averages between 2.2 and 2.4. The reason for using the latter group for comparison is that it represents a "safe" passing range in which the student is in no danger of suspension, but at the same time is not performing particularly well. It was suspected that students with much lower grades than this might show an exaggerated emphasis on academic achievement (assuming that they were motivated to remain in school). The difference between the "high" and "low" groups was significant ($r = +.36$); the former group also tended to score higher on independence ($r = +.27$), lower on honesty ($r = -.28$). (Since the list of honor students was obtained from the University Records Office, there is no reason to suspect contaminated results caused by the difference in professed honesty value.)

Other Value Scales

The differences between Greek and Independent students at the University of Colorado on the values of loyalty and social skills (see Table 9) may be taken as evidence for the validity of these scales, since it can reasonably be assumed (and other results of the present study confirm) that Greek organizations tend to stress these values. The remaining scales—kindness, status, honesty, intellectualism, and self-control—have not yet been subjected to "known groups" validation procedures, usually because it has proved difficult to think of groups that can reasonably be assumed, a priori, to value these traits to an extreme degree.

VALUES AND BEHAVIOR

The relation between an individual's moral concepts and his actual behavior at any given time may be problematical, but it would seem that over the long run there would be a tendency toward convergence. This is because values are conceived here both as justification for past actions and as guides to subsequent actions. The degree of correspondence will, of course, vary greatly from one person to another, depending upon such things as their facility for rationalization and self-justification, their capacity for deliberate, internally controlled action, and the intensities of their self-reward and self-punishment.

For the average student at the University of Colorado there was evidently some tendency toward correspondence between value and overt behavior. This was inferred from responses to a questionnaire in which a random sample of the student body reported on a variety of activities relevant to each of the twelve values measured here (see Scott, 1963, p. 575). Behavior appropriate to the value of loyalty, for example, was assessed by questions about frequency of attendance at meetings and amount of time devoted to organizations of which the subject was a member. Twelve such "behavior indices" were constructed from questions referring as much as possible to objectively reportable actions, in an effort to minimize unintentional response distortion. They were homogenized separately from the value scales, and the two sets of scales had no items in common.

Correlations between values and reported behaviors in the representative cross-section of the student body are presented in Table 5. They range from +.10 for the independence value to

TABLE 5
CORRELATIONS BETWEEN VALUES AND
REPORTED BEHAVIORS
(University Cross-Section; $n = 218$)

Value	
Intellectualism	.40**
Kindness	.12*
Social skills	.20**
Loyalty	.25**
Academic achievement	.17**
Physical development	.31**
Status	.21**
Honesty	.20**
Religiousness	.55**
Self-control	.16**
Creativity	.13*
Independence	.10

* $\alpha < .05$.
** $\alpha < .01$.

+.55 for the religiousness value, with a mean of .23. Eleven of the twelve correlations are significantly different from zero, and every value scale correlated with its corresponding behavior index to a greater degree than it correlated with at least nine of the other (non-relevant) behavior indices. Therefore, one can conclude with fair confidence that there is, on the average, some tendency for values and behavior (at least self-reported behavior) to correspond within the population of students represented here. Some of them showed much higher degrees of value-behavior congruence, some of them considerably lower.

When subjects report their own actions and preferences with reference to the same test items that they have rated for "desirability," the correlations between desirability judgments and self-reports are much higher (see Scott, 1963). This increased magnitude is, of course, partly due to similarities between the testing instruments, but it also suggests that correspondences between values and behavior might be somewhat higher than is indicated in Table 5 if identical behaviors were represented in both domains.

STANDARD SCORES

Throughout the analyses in subsequent chapters, we shall be reporting various group differences in single values and in patterns of values, as they were encountered in the longitudinal study of fraternities and sororities. To reduce the essential difficulty of these tables and to permit ready comparison from one value to another, it is useful to have a standard scale along which all value strengths are measured. Such a standard scale is certainly not provided by the raw scores obtained from the items checked "always admire," for there are different numbers of items per scale, and the items vary in popularity. It may even be considered illogical to seek standard scales for attributes that are measured by quite different instruments; this is something like trying to compare height and weight — asking, in effect, if a person is as heavy as he is tall.

Such a question can only be answered in terms relative to the distributions of all scores on the two variables that are to be compared. A "high" score is translated as "a score that is higher than most other people obtain," a "low" score as one that "is lower than most other people obtain," etc. In the present research, "most other people" were not accessible for measurement. We had to be content with a representative sample of the University of Colorado student body to provide a set of standards against which any individual's score on any of the twelve values could be compared. The sample was selected from the alphabetized student directory, in the fall of 1958, by starting with a random number between 1 and 40, and taking every fortieth name thereafter. Letters were sent to the designated students asking them to come to group testing sessions scheduled just before Christmas vacation. Delinquents were followed up by telephone immediately after the holidays, and questionnaires were secured from them either in individual appointments or by mail.[5] All told, 218 persons — 90% of those designated in the sample — completed their questionnaires, so the results can be deemed quite representative of the entire student body at that time. However, there is no assurance that they would be duplicated in another population.

The means and standard deviations of the twelve value scales, calculated from the university cross-section, are indicated in Appendix Table A-1. Unless otherwise specified, they provide the basis for all standard scores reported in subsequent chapters. Although these are not necessarily the same standard scores that would be obtained if another sample were used as the basis for calculations, they at least offer some improvement over the original raw scores, in that gross instrument differences (in means and standard deviations of the several scales) no longer contributes so heavily to the results as they would have if there had been no attempt at standardization.

SUMMARY

A personal value, or moral ideal, is defined as an individual's concept of an ideal relationship, which he uses to assess the

[5] This study was conducted with the collaboration of Robert Kassebaum and Leon Rappoport.

"goodness" or "badness," "rightness" or "wrongness" of actual relationships. A valued state of affairs tends to be conceived by the person as intrinsically, absolutely, and universally good. This proposed meaning has been theoretically distinguished from the related concepts, "attitude" and "motive." There is some evidence indicating that a majority of the college students tested do, in fact, conceive of their own values in absolutistic terms.

Short multiple-item scales have been developed for measuring twelve different prescriptive values that may be professed, to varying degrees, by students such as those used in this research. Though not sufficiently reliable for assessment of individuals, they can be expected to yield significant differences between sizable groups of subjects who differ in the values assessed. The scales are quite homogeneous in content and, though intercorrelated to some degree, are empirically distinguishable from one another. Investigations conducted so far indicate that "values" measured by this technique tend to behave empirically as one would expect them to if they were tapping attributes of the kind conceptualized here.

Since completion of this research on fraternities and sororities, improved value scales have been constructed. These are reported in Appendix A (pp. 249–257) for the convenience of researchers who may wish to use them.

CHAPTER 2

ORIGINS AND FUNCTIONS OF MORALITY

How do human beings come to value certain states of affairs — to regard some actions, or goals of action, as inherently desirable and worthy of pursuit, in contrast to other actions that are deemed blameworthy, others that are deemed optional, deserving neither praise nor blame? This question has captured the attention of philosophers and psychologists alike, some offering mystical answers embodying assumptions about the inherent nature and destiny of man, others offering theoretical interpretations that might be empirically verified.

Treated as an empirical problem, the question of the sources of morality may be divided into a number of subsidiary questions, focusing on different aspects of morality and on different kinds of sources. Considering values as conceptions of the desirable, one is led to inquire, "How do people come to hold the particular values they do?" and also, "How do people acquire their notions of a valued state — whatever it may be — as something inherently desirable?" Considering sources both from the standpoint of the individual and from the standpoint of the larger culture, one may ask either, "How does a person come to adopt values from those around him?" or "Why do the people around him hold those values in the first place?" In this chapter, we shall consider theoretical explanations bearing on each of these questions.

THE CONTENTS OF MORALS —
WHAT IS VALUED

Noting the diversity of value contents in various societies, and even within a single sub-culture (see Chapter 1), the social psychologist is inclined to attribute these almost exclusively to differences in experiences encountered by various individuals in the course of their socialization. The acquisition of value content is ordinarily described as a learning process, whereby the individual comes to anticipate reward or punishment following an approved or forbidden act, and develops some (approximate) conception of the standard that others use to reinforce his behavior.

McDougall (1909, p. 181) described four stages in the development of human conduct in terms remarkably congenial to contemporary formulations:

(1) the stage of instinctive behaviour modified only by the influence of the pains and pleasures that are incidentally experienced in the course of instinctive activities; (2) the stage in which the operation of the instinctive impulses is modified by the influence of rewards and punishments administered more or less systematically by the social environment; (3) the stage in which conduct is controlled in the main by anticipation of social praise and blame; (4) the highest stage, in which conduct is regulated by an ideal of conduct that enables man to act in the way that seems to him right regardless of the praise or blame of his immediate social environment.

Hill (1960) elaborates some mechanisms of generalization and vicarious reinforcement that may help account for the development of internalized guides to behavior: "The child is typically reinforced . . . for doing what others tell him to do. Hence . . . a generalized tendency toward conformity to verbal instructions may be expected to develop. With increasing intellectual development, this tendency should come to include conformity to fictional examples or to abstract ethical exhortations" (p. 320). Thus, the child's behavior may come to be guided, not only by the consequences of his own acts, but also by implicitly promised consequences that he has never experienced. The moral deficit allegedly encountered among "psychopaths" might be seen in these terms as an inability to anticipate consequences from the sorts of minimal cues that come to be sufficient for guiding most people.

Children appear to learn values not only from what they are told, but from observing the reinforcements that others — their "models" —receive for their acts. "If [the model] is frequently reinforced, the person should find it rewarding to resemble [the model] in general, including imitation of some of [the model's] behavior which the person has never seen rewarded" (Hill, 1960, p. 321).

Psychoanalytic formulations of Superego development (e.g., Freud, 1935) can be translated into equivalent terminology. Although the Superego is seen primarily as an accumulation of inhibitive, rather than prescriptive, morality — a codification of punishable, rather than rewardable, acts — these concepts of forbidden behaviors are seen as resulting largely from the experience of punishment and anticipation of punishment from the child's parents and other socializing agents.

The principle of reinforcement has been well established in experiments on the learning of habits, imitative behavior, and attitudes (see Miller & Dollard, 1941; Scott, 1957, 1959c; Staats, Staats, & Heard, 1960). It seems reasonable, therefore, that it should also apply to the learning of values, if values are conceived as a sub-class of attitudes. Leaving aside, for the moment, the feelings of absoluteness, etc., that accompany the person's concept of what is right, the value content itself can probably be acquired in much the same way as any other attitude or behavior. This includes acquisition via response reinforcement, the learning of expectancies, imitation, and generalization of these. But direct empirical evidence for this belief is scarce.[1] Perhaps because the category of moral attitudes has not commonly been

[1] Since this was written, I have seen Bandura and Walters' *Social Learning and Personality Development* (1963), which offers an excellent review of theories and research findings concerning the development of self-control in children. Their treatment emphasizes the importance of imitation, as well as reinforcement, in the acquisition of "morality," and suggests that a variety of different "moral" patterns may be acquired through these processes.

distinguished by psychologists, or because values are believed to be basically indistinguishable from other sorts of attitudes, the relevance of these learning principles to value acquisition has been established by logical translation, rather than by direct empirical inquiry. Implicit in the present study of value change in fraternities and sororities was the assumption that interpersonal relations in these organizations would provide numerous opportunities for imitation and reinforcement of valued acts and, therefore, that systematic changes in values over time could reasonably by attributed to interpersonal rewards and punishments. Yet this remained an assumption not directly tested, for we measured only the changes in values, not the kinds of interpersonal reinforcers that members encountered.

Psychologists have typically studied the development of values in children rather than in adults. In fact, it is an implicit assumption of much research in this area that moral standards acquired in childhood do not change appreciably in later life. Piaget's (1932) pioneering studies of morality in children indicated to him that by their early teens children tend to have developed views of morality that are not essentially different from the adult's view. Peck and Havighurst (1960) interpreted their study of thirty-four adolescents in "Prairie City" as showing that the level of morality attained by their subjects at age 16 could be quite well predicted by age 10, and almost perfectly predicted by age 13 (p. 156). These beliefs appear contrary to the assumption of the present study that concepts of morality may continue to be acquired well into early adulthood and, indeed, throughout life. Perhaps the contradiction is not so great if one distinguishes the specific content of the values professed or practiced from the moral attitude that accompanies any particular value. Piaget was chiefly concerned with the *way* in which values relating to rules, honesty, property damage, and the like were regarded by his subjects. He did not explicitly look for changes in *what* was valued at each age level. We may suggest that, even if the manner in which a value is held be fairly stable throughout the average person's life, the content of what is valued may change greatly as a result of his changing experiences. Rules of marbles may be important to children, rules of interpersonal conduct to adults.

The Peck and Havighurst study did not look explicitly for changes in value content either. Instead, these researchers seemed to have assumed a fairly constant standard of moral behavior that they themselves espoused, and assessed by ratings the degree to which their subjects met this standard at various times in their development. It is not clear from their report whether the ratings were made independently at the three age levels. If the same judges rated each level, it is likely that their memories for specific subjects introduced some spurious consistency. Since all ratings were arrived at through a conference among the judges, it is certain that the inter-judge agreement on particular subjects was inflated above that which independent ratings would have produced.

Even if considerable allowance is made for spurious consistencies in the ratings, it is still probable that their subjects did manifest a fair degree of stability in the level of moral character throughout the six-year period. But it should be noted that this occurred in the context of a more or less fixed criterion of morality and a relatively unchanging social surround provided for these adolescents in Prairie City. Results of the Nobles County (Minnesota) Mental Health Survey (e.g., Beilin, 1957, 1958) indicate less constancy in reputation over time; more important, they demonstrate that judgments of evaluated traits like "adjustment" and "character" depend heavily on the standards used by the judge. Elementary school teachers seem to be especially sensitive to social adjustment as a criterion; high school teachers to emotional stability and ambition; clergymen to dependability. Thus, one might expect that, if "maturity of character" were rated by different people at different stages in a person's life —

especially if he were undergoing substantial changes in social environment — these ratings would show less consistency than appeared in the Peck and Havighurst study.

This is not to criticize these researchers' use of a constant frame of reference in judging the level of moral behavior. Without a constant standard, change in the subject cannot be distinguished from changes in the raters' perspectives. It is important to note, however, that what is regarded as moral maturity by one group of judges will not necessarily be similarly regarded by another group. So any conclusions concerning constancy in this respect must be limited to the particular frame of reference used in judging. Peck and Havighurst present a fairly detailed description of their frame of reference. Unfortunately, it is impossible to tell from their study how successful some other group of judges would be in applying even these same criteria (independently) to the same subjects, for all of their ratings were arrived at through a conference of judges, and no tests were made of the reliability of independent ratings.

In the next chapter we shall consider in more detail some findings concerning value change among college students. The data in this area are ambiguous, and it has been concluded by some (e.g., Jacob, 1957) that value changes do not generally occur as a result of college experience, while others (e.g., Sanford, et al., 1962) claim otherwise. Considering the contents of morality — what is valued — alone, the present orientation suggests that value changes *can* occur at any time of life. Whether they do occur, and whether they occur in any particular direction, should depend both on the nature (and consistency) of social reinforcements in the person's surround and on the prior relation between his own values and those which are to be reinforced.

THE MORAL ATTITUDE —
HOW VALUES ARE HELD

The definition of a value proposed in the first chapter (p. 15) included as its essential characteristic the person's belief that the valued state of affairs is inherently and absolutely good, independent of his own appraisal, also that it is universally applicable, and hence should be admired by all "right-thinking" people. This definition limits the term to the person's conception of "absolutes" and explicitly excludes preferences that, for him, are a matter of option. Of course, the absolute-vs.-preferential nature of a particular state may be only a matter of degree, but we are interested in studying those attitudes which carry a considerable degree of this absolutistic moral flavor.

The results of Piaget's (1932) studies are often interpreted as showing that an absolutistic morality characterizes the young child, but not the older child, much less the mature adult. Since our point of view is rather different — asserting, in effect, that most morality carries an absolutistic flavor — it is important to consider Piaget's research somewhat more carefully. He studied children's conceptions of a game of marbles with particular reference to how they viewed the rules of the game. Among younger children he found "an almost mystical respect for rules: rules are external.... It is forbidden to change them, and even if the whole of general opinion supported such a change, general opinion would be wrong" (Piaget, 1932, p. 52). Among older children (above age 10), however, "consciousness of rules undergoes a complete transformation. Autonomy follows upon heteronomy: the rule of the game appears to the child no longer as an external law, sacred in so far as it has been laid down by adults; but as the outcome of a free decision and worthy of respect in the measure that it has enlisted mutual consent" (p. 56). "The child ceases *ipso facto* to look upon rules as eternal and as having been handed down unchanged from one generation to another.... His ideas on the origin of the rules and of the game do not differ from ours" (p. 57).

Heteronomy, the conception of rules as externally given, is equivalent to our definition of the moral attitude as ultimate, absolute, and universal in concept. It is an aspect of "moral realism," which Piaget defined as "the tendency which the child has to regard duty and the value attaching to it as self-subsistent and independent of the mind, as imposing itself regardless of the circumstances in which the individual may find himself" (p. 106). This he distinguishes from the adult's (and older child's) view, which is characterized by autonomy, or the belief that rules are the product of consensus among free, equal-status individuals. Other aspects of moral realism are said to be the assessment of guilt according to the consequences of the act, rather than according to the intent of the actor, and the notion of imminent justice (that punishment follows immediately as a direct consequence of moral transgression). Piaget found that these manifestations of moral realism decreased with age, and some subsequent research reported by Johnson (1962) and Kohlberg (1963) has tended to confirm many of these trends.

According to Piaget's interpretation, the moral absolutism of the young child derives from his subservience to rules imposed by his parents, while autonomous moral conceptions are said to derive from the peer group, in which differences in power and subordination are less extreme.

The main factor in the obligatory conformity of very young children is nothing but respect for age — respect for older children, and, above all, respect for adults. And if, at a given amount, cooperation takes the place of restraint, or autonomy that of conformity, it is because the child, as he grows older, becomes progressively free from adult supervision. . . . As soon as the individual escapes from the domination of age, he tends towards cooperation as the normal form of social equilibrium (pp. 98-99).

Since the results of his research are so often interpreted as evidence of a pervasive transition from "moral absolutism" in children to "moral relativism" in adults, it is important to recognize that Piaget himself qualified the generality of this trend:

After having tried to describe the child's mentality as distinct from the adult's we have found ourselves obliged to include it in our descriptions of the adult mind in so far as the adult still remains a child. This happens particularly in the case of moral psychology, since certain features of child morality always appear to be closely connected with a situation that from the first predominates in childhood (egocentrism, resulting from the inequality between the child and the adult surrounding which presses upon him) but which may recur in adult life, especially in the strictly conformist and geronto-cratic societies designated as primitive . . . . A given individual may, for example, have reached the stage of autonomy with regard to a certain group of rules, while his consciousness of these rules, together with the practice of certain more subtle rules, will be coloured with heteronomy. We cannot therefore speak of global or inclusive stages characterized as such by autonomy or heteronomy, but only of phases of heteronomy or autonomy which define a process that is repeated for each new set of rules or for each new plane of thought or reflection (pp. 77-78).

This qualification would appear to render meaningless the developmental interpretation applied to general conceptions of morality, and instead restrict its application to specific contents of morality as they are adopted successively throughout life. Though this is not the way in which Piaget's interpretation is usually understood, we find it more congenial to the present view: namely, that the *moral attitude* tends to be absolutistic, though what is valued — the content of morality — changes with experience. For any specific content that one may assess, sub-jects will differ in the degree of moral absolutism attached to it; and, for simple situations such as Piaget studied, the degree of absolutism tends to decrease with age (within the range from childhood through adolescence), for this is a period in which broader perspectives on games and truth-telling are being ac-quired. At the same time, however, new moral contents are probably being developed, which may partake of an absolutism no less than that which younger children apply to rules of the marble game. For instance, the notion that harmful acts should be judged on the basis of the wrongdoer's intent is regarded as a "mature" form of morality, but this very conception is gen-erally held as an absolute "good" by those who profess it. One *should* judge acts by their intent, because this is the right way. One should have respect for his fellow men because this is right (or because it is necessary for social living, which is an absolute good), and so on. The moral attitude of absolutism, universality, and ultimacy of the valued state may thus be applied to a variety of contents. With increasing experience, it may be relinquished (in favor of relativism) with respect to one domain of activity, but re-applied to another domain.

We have reported in Chapter 1 (p. 17) two studies of college students in which a majority of the subjects seemed to display various signs of absolutism in the way they professed their personal values in response to open questions. In another study (p. 31) substantial correlations were shown between the degree to which subjects admired twelve specified traits and the degree to which they regarded these as universal absolutes. Correlations cannot conveniently be reduced to numbers describing the percentage of absolutists, but the inference here is that most subjects tended to take an absolutistic view of their own moralities. Though these college students are hardly representative of the average adult population, their presumed exposure to more divergent values than are typically encountered by other people their age might make them more relativistic than average.

It seems, at least, that the proposed definition of values as moral absolutes has meaning for a substantial proportion of the college students assessed here. This calls into question any blanket interpretation of Piaget's data as indicating that the stage of moral realism is normally passed by early adolescence. It seems to persist, for a sizable number of people, well into maturity. The reasons for this can only be conjectured at present. In terms of Piaget's theory, one might infer that these college students were still under strong authoritative pressures from powerful adults (parents, teachers, housemothers, etc.), and had yet to move decidedly into a peer group of equal-status individuals. More plausibly, though, it may be proposed that, for the most part, the current peer groups tend to support the same sorts of values that the adult culture prescribes, or in any case to maintain their own values in an equally absolutistic fashion. There are undoubtedly differences among groups, and among individuals within a single group, concerning *what* values are important, but (for reasons that will be suggested presently) these differences either go unrecognized by the individual or else provide him with grounds for rejecting as morally defective the dissidents he knows about.

Basically, the very concept of "right" or "good" precludes, for many people, the legitimacy of alternative moralities. Either something is right or it isn't. The failure of respectable others to assent to the person's own values would deprive these values of their real, external character, which serves to justify the person's own orientation toward them. Just why should such a moral realism be an important component of many people's ethical conceptions? We shall speculate on some possible reasons by considering the functions that absolutistic values may perform for the individual's self-maintenance.

PSYCHOLOGICAL FUNCTIONS OF MORALITY

Perhaps the most significant function of moral values for human behavior is the capacity they lend the individual to sustain his endeavors in the face of adversity. A concept of morality may enable the person to remain temporarily independent of environmental reward, to contradict social norms or other situational pressures for a time. The quality of moral courage is often attributed to one who knows what is "right" and steadfastly pursues it. People tend to regard as important the things they do — at least some of the things. This attachment of value probably arises out of the activity itself but, once established, it serves to sustain the activity, even when it is no longer forced on one, no longer prized by one's associates, no longer a means to immediate prestige. The person convinced of the inherent value of an endeavor will tell himself — if he is religiously inclined — that, though temporal rewards may not be forthcoming, eternal rewards will be. The non-religious but historically oriented person will tell himself that, though he — like Gauguin or Schoenberg — may not be appreciated in his lifetime, posterity will recognize his contribution. This amounts to providing for oneself a kind of imaginary reference group whose approval one can anticipate at a time so far in the future that disappointment is impossible. The non-religious moralist will tell himself that he is abiding by his principles simply because they are right. All of these professions of faith serve to console people during unpopular pursuit of their values; no matter what the rationalization chosen, the value helps sustain consistent, directed action.

Some empirical support for this point may be extrapolated from a study of resistance to attitude change (Scott, 1959b). The attitudes of college students toward three campus issues were assessed, together with the evaluative considerations that subjects saw as relevant to them. Some subjects' attitudes toward the issues were quite consonant with the way in which they viewed them in relation to their own professed values; such subjects were called "cognitively consistent" (though a more appropriate term might have been "evaluatively consistent"). Another group showed less consistent attitudes, in that their opinions about a particular issue could not be well predicted from the way they saw the controversial event in relation to their values. When put under pressure to change their attitudes (by being induced to support in debate the side opposite from their own and then being rewarded for their performance), the consistent subjects tended not to change their original attitudes as much as the inconsistent ones did. This finding may be interpreted to indicate that values serve the function of sustaining attitudes that are subjectively relevant to them; by extension, one could suggest that behaviors based on value considerations would be more resistant to extinction than behaviors without such a value base.

Besides their energizing, sustaining qualities, personal values, by providing the concept of an "absolute" good, lend subjective rationality to man's behavior. If one thinks of himself as a rational being, one requires "objective" reasons for behaving as he does. Many utilitarian actions can be readily justified on empirical grounds; evidence from the person's senses informs him of the physical structure of the world to which he must respond. Other actions cannot be justified empirically, but the notion of a moral absolute provides a comparably "external" reality to which one "must" respond because that is the only reasonable thing to do.

On those occasions when one is able to match his actions to his values, he experiences the joy of moral virtue. Another, less complimentary, name for this emotion is self-righteousness. Conceiving a valued state of affairs as universally and absolutely good, the person is inclined to assume that his conception is shared, or potentially sharable, by all other human beings — unless they be morally defective. Just as the typical naive realist assumes that his sense impressions are shared by others, so the typical moral realist assumes that his conceptions of the desirable are available for others to recognize as well.

When Mark Twain observed that "nothing so needs reforming as other people's habits," he was referring to a common tendency among moralists to condemn others' actions more readily than their own. Few of the morally righteous are found to obey the Confucian admonition to "reform thyself first." The characteristically outward direction of moral blame may stem from at least three sources: first, from the need to maintain one's own self-esteem; second, from the relative ease of interpreting others' behaviors in morally unambiguous terms, since information about the circumstances of their violation is more fragmentary than it is for one's own violations; and third, from the fact that another's violation of a cherished value threatens to deprive the value of its absolute quality; this threat can be fended off if the violator is relegated to the category of the unholy, so that his violation of the value does not provide a respectable exception to its assumed universality. For all these reasons the greatest moral fervor may generally be directed against transgressors other than oneself, particularly against persons about whom one has little information, and to whom one has no particular reason to feel emotionally attached.

Morality may even help one to justify hurting those he loves — for instance, his children. Much of a child's behavior is bound to interfere with its parents' own goal-oriented action. Given the unequal power structure of the relationship, the parent can readily block the competitive behavior — if necessary, by punishing the child. But his own love for the child, combined with his self-concept as a rational being, demands that this thwarting be explained in terms other than self-interest. A reasonable justification is that the child's behavior is "wrong," and must be stopped. The temporary hurt of punishment is justified on the ground that it will benefit the child in the long run, because it will lead to some desirable state of affairs. Without such an absolute justification, the parent would be forced to admit that his own action was selfish and his love for the child was less strong than self-love. Value-inspired justification of one's own acts may thus serve to maintain one's self-picture as a rational, progeny-loving being.

Not only, therefore, are dependent children subject to an absolutistic morality through subordination to more powerful adults, but the controlling adults themselves may continue to believe in the absolute goodness of the value, because this belief helps justify occasional punitive actions toward their beloved children. Modifying Piaget's formulation, then, we may propose that moral realism is sustained first by subordination in a dependent relationship, and later through the exercise of omnipotent control over others, where justification of one's control procedures is implicitly demanded. Of course, there are available to the average person, besides such relationships of subordination and absolute control, a number of equal-status relationships, where standards of conduct have to be worked out on the basis of reciprocity (bargaining). But many people find it possible to avoid such relationships for the most part, and thus can maintain a fairly absolutistic view of whatever morality they adhere to.

INDIVIDUAL SOURCES AND
CULTURAL SOURCES

Thus far, we have considered the acquisition of values as essentially a matter of individual learning. It has been proposed that the person acquires, via social reinforcements, his concepts of desirable states, and that these may come to be interpreted by him as absolutes, partly because he seems to find them universally professed, partly as a consequence of the kinds of power relationships he habitually participates in. In addition, an absolutistic morality is seen to serve certain functions for self-maintenance — in the stabilization and rationalization of the person's behavior.

This explanation, insofar as it presumes learning mechanisms, simply asserts that the individual will acquire whatever values are reinforced in his social environment. It does not confront the problem of how the surrounding values came to be — of why one group's values are different from another's. This question is difficult to answer in a historical way, for it apparently leads to an infinite regress: The group members acquired their values from their own socializing agents, and so on back through time. Such an explanation is unsatisfactory because of its redundancy; furthermore, it implies that individuals have a single dominant source of values (usually during childhood), and do not change these values once they are internalized. This degree of stability from childhood through adulthood is improbable, unless later influences remain fairly constant in value-orientation; one must still account for the constancy of later influences.

Perhaps because sociologists can rarely observe the origins of the group phenomena they study, they tend to seek reasons for persisting patterns in the contemporary consequences of those patterns for the group and its members. Such a functional approach to the explanation of behavior may add new understandings, because it focuses on the adaptive significance of behavior patterns. It suggests that behaviors will persist only insofar as they are functional for the behaving entity. From a psychologist's perspective, the behaving entity is an individual person. From the sociologist's perspective, it is a collectivity. For either unit of analysis, one may designate two broad classes of functional requisites — that is, needs or requirements of the behaving unit. They are performance and maintenance. Performance refers to the unit's impact on its surround. The most important surround for a social man is other people. A group is surrounded by other, larger collectivities — ultimately, by a geographical and physical environment; it must adapt to these.

Maintenance of an individual person is ordinarily interpreted largely in terms of need satisfaction, but it may also include preservation of an established habit repertory, a self-concept, an ego-ideal, and so on. Maintenance of a social system consists, analogously, in preserving intact those shared interpersonal orientations designated as social norms and role systems.

SOCIAL FUNCTIONS OF MORALITY

Within a social functional analysis, one would seek the contemporary sources of collective values in the functions they serve for group performance and maintenance. One would ask, "What do these particular values permit the group to do, that it could not do without them? How do these values facilitate the group's survival and the performance of its tasks?" At a general level, applicable to nearly all groups, one might say that a shared value system provides a group, first of all, with a *raison d'être* — a justification for its separate definition, an appeal for recruiting new members, a "cause" that orients its members toward it. This is essentially a maintenance function, for the professed morality serves to perpetuate the group.

A shared morality also serves to deter deviant behavior

among members, for it induces them to *want* to do that which they *must* do in order to avoid punitive sanctions. As Clyde Kluckhohn (1951) has put it: "A social life and living in a social world both require standards 'within' the individual and standards roughly agreed upon by individuals who live and work together. There can be no personal security and no stability of social organization unless random carelessness, irresponsibility, and purely impulsive behavior are restrained in terms of private and group codes" (p. 400). Though additional mechanisms of social control are normally provided too, it is hard to imagine one as efficient for a group as common values internalized in all members. These discourage potential violations of norms before they occur, and lessen the need for special procedures for detecting and punishing actual deviancy.

Another group-maintaining function of shared values is the limitation of intra-group conflict. Though common motives may impel members to compete for limited resources, and incompatible motives may direct them toward conflict, the shared value system prescribes priorities among goals and sets standards of appropriateness for selecting means to attain the goals. If members accept these standards as absolutes, their common values can exert more influence on their behaviors than the potentially conflicting motives do.

Shared values also serve to justify sanctions against deviants. If, in a small minority of members, disruptive behavior should appear, the majority can point to an alleged violation of shared values in confident expectation of enlisting the moral indignation of the entire group, so that punishment of the offender will be sanctioned. A source of major threat may be eliminated, either through execution or permanent incarceration; minor violators may be subjected to rehabilitative measures, or more commonly to some form of punishment through social isolation. The ease with which shared values permit the assignment of blame, and distinguish the "guilty" from the "innocent," means that isolated disruptive action can be choked off without any essential alteration of the institutional structure. It is unnecessary to spread blame in all directions or to demand corrective action on a large scale.

In all these ways, then, shared values in a society or group promote the stability and continuity of the group. This does not mean, however, that they cannot also be used as instruments of change. A great many social practices arise in a rather unplanned way, as unintended consequences of other actions, and hence may not be seen from the start as having any particular moral significance. However, the unintended conditions may threaten the self-interest of a sizable number of less powerful members, and also become a focus of concern for people who are prepared to act on the basis of relatively disinterested values. Urban slums, which arose as a consequence of industrialization and migration, posed a condition that had been neither intended nor anticipated; it was only after they were well established that their moral significance became apparent.

Direct action to alter the offending conditions is probably most potently impelled by self-interest of the affected persons. But such persons may be incapable of devising appropriate corrective measures — because they are unaware of them or lack the power and skills to carry them out. If the deprived group, by itself, were to institute corrective action, this action might neglect or infringe upon other community interests whose welfare was not adequately considered because of the narrowness of the planners' perspective. In his frustrated state, the deprived person is perhaps even less capable than he might otherwise be of planning remedial action that would reconcile, rather than exacerbate, conflicting interests.

Though self-interest may provide the strongest motivation to action, a value-interest is at least capable of generating support for another's cause. If the cause can be framed in moral terms, other community members may be stirred to concerted action themselves, provided the effort is not too great or the consequences to themselves too dangerous. If well informed people of secure status, broad perspective, and social power can be enlisted in a cause, the actions they propose are more likely to be solution-oriented, rather than frustration-generated, and to be effective in solving the problem, because they take account of a greater variety of societal interests and because they can command the assent, on moral grounds, of the preponderance of the community. It is in this way that shared values may, on occasion, serve the ends of social change, rather than those of social stability. Needless to say, there is a limit to the scope of such peaceful change. It must generally deal with a morally offensive problem that was created without intent of the dominant group, and the solution proposed must be one that does not greatly disturb other powerful interests.

The social functions of values are closely interwoven with their psychological functions. The psychological impetus of morality depends, in part, on its social significance, and the reverse is equally true. Only through evidence of consistent responses from others can the individual arrive at, or maintain, his impressions of the universality and absoluteness of his own values. Take away the consensual reactions from the earliest periods of socialization onward, and the moral attitude is deprived of its very basis for development. The guilt that accompanies value violation, and the self-righteousness that accompanies value conformity, both presumably reflect anticipation of sanctions or rewards from one's reference group; this anticipation is warranted to the extent that the value is in fact shared. Violation of a community value elicits concerted social sanctions in part, presumably, because the violation threatens the majority members' concept of an absolute, which has served to sustain their own behaviors and self-concepts. Values can be effective instruments for ameliorative social action largely because the sense of right of individual moralists is outraged by the offending conditions. This outrage can be sustained and translated into effective action only if the relevant values are widely shared in the community.

Such considerations as these are relevant to the question why *some sort* of morality is likely to be shared by members of any social group: A shared morality serves the function of group maintenance, no matter what the group's external purposes may be. But in order to deal with the fact of differences in value content from one group to another, one must consider the different problems they face and the different activities they perform in order to meet the needs of their members and clientele.

From a functional point of view, one would say that distinctive values arise out of those adaptive activities which characterize a group; for values serve to justify the members' actions to themselves and to sustain their endeavors on behalf of the adaptive function. The value that businessmen place on profit justifies their dedication to money-making, just as a college professor's evaluative emphasis on knowledge, skills, and achievement justifies his overt orientation toward the acquisition and dissemination of knowledge.

A campus fraternity's functions are rather diffuse and inexplicit. They may be described by the organization's charter in terms of "character development," by some alumni and current members in terms of developing interpersonal skills, by other members in terms of providing board and room in a congenial group. Basic to these stated objectives would seem to be the satisfaction of interpersonal needs of its membership. Therefore, it is to be expected that fraternity members will value interpersonal relations to a pre-eminent degree. In this kind of organization, the members themselves constitute the clientele for which the services of the organization are performed. Group maintenance and performance functions are thus nearly identical, in that simply by maintaining the internal system (i.e., the group structure), the external system (consisting of the individual members' needs) is served.

This is not to say that the value systems of these various institutions — business, academic, and social — are contradictory. To a very large degree each of them is dependent on the others, and their personnel overlap to some extent. They are all em-

bedded in a wider culture that tends to emphasize certain pervasive values. So one group's dominant values will rarely be
explicitly contradicted by another group. Rather, the different
organizations will tend to develop differences in emphases,
which mean that if a conflict is posed, choice of action will be
in the direction of the particular group's dominant pattern.

Concerning the social sources of morality, then, we may
propose that the contents of values are intimately related to the
group's performance functions. What the group is explicitly
set up to do, or what it actually accomplishes for its clientele, will
presumably be adopted as values by its membership. Treating
these values as absolutes serves the function of group maintenance
in that contributory activities can be rewarded, and disruptive
activities punished, "for just cause."

LIMITATIONS OF A FUNCTIONAL ANALYSIS

In order to account for the persistence of values within an
individual or group, we have repeatedly appealed to functional
explanations — asserting that values are maintained because they
serve the needs (or functional requirements) of the behaving
system, be it an individual or a group. Such an explanation appears unsatisfactory from traditional conceptions of causation,
because it seems to posit the "cause" of an event in its consequences. When one attempts to explain X on the ground that it
contributes to Y, he is asserting two kinds of causation. On the
one hand, he proposes that X causes Y, e.g., that an absolutistic
morality (X) enables the person to maintain his self-concept as
a rational being (Y), or that a shared morality (X) enables the
group to deter deviancy (Y). More important, however, such
functional statements imply that the *reason* X occurs is that it
contributes to Y—that Y, in a sense, causes X, for without Y
as a consequence there would be no need for X.

Since "cause and effect" is essentially a human formulation,
humans can construct the relationship in any way they wish;

there is no inherent reason why a cause must temporally precede its effect. But a more essential problem lies in the amenability of functional propositions to empirical testing. An X-causes-Y statement can, in principle, be investigated experimentally by manipulating X to note its effect on Y. But the reverse, Y-causes-X, proposition — which constitutes the essence of functional analysis — is less easily tested. One might, in straightforward fashion, propose a manipulation of the consequent, Y, to see what effect this would have on the antecedent, X. This is impossible to do for some Ys, for they deal with the very maintenance of the system. If the system were eliminated, its component Xs would be necessarily eliminated as well, and the empirical proposition would immediately become an experimental tautology.

Other Ys are, in principle, manipulable without contaminating the X components. One may, for instance, alter the performance functions of a group — change it, say, from a profit-making corporation to a skill-imparting educational institution — and see what impact this change has on the values of its members. Aside from the practical difficulty of such a manipulation, it is still likely to prove ambiguous as far as functional theories are concerned, because of an escape clause built into most of them. Most functionalists would maintain that a given structure (X) may serve many different functions (Ys), so that altering one function will not necessarily alter the structure that contributed to it. This is an unsatisfactory formulation for purposes of experimental testing. Applied to an organization's dominant values, it might assert that the values would not necessarily disappear when the function they apparently serve is eliminated, for they may still serve some other function (e.g., for the individual members, rather than for the organization as a whole, or for the larger society in which the institution is embedded).

Though recognizing this defect of a functional analysis, we shall not attempt to patch it up here. In fact, no experimental manipulation of functions was attempted in the present research on fraternities and sororities. Rather, the approach was one of "systematic assessment" (see Scott & Wertheimer, 1962), in which groups were taken as they were found. Given the postulated function of fraternities and sororities — to further interpersonal relations of their members — it was simply predicted that various processes within these organizations — such as recruitment, status differentiation, maintenance of member loyalties, influence, and attrition — would reflect this function in the kinds of values they brought into play.

VALUE CONFLICT

This functional analysis has implied the presence of compatible values, both within the individual and among individuals of a given social group. But such conditions are unlikely to obtain to more than a moderate degree, given the fact that an individual's experiences are complex and only partially interconnected, and given also that one person's experiences are not completely shared with all other members of his group. People may thus develop quite unrelated, or even antithetical, values, which may generate conflict at either an intrapersonal or an interpersonal level. The expression "conflict of values" is elliptical, for it is actions that conflict, not values.

Intra-individual Conflict

Any single action of the individual is potentially relevant to several different value states, furthering one and impeding another. An action that might facilitate one value precludes other action pursuant to a different value. In circumstances requiring choice, intra-individual conflict may occur, particularly for choices interpreted as morally relevant, because the person views each value as an "absolute" that "ought" to be pursued. The person with too many different values to contend with may become indecisive, or even perhaps be driven to a neurotic anxiety over the impossibility of pursuing all of them.

But cognitive mechanisms are usually available for reducing

the conflict. Aside from the drastic solution of relinquishing the moral absoluteness of one of the conflicting considerations, the person may so narrow the focus for interpreting a decision that it becomes subjectively relevant to a single value; then the selection among alternatives is readily made. A variety of evaluative bases for justifying or condemning any act are generally available in the person's culture. By appropriate narrowing of focus, one may select that value which supports a decision he is compelled to make on other grounds (such as self-interest or normative pressures from a reference group). This formulation implies that the value is generally a tool of exigencies, and indeed this would appear to be a prevalent solution to intra-individual conflict, particularly among persons who are widely acquainted with diverse cultural values, and who are sufficiently facile of wit to interpret the alternatives opportunistically.

There are, of course, other circumstances in which morality (rather, a particular morality) wins out, by the person's suppression of self-interest (or by altering his definition of self-interest, if that is possible), by his ability to convince the reference group of the propriety of his favored action, or by his determination to ignore the reference group's pressure. Needless to say, prolonged pursuit of an idiosyncratic morality, in conflict with self-interest (as, for example, in fasting for a political end) or in conflict with group standards, will threaten the individual's biological survival or his continued social membership. Consequently, no person has unlimited opportunity to pursue an idiosyncratic morality, and the man concerned with his own survival as a biological and social organism will select the occasions for such pursuit carefully.

Social Conflict

Even in a culture as homogeneous as that of a university student body, notions of the desirable are by no means universally shared. Florence Kluckhohn (1954) has described this diversity in terms of dominant, variant, and deviant values — dominant values being those held by a majority of the group or by the most prestigious elite, variant values those which are adhered to by minority segments and permitted by the majority, deviant values those which are generally disallowed and, when detected, punished. Such a formulation would appear to express the perspective of the majority, or elite, who define the "dominant" values; dominance is thus only a statistical concept or a concept that depends on the status of the group that holds the value. From the standpoint of a minority sub-group, the designations may be quite different: What is a variant or deviant value from the elite's standpoint may be dominant within the sub-group. In other words, except in terms of a statistical average, dominance, variance, and deviance do not describe any particular valued state of affairs; rather they characterize a particular person's view of the state. The dimension of values previously proposed (p. 13), degree of absoluteness, is intended to represent this aspect of the person's subjective view of the required, permissible, or proscribed nature of any behavior.

Given intra-cultural diversity of values, any single event may be evaluated quite differently by various people, depending on which values they choose to bring to bear. Conflict will typically center upon the event itself (an action or decision), rather than upon the surrounding values. To the extent that there is an overriding consensus concerning the legitimacy of diverse values, or to the extent that disputants are concerned over mutual face-saving, they will be unlikely to oppose one another's values directly, but instead will argue about the differential relevance of various values to the issue. Thus, in a relatively consensual society (one in which certain values are legitimized, though not necessarily espoused, by most members), "value conflict" does not take the form of a direct confrontation of moralities. One disputant will rarely deny another's value. Rather, he will affirm the pre-eminent relevance of a different value. The most one will say is that his opponent's value is not central to the issue, or is offset by other considerations—not that it is "wrong."

In the twelve value scales developed for the present research (see Appendix A), subjects were to indicate if they always admired each trait, if they always disliked it, or if it depended on the situation whether or not they admired the trait. They rarely checked the "always dislike" category, but instead indicated their indifference to a trait by checking the "depends" response. In another part of the questionnaire, a summary statement of each value (see p. 24) was presented with instructions to rate it on a five-point scale (admire very much, admire somewhat, neither admire nor dislike, dislike somewhat, dislike very much). The two "dislike" categories were infrequently used, and the mean ratings for all of the values were above the scale midpoint (3) — 11 of them substantially so (see Table 6). Thus, there was little tendency in this population to reject explicitly any of the twelve values; instead, they all seemed to enjoy a fair degree of "cultural legitimacy," in the sense that even those individuals who did not themselves profess a particular value usually expressed a tolerance for it.

In a community whose members have exceedingly diverse

TABLE 6
MEAN RATINGS OF
SUMMARY VALUE STATEMENTS

Value	Mean Rating[a]
Social skills	1.27
Status	1.51
Creativity	1.63
Academic achievement	1.75
Loyalty	1.78
Physical development	1.81
Religiousness	1.85
Self-control	2.03
Intellectualism	2.04
Honesty	2.08
Kindness	2.11
Independence	2.52

[a]Low numbers indicate high value strength (admiration) on the five-point rating scale; 3 is the scale mid-point.

interests and backgrounds, and where value diversity is not so legitimized, a more direct form of "value conflict" may appear, in which one participant to a dispute challenges another's value. Such a circumstance does not represent a marked discontinuity from the relatively consensual state just described; rather it is a matter of extreme degree. (In fact, even in a relatively consensual culture, if one sub-group consistently denies the relevance for successive decisions of the values that another group espouses, the resulting conflict will be indistinguishable from the direct opposition of values.)

In the face of such explicit value conflict, it is the subjective absoluteness of each value for its defender that heightens the dispute to extremes of acrimony and distrust. Each disputant has difficulty understanding how the other can fail to recognize the self-evident absolute; unwitting or purposeful moral distortion seems to provide the only explanation. Conflicts between nations seem to develop readily into such a moral confrontation. Since the members have grown up in different cultures, faced with different problems of adaptation, the contents of their dominant values are likely to differ in major ways. For an American capitalist, for example, individual freedom is an absolute good, and revolutionary violence an absolute bad. By contrast, a Russian communist will see creation or perpetuation of underprivileged classes as absolutely wrong and distribution of wealth according to need as absolutely right. At this point, there is no explicit value conflict, but simply an emphasis on different goals—perhaps complementary or orthogonal, rather than antithetical. However, the former antagonist is apt to view capitalism as an essential means toward attainment of his goals, whereas the latter will see communism as an indispensable means to his value realization. At this point, the cathexis on unique means introduces, in effect, two value-like alternatives that are necessarily incompatible, and an impasse is reached. The ultimate values (individual freedom vs. distribution of wealth) are, by extension, deemed inconsistent, and each side accuses the other of immorality by its standards.

With the conflict defined in moral terms, a resolution becomes impossible without one or the other's morality being relinquished.

Within a relatively homogeneous culture, with centralized monopoly of the means of violence, morality exerts a stabilizing influence, an efficient mechanism for maintaining community integration. But in a heterogeneous culture, with dispersed control of the means of violence, morality may exacerbate the disruptive forces that inhere in normal conflict of interest, because differing conceptions of the desirable are treated by their protagonists as absolutes from which there can be no retreat, over which there can be no compromise. This conflict of absolutes can only be avoided if the major opponents adhere to a superordinate value that asserts the legitimacy of alternative moralities. Such a belief would appear unreasonable to some. Yet the absoluteness of any value is only an apparent quality for its host, which, when pressed under hypothetical circumstances, is bound to evaporate. So an absolute that over-rides other absolutes is certainly not psychologically impossible.

A passionate, committed ideologist, who will not tolerate the pursuit by others of values different from his own when such values consistently lead to incompatible actions, will contribute to the magnification of conflict in the community, and thus threaten its stability. There is, of course, no inherent reason why stability of the social structure should be viewed as a necessity. Passionate, committed ideologists may be responsible for changes that future generations will agree have been desirable. Their single-minded pursuit of a central value may, if successful, create an imbalance in the society which is subsequently rectified by another successful single-minded absolutist, and the resulting state may permit the easier pursuit of many different legitimate values.

ALTERNATIVES TO MORALITY

The persistence of morality as an individual and cultural process has been interpreted by reference to certain alleged functions that it performs for the maintenance of personality and social systems. Basically, values enable a person to view his own behavior as rational, and they justify concerted action to stabilize the social structure. Admittedly, these are not absolutely essential functions, and it would be easy to dispense (theoretically) with values simply by positing personality and social systems in which these functions need not be performed. Man might hypothetically (even actually) be constructed so as not to require rational reasons for his behavior: He could be taught to look for explanations in antecedent circumstances, rather than intended consequences, of his actions. A social system might be constructed primarily as an adaptive arrangement aimed at flexibility and change, rather than at self-maintenance. But these are not men and society as we know them, and such wishing away of the functions seems altogether too glib. Morality may be regarded as a fairly successful mechanism for individual and societal maintenance. It is by no means an exclusively appropriate mechanism, however; other processes may be found which can fulfill essentially similar functions.

Rational Hedonism and Opportunism

One psychologically feasible substitute for morality is a conscious, purposeful hedonism, in which the individual explicitly undertakes to maximize his own motive satisfaction and assumes that others will do the same. This amounts to phenomenological acceptance of what is now regarded by many psychologists and economists as describing the fundamental motivating principle of individual and collective mankind. No justification of motives is sought; they are simply accepted as given (whether inborn or acquired) in the present individual. The conscious intent to satisfy these motives provides sufficient rationalization for one's own actions. An irrational identification with one's children or with other fellow humans may even be accommodated within this motive pattern; all that is required is recognition of this feeling and an explicit attempt to take it into account as one of the motives to be satisfied in planning one's actions.

The basic criterion against which action is assessed under such a non-morality is its effectiveness in attaining the intended goals. Long-run, as well as short-run, satisfaction must be taken into account, and the individual must be prepared for erroneous predictions caused by insufficient information about alternative means and unanticipated consequences of the chosen course. Thus, there is ample room for individual growth and broadening under this orientation; there is also no intrinsic reason why opportunistic hedonists should not come to regard consideration for the evident motives of others as an indispensable means to their own motive satisfaction.

The function of social stability could, in principle, be achieved in a society of opportunistic hedonists, through an explicit recognition of the symbiotic interdependence of group members, and through the attempt to reconcile conflict in such a way that motive satisfaction could be maximally widespread. This would consist, essentially, of political resolutions to conflict. Such a mode of conflict management occurs constantly in legislative bodies and other political institutions: The legitimacy of the contending interests is seldom questioned; rather a solution is sought (e.g., in "pork-barrel" appropriation bills) which will satisfy all interests to the utmost. It has been said that morality cannot be found among thieves and prostitutes. This is far from the case, if the present conception of morality be accepted. But the place where one is less likely to find morality is among politicians, whose central concern is with maintaining power through gratification of relevant interests, rather than with judging the legitimacy of those interests.

It is clear, however, that the motives of some individuals are incompatible with such a hedonistic symbiosis — for example, the desire to attain unlimited power over all other men or the wish to destroy life and property of others. It takes considerable intellectual capacity and wide experience to recognize the relevance of other persons' interests for one's own motive satisfaction and, especially, to devise courses of action that will promote one's self-interest without threatening others'. There are not enough people in any group who are capable of such reasonable fore-thought to make a rational symbiosis work by itself. Some other social mechanism must be provided to control conspicuous deviants who are not symbiotically oriented. One such mechanism is a hierarchical power differentiation, with threat of punishment for encroaching on a superior's self-interest. Something like this is found in most societies, but it doesn't work too well if power is distributed widely, and it may even be quite unstable if there is unregulated competition for power.

A social stabilizer which may be effective under various forms of power distribution is the inculcation in all group members of an attitude which encourages their taking into account others' self-interests in pursuit of their own motive satisfaction. This amounts to a morality to the extent that it asserts the absolute legitimacy of other's interests; but the attitude may also be taught simply as a sophisticated hedonism — the generalized expectation that others' expressions of self-interest might possibly be relevant for one's own motive satisfaction, so that it would be prudent at least to understand them, and to take them into account when convenient.

Postulational Morality

Another alternative to an absolute moral ethic is the inculcation in people of the habits of postulational thinking. If, instead of learning that certain favored states are "good," the individual is taught to inquire, "Good for what?", he will ultimately be faced with the need to clarify his own assumptions about the ultimate state that is to be achieved through moral behavior. But his attitude toward this state need not be that it *is* an absolute, universal, and final end; rather he will tentatively choose to regard it so, in order to undertake consistent, relevant action. Thus, the need to appear rational to oneself may be filled by justifying one's actions on the basis of postulates and by justifying the tentative nature of the postulates by admitting insufficient thought or inadequate information about alternative states.

In social decisions, the postulates would generally refer to some existing or desired social structure. One would propose, for example, that "Our ultimate goal here is to maintain an academic institution in which people seek truth. Moral codes consonant with this aim include the promotion of free inquiry, the reward of knowledge acquisition, and the prohibition of attempts to gain status through other means." Such a proposed morality represents a logical derivation, based on available knowledge, of functional requisites for the social structure that is postulated as an end-state to be maintained (or created). Of course, the derivations may be in error, but they can be checked, either through systematic experimental inquiry or through informal experience with the consequences of the morality for the institution.

Under such a postulational morality, the mechanisms for social control and social change would appear little different from those found under an absolutistic morality, with respect to people who remain within the social system. But the maintainers of the system would be more likely to recognize the postulational, non-absolute nature of their morality, and hence to banish offenders or transfer them to other social structures as a defense against normative erosion. Perhaps people would also give thought to the creation of different social structures in which alternative moralities would be appropriate, so that a deviant in one might find adjustment in another. It is possible that quite distinct social structures could readily exist in the same community, given that the participating individuals (1) treat their circumstances as postulates, (2) have freedom of movement to seek social structures with moralities more congenial to themselves, and (3) have the opportunity to invent new structures under different postulational systems where alternative moralities may prevail. The alternative moralities of alien societies would have to be accepted just enough to permit necessary symbiotic interaction with them.

In any culture one is likely to find, along with moral processes, at least rudimentary forms of alternative mechanisms such as these. They may be deemed alternatives to the extent that they are capable of filling the essential psychological and social functions that morality fills. Whether they *could* fill these as well, or whether morality is indeed a necessary feature of human social life, cannot possibly be decided on the basis of present knowledge. But the social planner, as well as the social scientist, might well remain alert to the emergence of such alternative guidance and control mechanisms, so that their potential significance as functional substitutes for a (temporarily or permanently) vanished morality is not overlooked.

SUMMARY

A variety of approaches to "explaining" the appearance of human morality have been considered. Some of these explanations refer to the individual's acquisition of particular value contents; others refer to the reasons why any particular content is regarded by the person as a universal and absolute good. Reasons may be sought in the individual's own history of learning from social groups that are important to him; they may also be sought in the functions that the "moral attitude" and particular moral contents fill for the group that transmits the values.

It has been assumed, broadly, that any value content may be acquired by an individual, given sufficiently consistent reinforcement from his social surround. The very fact of participating in an activity seems to be sufficient for many people to develop a positive attitude toward it. But the reason why this positive cathexis should be converted into an absolute, universal "ought" is obscure. A large number of people evidently do regard their own evaluative standards as absolutes which others ought to share. It has been proposed that this "moral attitude" serves certain functions for the individual's self-maintenance, helping to support his self-concept as a rational human being and helping to justify the hurt he must often cause others.

It is also commonly contended that internalized standards of right and wrong serve the functions of group maintenance and adaptation. They help a group to justify its own existence and activities; they help to deter deviancy and to justify the application of sanctions when deviancy does occur.

These views of morality as serving the functions of self-maintenance and group maintenance inevitably assign a subordinate position to moral processes — conceiving them as consequences of individual and collective efforts at adaptation. Yet, once established, conceptions of morality may serve to guide and sustain either individual or collective activity, thus becoming determining factors in their own right. An individual, guided by a concept of absolute good, is in a position to reward himself for conformity to his own standard, and thus to sustain activity in pursuit of that standard even in the face of adverse circumstances, and in the absence of group approval. Just how such an independent, self-sufficient morality comes about, and the conditions that may help to maintain or extinguish it, are problems that need further study.

CHAPTER 3

PERSONAL VALUES IN THE
COLLEGE ENVIRONMENT

There are enormous differences among American colleges — differences in size, nature and quality of academic programs, competence and dedication of staffs, excellence of students, culture of the academic community, and so forth. The University of Colorado, where the present research was undertaken, can scarcely be taken to represent this diversity — nor could any other single institution. Yet in many respects it shares the characteristics of other large, state-supported universities with heterogeneous student bodies and diverse functions.

The dominant function of a university would be described by most as the acquisition and dissemination of knowledge. But, like so many other large institutions in a complex society, the university incorporates a number of programs and activities quite tangential to its main focus. Since a large proportion of the students live on campus or in boarding houses away from home, it is not surprising to find the university filling for them many features of "total human life" which they might have continued to find at home. Group living, recreation, mating and dating, food, health, and religious services, personal counseling — these and many other activities that, for most adults, would normally be scattered throughout a variety of social institutions — are all found on campus, under the more or less direct supervision of the university administration.

This accretion of diverse functions within the scope of a

single large institution provides a temporary delay in the maturing adolescent's weaning toward the larger, complex society with its more highly differentiated institutions. From the students' perspectives, such a multi-functional institution may help prevent feelings of fragmentation and anomia which might result if they were forced to gratify their diverse needs in many different places. From the university's perspective, this arrangement approximates the condition of a "total institution" (cf. Goffman, 1961), with diffuse responsibility for the welfare of its inhabitants and immense potential for shaping their lives and personalities.

Not all colleges are like this. In one direction of departure are many city colleges and technical schools, which function essentially as commuter colleges and hence are more restricted in the amount and scope of contact with students. In the other direction of departure are the small community colleges, often under religious auspices, with more homogeneous clientele and more integrated programs of activity in which larger proportions of the student body participate.

With an undergraduate enrollment of about 8,000 and a total student body of over 12,000, the University of Colorado has a tremendous diversity of orientations among its students, and varying proportions of them are involved in the different aspects of campus life.

VALUE CHANGE IN COLLEGE

In a sense, any college or university represents an extension into young adult life of the period of intensive socialization that in former times or in other societies would have terminated in late childhood. Thus, it should provide ample opportunity for continued development and change of personal values. According to the view proposed in the preceding chapter, the contents of values are subject to change throughout life, given a change in the circumstances to which the person must adapt. Particularly within an almost-total institution of enforced socialization, the impact on the members' values might be expected to be more pronounced than in other circumstances of adult life.

Yet the large body of research evidence on value changes in college reviewed by Jacob (1957) led him to conclude:

This study has not discerned significant changes in student values which can be attributed directly either to the character of the curriculum or to the basic courses in social science which students take as part of their general education (p. 5).

The weight of evidence indicates that actually very little change occurs during college in the essential standards by which students govern their lives. The values with which they arrive, and which are integral elements of their personality, are still there when most students leave (p. 53).

On the face of it, this conclusion seems to contradict flatly the common-sense expectations of most educators and community members, as well as the assumptions underlying the present investigation. Before accepting the conclusion, however, it would be well to note two kinds of limitations in the studies reviewed by Jacob — relating to the kinds of changes measured and to the groups in which these changes were sought.

Many of the studies used the Allport-Vernon Study of Values, or the American Council on Education's Inventory of Beliefs, or the Cornell Values Survey as the instrument for measuring the impact of college. These are quite heterogeneous in content, measuring a variety of attitudes and beliefs (most of them not "values" in the present sense), in which there is no particular reason to expect change during college. College curricula are not normally designed explicitly to affect students' orientations along the dimensions that these instruments measure.

A later review by Webster, Freedman, and Heist (1962) finds some tendency toward decrease in "religious value" during college; perhaps this reflects most college faculties' rationalist approach to their subject matter, which is somewhat antithetical to traditional religious orientations tapped by the measures used.

These authors also found a tendency toward reduction in eth-

77

nocentrism, usually measured by the California E scale (Adorno, et al., 1950). This trend may represent in part an increasing skepticism that results in less willingness to agree to any extreme stereotyping statement of the kind included in the E scale, but it is also reasonable to infer that the college experience actually does tend to increase students' tolerance of ethnic differences. Religious heterodoxy and ethnic tolerance probably characterize the average faculty viewpoint at most colleges. On the other hand, it is unlikely that a major portion of their instruction is devoted to the propagation of these views. Thus, changes in these attitudes are probably not as great as might be achieved if the college intellectual climates were oriented specifically to induce such changes in students.

If substantial value changes are to be found, they must be measured along dimensions that, a priori, are likely to be affected by the particular college environment. In Newcomb's (1943) investigation of the impact of Bennington College on its students during the 1930's, he constructed a scale aimed at measuring the general attitude of "liberalism" (Newcomb referred to it as "non-conservatism"). This scale was peculiarly appropriate to the Bennington setting of that time, because a well-advertised "liberal" ideology pervaded the entire campus, students and faculty alike; at the same time, Bennington tended to recruit new members (i.e., freshman students) from more conservative backgrounds. Thus, there was considerable room for movement and a fairly concerted effort to bring it about. In fact, Newcomb found rather consistent (though small) mean shifts in a non-conservative direction the longer the students remained in school.

It is unlikely that many colleges today would be found to exert the kind of "liberalizing" influence found at Bennington in the thirties. In fact, the very meaning of "liberalism" is obscure at the present time, for the term is used by different people to refer to quite different attitudes that do not hang together very closely. Nevertheless, the strategy of assessment used in that study should remain applicable: The researcher must seek changes in specific values (or attitudes) that are fairly uniformly stressed by the college in a direction away from where the students begin. The particular values that fit this criterion might be expected to differ from one college to another.

This brings up the second qualification that must be applied to the studies reviewed by Jacob—referring to the groups in which value changes were sought. Almost without exception, these were studies of the average impact of formal educational processes — of teachers, teaching methods, social science curricula, and complete university cultures on all students exposed to them. It is possible that these are not the appropriate units within which to seek systematic value changes.

In a large university, campus life is exceedingly complex. Though academic affairs may consume the single largest portion of students' waking hours, a variety of subsidiary activities invite their attention: Fraternities, coop houses, recreational programs, religious activities, the college newspaper, the student senate, and so forth. Though no one student participates in all of these, the activities that he does get involved in are likely to provide potent sources of values for him. Intense involvement and immediate interpersonal gratification may be more readily available here than in the more formal aspects of the academic curriculum. Most individual teachers, courses, or teaching methods contact students for only a minor portion of their time. These are ordinarily not aimed explicitly at ideological indoctrination, but even when they are, the ideology of one source will be contradicted by that of another. Except in a small, homogeneous campus, the total college experience presents such a variety of potential value-influencers that the effect of any one of these on the total student body — or even on the sub-group exposed to it — is likely to be cancelled out by competing forces.

Of course, students do not expose themselves indiscriminately to all these sources of influence. Their pre-existing values may direct a purposeful orientation toward one source; a chance encounter may arouse interest and intense involvement in an activity which thereby becomes a new source of value influence. But these individually determined directions of influence cannot be well predicted from the student's membership in transient or arbitrarily determined groups such as classes or curriculum programs. While a small proportion of the exposed students are intensely stimulated by a particular teacher or course, the remainder are relatively unaffected by it, for their dominant orientation is toward other sources of influence.

There is tentative evidence from the present study that the values of students *do* change during a single year at the University of Colorado. Table 7 presents the aggregate data from all subjects in the present longitudinal study ($n=462$) who remained in the same status — Greek or Independent — throughout the year and were still enrolled in school the following fall. The degree of similarity between their pretest and posttest values is

TABLE 7

STABILITIES OF VALUE SCORES OVER A ONE-YEAR INTERVAL
AND OVER A TWO-WEEK INTERVAL

	Intra-class Correlations between Test and Retest		
	(1)		*(2)*
	One Year		*Two Weeks*
	Apart		*Apart*
Value	*($n = 462$)*		*($n = 208$)*
Intellectualism	.55		.63
Kindness	.43	**	.68
Social skills	.50	**	.73
Loyalty	.44	*	.57
Academic achievement	.45	**	.67
Physical development	.53	**	.71
Status	.41	**	.70
Honesty	.41	**	.72
Religiousness	.64	**	.77
Self-control	.53	**	.72
Creativity	.43	**	.66
Independence	.42	**	.73

* Adjacent columns significantly different at $\alpha < .05$ (via z transformations).
**Adjacent columns significantly different at $\alpha < .001$.

reported by the intra-class correlation coefficients in the first column. These may be compared with the reliability coefficients of Column 2, which represent intra-class correlations based on a two-week interval between test and retest administered to a General Psychology class.[1] In nearly all cases the first column figures are significantly lower than their counterparts in the second column, indicating that changes of values during the entire year were larger than would be expected solely from unreliability of the scales. The important research question raised by these findings is: Can changes in individuals' values be explained on some systematic basis?

THE "STUDENT CULTURE"

One possible source of value influence which has not been well studied is the primary living group, as represented in this study of ten fraternities and sororities.[2] When a student spends a great deal of time in a living group of his own choice, and is dependent on its members for much of his security and satisfaction, he should be vulnerable to potent influence from this group. His values may be affected, first, because the group's members provide cues concerning what notions are "universally shared"; second, because they induce the person to engage in behaviors that he may subsequently be called upon to justify to himself or to others; third, because the group members are in a position to punish serious deviation from their norms by withdrawing

[1] These statistics are based on the same data that were used for Col. 5 in Table 1. Here, however, we report intra-class correlation coefficients (Haggard, 1958), instead of product-moment correlation coefficients, since it is important to consider shifts in group means and standard deviations from test to retest. That such over-all group shifts were very small is indicated by the close correspondence between the product-moment rs (Table 1, Col. 5) and the intra-class ρs (Table 7, Col. 2).

[2] Actually, these campus organizations are local chapters of national men's and women's fraternities. To varying degrees, some of their distinctive characteristics may depend on the national organizations with which they are affiliated. Here we are concerned only with their local features and, for the sake of brevity, refer to them throughout this book simply as "fraternities" and "sororities."

emotional support from the offender. (Notice how few of these sources of potent influence are provided in the typical classroom.)

Within fraternities and sororities, members have quite pervasive contacts, so that the scope of their relations is diffuse. These organizations attract strong member allegiances, so that the individual is amendable to influence. They distinguish clearly between members and non-members and accord differential treatment on this basis. It may be expected that shared conceptions of what is right and wrong will serve as standards for justifying the members' actions toward one another and toward the outside world. Older members may exert pressure on noviciates to adopt the prevailing values, ostensibly and primarily because they feel them to be "right," but latently also because shared values facilitate group interaction and serve to reassure each person as to the moral absoluteness of his own standards.

For all of these a priori reasons, fraternities and sororities were selected as a setting for the present study of value development in college. It was felt that, of all the sources of systematic value influence that could be independently identified in this complex college environment, this source would be the most potent and therefore have the greatest chance of showing a uniform influence on the students exposed to it.

To this point there might be ready agreement from many sides, but the issue that divides protagonists and antagonists of the Greek system concerns the desirability of the value changes that may be induced by these organizations. On the one side are those who praise their contributions to certain basic values of the society — loyalty to the group, concern for other people and ability to get along with them, concern for the esteem of others. Antagonists, on the other hand, point to the detrimental effects that these organizations may have on other significant values — such as academic achievement, intellectual development, creativity, and independence.

Many observers of contemporary American college life allude in one way or another to a presumed conflict of cultures within these institutions. On the one side, they suggest, is the academic intellectual culture promoted by the faculty and a few outstandingly involved students. On the other side is the mass student culture, oriented perhaps toward recreation and social activities, but at least alienated from the academic goals and tending to regard education in wholly instrumental terms. A recent volume on *The American College* edited by Sanford (1962) contains many references to this alienation. Bushnell (1962), for example, in describing the "Student Culture at Vassar," claims that "the usual course of action is for students to keep faculty at a distance and to rely on each other for counsel and support" (p. 512). Complementarily, in the same volume, Brown (1962) reports that teachers at Vassar nominate as superior students those with high grades who are "low on conformity and integration into the student peer culture" (p. 544).

In a similar vein, Hughes, Becker, and Geer (1962), summarizing their study of a medical school, conclude that the student culture there provides the basis for a modus vivendi between the students and their superiors, providing a perspective from which students can build consistent patterns of response enabling them to fit into the activities of the school and hospital . . . it provides them with sufficient collective support to allow them to direct their effort in quite different directions than those suggested by the faculty (pp. 528-529).

Bay (1962) concludes this volume with a generalized assertion:

In the vast majority of the colleges [peer-group] norms are primarily nonintellectual as well as nonacademic. . . . One reason for this nonintellectualism may be that students with social skills almost inevitably acquire more influence in the shaping of peer-group culture than do those with intellectual skills (p. 989).

Though descriptions such as these may well apply to a great many campuses (with certain notable exceptions), the data on which they are based are mostly impressionistic. *The American College* reports little systematic data to support the view that the typical student culture — even that at Vassar — is primarily alienative with respect to intellectual academic values. One even suspects that it would be hard to find clear evidence one way or another on this question. For the very definition of a "student culture" and its counterpart, the "faculty culture," poses an enormous problem, heterogeneous as these two groups of culture-carriers are on most campuses. Any single student is likely to be oriented simultaneously toward a number of different sources of influence, among which are one or more faculty members. Since intellectual values and interpersonal values are both legitimized in the composite culture, it is unlikely that he will explicitly reject either, but at most give predominant weight to one or another consideration in any particular action choice.

Impressionistically based conclusions in the other direction may be cited as well. Etzioni (1961) regards universities as a predominantly "normative" type of organization (though not a pure exemplar of this type) in which members manifest a moral involvement in the collective enterprise. In typical normative organizations, he asserts,

High commitment of lower participants to the organization allows the organizational elites to develop leadership over them; consequently, leadership outside the organizational power structure is infrequent. In less typical normative organizations . . . special efforts are made to encourage formal expressive leaders, in order to reduce the dysfunctional effects of alienated informal leadership (p. 112).

Thus the university leadership (faculty and administration) would normally try to see to it that key charismatic leaders outside the regular academic hierarchy — such as football coaches, housemothers, resident advisors — share, and in any case do not subvert, the academic values.

Citing Newcomb's (1943) Bennington study, Etzioni argues that college students usually accept expressive leadership of their instructors. "It is only in the relatively coerced special and vocational schools that the students tend to have an extensive subcollectivity of their own, controlled by informal student leaders" (p. 105). Indeed, Stern (1962) reports that, over a sample of 43 colleges and universities that were systematically studied with his student Activities Index and College Characteristics Index, the typical orientations of students in any particular institution tended to be compatible with the kind of campus environments the school provided. Though some entire campuses — administration, faculty, and students alike — might be judged alienated from intellectual values, it is doubtful whether this alienation could be traced primarily to the student body.

Thus run the conflicting views regarding "student culture." At the core of many people's image of the alienative student culture lies the fraternity-sorority system, and it has been the target of many efforts to improve the intellectual atmosphere on campuses. Corrective action has ranged from banishment of the organizations to more gentle attempts to get the houses to participate explicitly in academic functions by establishing reading libraries and substituting intellectually oriented activities in place of their traditional homecoming displays.

Yet the choice of these Greek organizations as a major target for academic and intellectual improvement stems more from the faculties' preconceptions about their alienative role than from systematic data on just what their actual role is in the total campus culture. In fact, their role is probably a complex one, and only some aspects of it would seem, a priori, to be alienative; other aspects appear quite congruent with professed academic values. Grade-point averages of fraternity and sorority members at many schools tend to be higher than those of Independents. Summerskill (1962) cites several studies showing that persistence and graduation rates are higher among fraternity and sorority members than among non-members. Of course, these data are ambiguous with respect to the present issue, first of all because grades and graduation are not necessarily the best measures of involvement in the intellectual academic culture. Second, of course, the very recruitment of members to these organizations is likely to *depend* on previous grades and on certain individual characteristics that would predispose them to complete their schooling. When academic aptitude scores and first semester grades of members and non-members are equated, the Greeks may show some decrement in academic performance relative to Independents during their subsequent school years (Faguy-Coté, 1960).

ORGANIZATIONAL PROCESSES IN FRATERNITIES AND SORORITIES

Implicit in the selection of variables for assessment were certain theories about how such voluntary social organizations work and how their members participate in their organizational processes. Implicit also were certain assumptions about the characteristic functions of fraternities and sororities and about their dominant foci of interest. An explicit statement of these theories and assumptions will provide a rationale for the particular research questions asked concerning the relations between organizations and values; it will also help justify the treatment of these particular groups as instances of a larger class in which similar relationships presumably obtain.

Without attempting to define the term formally, we may designate an organizational process as any practice, regularly engaged in by members, which is relevant to the functioning of the organization. This means that it will be performed, regardless of who the participating members are, so long as the group's functions remain essentially the same. (This kind of definition begs the question of what the group's "functions" are and of what is meant by "relevant." These are hard to specify in general terms; instead, we shall simply enumerate functions deemed relevant to these particular organizations.) It is in the organizational processes that one would expect to find the group's shared values expressed.

Among the processes assumed relevant to the functioning of voluntary organizations are: (1) recruitment of members, (2) maintenance of member allegiance, (3) establishment of inter-member communication, (4) effective adaptation to the wider culture in which the organization is embedded, (5) socialization of members into the group's normative patterns, (6) differential reward of members for differing degrees of contribution to the organization's functioning, (7) role differentiation, or division of tasks among members, according to priorities of function and according to member abilities and interests. All of these processes have to do with group maintenance, with holding the group together as a normatively regulated entity, regardless of the functions that it may perform for its members or for the culture external to it. Unless these system-maintaining processes are accomplished somehow, it will not be a *group* that is performing the external functions, but a collection of individuals acting independently or in parallel.

Each of the processes may be described either from the perspective of the organization or from the perspective of the individual members who are affected by them. Thus, recruitment has two aspects — from the standpoint of the current organization, it entails selection or enticement of new members; from the standpoint of the person outside, it involves deciding whether or not to join and, if so, deciding how to gain entrance. From the group's perspective, the maintenance of member allegiance may be seen as the establishment of group cohesiveness; from an individual member's perspective, it involves his feeling of loyalty to, or alienation from, the group. Inter-member communication consists both in individuals talking to one another and in the cultural development (or adoption) of a system of shared symbols which makes communication possible. Adaptation to the surrounding culture serves to ward off potential external antagonisms, so that the group's existence is not threatened; it is accomplished, in part, by the things individual members do to gain community acceptance. Socialization is, at once, learning (intentional or unintentional) on the part of new members and teaching (intentional or unintentional) on the part of the old ones. Role differentiation involves individual members' choices of the ways in which they wish to contribute, and also the allocation of tasks so that what must be done gets done. Differential reward may be seen as the allocation of high or low status to participating members, also as the individual's incentive for participation. Attrition of membership takes place both as forcible ejection of undesirables and as voluntary disaffiliation by the disaffected. The perspective that is used in describing a particular process will depend on whether the focus is on a relatively enduring organization or on a relatively enduring individual personality.

In describing processes such as these, "the organization" is simply a reified shorthand for some undesignated consensual group (or relatively consensual group) within the total, which manages the processes. This relatively consensual nucleus need not be constant, and it may vary from one process to another, but generally it consists of the senior members who have an established interest in group maintenance, and who are also principal contributors to the group's external functioning. In each case, one might ask, "Who are the agents of the particular organizational process being described?" These are questions generally overlooked in organizational sociology, and we shall tend to gloss over them in the present analysis.

The way in which these group processes are managed presumably depends to some extent on the functions the group performs. For instance, members will be recruited who are viewed as likely to contribute to the organization's goals; the content of norms will ostensibly be aimed at promoting manifest group functions. The plurality of "functions" should be emphasized, for any organization is set up to accomplish more than one thing; hence independent, or even conflicting, considerations may enter into each of the processes. In secondary groups, it is usually possible to specify some hierarchical ordering of the several functions performed, so that one may be judged dominant over the others, and expected to "win out" in any conflict of purpose. In primary groups, the designation of dominant and subsidiary functions may be much more difficult, for the intense and diffuse nature of interpersonal relations tends to engender many inter-locking reasons for participation, which may differ greatly from one member to another. Some major functions of a primary group are apt to go unrecognized by most of its members, since they develop out of interpersonal experiences, rather than having been planned as explicit goals from the start.

THE SURROUNDING COMMUNITY

No organization exists in isolation. The very designation of functions implies some external system for which the functions are performed. And the manner in which these functions are performed will be affected to a greater or lesser degree by the cultural surround in which the organization is embedded. Certain groups are exceedingly dependent on, and therefore responsible to, their social environments. They are directly supported by, and operate at the sufferance of, the surrounding community. Such is the status of fraternities and sororities at the University of Colorado. This is in marked contrast to the status of a monastery, for example, which may be quite independent economically, and — more important for present purposes — is less subject to constant disruption of membership through environmental pressures.

Fraternities and sororities are intimately dependent on their academic surround. Their recruits must be students in good standing; their practices must not violate university norms. They must constantly attend to community relations, especially *vis-à-vis* the professors and university administration, in order not to invite crippling restrictions on their activity. Not that the organizations uniformly succeed in these processes of adaptation, but powerful weapons can be used against them if they do not — probation (which prohibits further recruitment), selective expulsion, or total banishment of all social organizations from the campus. With this degree of external control over membership and activities, fraternities and sororities at Colorado can hardly be considered as even semi-autonomous institutions. All of their processes, from recruitment through socialization to elimination, are performed with an eye to their cultural surround.

The university bureaucracy's own organization processes tend to be conducted in such a way as to serve its primary function. Selection processes are aimed at recruiting students who have the capacity and motivation to acquire the knowledge that the university is prepared to disseminate. Students maladapted to this aim are eliminated. Those who remain are subject to constant acculturation pressures. Status differentiation, through the grading system, is based on differential performance according to academic criteria. Reward for performance is an impersonal "A" grade (rarely achieved by most students), rather than signs of personal affection or esteem from one's professor. Methods of attaining status without acquiring knowledge — by cheating, plagiarism, or sycophancy — are proscribed. The faculty, too, operate under comparable normative standards. Selection, retention, and promotion all depend to a pre-eminent degree on the faculty member's success in acquiring and disseminating knowledge through research and teaching.

The norms of the academic portion of the university community, then, are essentially achievement-oriented, they are intended to apply impersonally to all participants, and considerations of friendship or compassion are not expected to play a dominant part in academic decisions. Such a normative pattern presents the antithesis of a typical primary group culture.

VALUES IN ORGANIZATIONAL PROCESSES

Recognizing the complex individual and social needs that they serve, we may nevertheless propose that the principal function of campus fraternities and sororities is the establishment and maintenance of friendships. They provide a home-away-from-home for students, a group to which they belong, a place where they are fairly sure to find sympathy and understanding, to find people who will accept and support them under any circumstances. It does not take a high level of performance to elicit friendly responses from one's fellow members. These primary groups thus provide a welcome contrast to the impersonal, achievement-oriented academic institution, and it is hardly surprising that many students seek their principal gratifications here rather than in the classroom. Certainly other mechanisms might be found to perform a similar function for students — many small colleges attempt to combine academic and primary-group functions within the single institution — but since these particular groups are available, they tend to fill their members' needs for primary-group affiliation, and thereby lessen the pressure for this kind of service from the rest of the university community.

If the establishment and maintenance of friendships is the dominant function of campus social organizations, there are nevertheless subsidiary functions which they fulfill — indeed, many of these would be proclaimed by the organizations as central. Usually, explicit concern is expressed for developing "the whole man," which may imply various things, such as interpersonal skills, intellectual and aesthetic appreciations, honesty, creativity, self-development — the sorts of virtues that are admired in the wider society and emphasized to varying degrees in other aspects of university life. Since these organizations are embedded in the university culture, they are compelled (they may even desire) to stress academic achievement as a value. In this context, academic achievement implies mainly the attainment of acceptable grades, for these signs are unambiguous, and failure to acquire them will result in loss of individual members or in probation for the entire house. Participation in political, social, athletic, and intellectual activities on the campus may also be prized, for it is through these that the organizations acquire community prestige, attract more desirable members, and maintain favorable impressions among the faculty, who have a potentially strong hand in determining their fate.

But such functions as these are probably subsidiary, stressed intensely by a minority of the organizations and performed by the rest just to the extent required for their own maintenance. The principal function, which is the *sine qua non* of fraternity living, is the furtherance of interpersonal relations. This function should therefore affect all of the organization's essential processes to some degree, and it should contribute to distinctive selection and emphasis within the houses among the range of values that are differentially pertinent to them.

Keeping in mind the allegedly dominant function of these organizations and the limitations imposed by the academic surround, we may speculate about how certain of their organizational processes operate and the ways in which personal values may be relevant to them. These expectations served to guide the empirical analyses reported in subsequent chapters, and they determined the kinds of variables assessed by the research instruments. Not all of the organizational processes mentioned above could be adequately studied in a single investigation. Consideration here will be limited to those for which systematic data were collected.

Recruitment

Initiation to full-fledged membership in the organizations is restricted to students in good standing. The academic community makes the final determination of who is in good standing, so fraternity and sorority selection practices must operate within this limitation. Other things being equal, they try to attract members who are likely not only to maintain good enough grades to remain themselves as members, but also to help raise the grade-point average of the entire house — for thereby is organizational prestige enhanced.

Given the minimum requirement that pledges be academically capable of maintaining membership, the organizations selecting them are likely to pay attention to two kinds of qualities in potential members: First are those that will suit them to the general function of acquiring and maintaining friends — an interest in other people, skill in relating to them, and, perhaps most important, an orientation toward group life which will dispose them to establish and maintain friendships within the house. The potential member's degree of physical attractiveness is probably important only insofar as it facilitates or impedes his successful interaction with others, though this quality, like outstanding academic aptitude, will probably be stressed by organizations that can afford such emphasis.

The other kind of attribute sought in pledges is not so clearly specifiable. It consists in the ability and inclination to fit in with the dominant orientation of the house, whatever that may be. Some houses may tend to stress a small range of virtues — athletics, or social poise, or political leadership. Others may be somewhat more eclectic, preferring a range of member orientations that can, in combination, advance the organization's prestige on a variety of fronts. Thus, different kinds of pledges may be seen as appropriate in different organizations. It can only be predicted, rather generally, that the traits aimed at in selecting pledges will be those that approximate the present members' actual or desired traits.

Recruitment also depends on the willingness of available freshmen to join the particular organization. (Pledging at Colorado usually occurs early in the first year, though some students may join at a later time.) Some students enter college with explicit intent not to pledge, or else they are reluctant to try, for fear of being rejected. The remaining students (about half of entering freshmen males, and 60% of females at the University of Colorado) declare themselves interested in joining some social organization, but they may have rather specific preferences in the matter; some will prefer not to join if they cannot enter a house of their choice.

Presumably the desire to establish and maintain friends is a predominant motive for the potential pledge. But, depending on the person, he may have other things in mind. Some consciously want to join a prestigious house to enhance their own personal status. Others are explicitly seeking an opportunity for self-development along lines reputedly emphasized by one or another of the houses — be they athletics, social skills, or scholarship.

Thus, both sides of the transaction — present and aspiring members — aim at matching dominant orientations. To the extent that personal values are significant determiners, or manifestations, of these orientations, and to the extent that evidence of the values is available to both parties, one would expect the results of recruitment to yield some degree of matching between new and old members' values — a matching with respect to values that are common to all fraternities and sororities, and a matching with respect to values that characterize a particular house.

Maintenance of Member Allegiance

For an organization to function optimally, a considerable degree of group-orientation must be required of the members. At least they must want to stay in it enough to keep paying their dues, board, and room. Moreover, the organization is in no position to influence members' behaviors unless they are motivated to belong and to be accepted by the group. It cannot arrive at consensual decisions concerning joint actions, and confidently expect that they will be carried out, unless membership loyalties are strong enough to over-ride minor reservations which some individuals may feel.

The potential for organizational cohesiveness is present at the time of recruitment to the extent that new members are motivated to belong to this particular group and to the extent that they are capable of displaying loyal sentiments in action. However, group-oriented feelings will not persist unsupported. There must be continued gratification, or promise of gratification from membership, and this must be strong enough to counterbalance the centrifugal forces that inevitably come to bear. Group-oriented newcomers will be demoralized if they find old members going their own independent ways and apparently being rewarded for doing so. In the normal course of academic life, students are likely to find an increasing degree of social support outside their living groups as they attain seniority and secure status in the wider community. Moreover, they can't help becoming aware of anti-fraternity sentiments among some faculty members whom they respect, so that there will be constant pressures toward disaffection from the group and a consequent deterioration in its cohesiveness. Unless mechanisms are available to counteract such centrifugal forces, the group cannot endure.

One of the major mechanisms is, of course, continual recruitment of new members who may be more disposed toward gaining gratifications from the group. But other devices are used to maintain allegiance. Ingroup-outgroup distinctions are emphasized in many (though not all) houses through closed meetings and secret rituals. *Intra*-house rivalry — for dates, political office, or other marks of status — is suppressed in favor of *inter*-house rivalry, which occurs in athletics, homecoming displays, and even in social service enterprises, such as donations to the Community Chest. Group activities, from formal dances through political campaigning to stuffing crepe paper in chicken wire, serve as frequent reminders of the members' common affiliation.

The role of personal values in the maintenance of member allegiance is a circular one. A basic value promulgated in the wider society is loyalty to one's own membership group, whatever that group may be. To the extent that individual members value loyalty, they should be willing to devote time and effort to the organization. Their desire to do so will presumably be increased if they find colleagues who share their own values in other ways, and whom they can therefore admire and work for willingly. Feelings of attraction to the group should, in turn, enhance the degree to which a member may be influenced by his colleagues, and thereby come to adopt their values.

Socialization

One important feature of group living is its potential for exerting changes on individuals. If the members are dependent on the organization for emotional support, and if they spend a preponderance of their time with each other and in the house, the pressures toward personality change may be great. Some freshmen join fraternities and sororities with the explicit intent of "self-improvement"— to acquire the characteristics of successful social beings. Indeed, this may be the chief reason for their coming to college. Many of the old organization members, too, undoubtedly view incoming pledges as malleable material which, with proper guidance and example, can be turned into worthwhile young adults. Even when the intent to change is not explicit on either side, the demands of group life generally require some degree of personal modification. In order to develop gratifying relationships with other members, the individual must share their language, interests, and perspectives to some extent.

The potential for influence is, however, limited by a number of other organizational processes. First of all, the aim of recruitment is generally, from the group's side, to select new members who already possess to a substantial degree those traits which the old members value. To the extent that they are successful in doing this, there will be less need for subsequent socialization and, correspondingly, less room for change of new members in the direction of group norms. As Etzioni (1961) states the matter,

All other things being equal, socialization and selectivity can frequently substitute for each other. . . . If the number of potential participants is close to that of actual participants, the degree to which selectivity can be increased is limited and the organization will have to rely on socialization to attain a given level of quality. A very large number of potential participants and a very high degree of selectivity may be required to recruit participants who do not need any socialization at all in order to fulfill organizational requirements (pp. 158-159).

The degree to which value-socialization pressures operate within fraternities and sororities is, therefore, limited by the degree to which new members' values differ from the old members' norms. Some high-prestige organizations, with many more applicants than they can admit, may operate primarily as selecting, rather than as socializing, agencies.

Another intra-organization process that limits the group's potential for effective socialization is the level of allegiance maintained among its members. The more a member is oriented toward the group as a primary source of gratification, the greater is the group's potential for influencing him. As older students find other sources of gratification on campus, they may become relatively disaffected from their fraternities, and thus be less subject to influence themselves. Moreover, with normal displacement of members through graduation and disaffiliation, the remaining members become norm-setters rather than norm-followers, the influencers rather than the influenced. In general, then, we would expect whatever distinctive value influence that occurs within these organizations to take place primarily within the first year or so of membership, for at this point the member's allegiance is relatively high and he is in the position of norm-follower rather than norm-setter.

Finally, the amount of normative influence that can be exerted on members depends on the degree to which the organization provides clear rewards for conformity and punishment for deviancy. Probably the most potent kind of reward within these campus fraternities is a favorable personal response from other members. This means that reward consists in being well-liked and punishment in being disliked by others. We consider this interpersonal process in the following section as a means of status differentiation within the groups. However, any kind of status differentiation within a group may be either clear or ambiguous. Ambiguity of status based on friendship occurs when there is little consensus among members concerning who is liked and who is disliked. To the extent that this ambiguous condition obtains, any particular member is not being uniformly rewarded or punished by his colleagues, for some of them like him and some do not. Such a fragmentation of the group into cliques should tend to limit the degree to which any given member can be induced to conform to the group's norms.

The main reason why most people join the university community is their desire to gain the intrinsic or extrinsic benefits offered by its academic aspect. Though fraternity and sorority life is an important part of their college experience, it may generally be presumed that they realize that ultimate success or failure in this stage of their lives depends more directly on academic performance. Thus members are oriented in major respects toward their studies; in fact, this is undoubtedly the major focus for most of them. Eighty-nine per cent of the organization members included in the present study claimed that if house activities were to interfere seriously with their academic performance, they would give up the former.

Professors and other features of the academic environment — textbooks, visiting lecturers, advisors, intellectual bull-sessions — have a sizable potential for impact on the members, and an important part of socialization is accomplished outside the organizational context. Undoubtedly, academic socialization leads to widespread acquisition of relevant skills and knowledge. That it regularly induces systematic changes in non-intellectual aspects of personality (including moral ideals) is less well documented. The present longitudinal study was not at all concerned with assessing the effect that professors and other academic sources of influence might have on students' values. Focus was exclusively on the primary groups' influence, where the expected directions of change could be specified more easily. However, the impact of these organizations on their members' values is limited by their academic surround: There are some values that cannot be professed openly, for the academic community would not tolerate them. Moreover, if members find potent sources of influence outside their organizations, the effect of the organization itself is likely to be correspondingly reduced.

Status Differentiation

Ranking of a group's members according to prestige seems to be an inevitable feature of social life. The marks of prestige vary from one society, and one group, to another. In some they may be wealth, in others political power, merit badges, or knighthood. Some sociologists maintain that status differentiation fills the necessary function of orienting members toward dominant values within the group, and encouraging contributions to these values. Regardless of whether or not stratification is a functional requisite of social systems, one may suspect that, when it does occur, it tends to bear some correspondence to recognized differences in members' contributions to the organization. There are at least two reasons for this: First, some method is generally found for rewarding members who are conspicuous contributors to the group's goals, and punishing (or depriving) those who conspicuously impede them. Second, people's judgmental processes seem to work so as to maintain some degree of "cognitive balance" (see Heider, 1946) between perception and affect. One will tend to like and respect those whom he perceives as engaging in valued activities; conversely, he will tend to interpret the behaviors of prestigious persons as justifying their prestige — as, in fact, worthy of the esteem accorded them. To the extent that members share a common understanding of the group's functions, they will therefore tend to distinguish between contributors and non-contributors, and to make this perceptual distinction correspond to the status distinctions they recognize.

Given our assumptions about dominant and subsidiary functions of fraternities and sororities, and assuming that members are somewhat aware of them, it is to be expected that persons of high prestige within the house will be more likely than those of low prestige to behave in ways that further the central primary group values — friendship, loyalty, and interpersonal competence. Assuming that they pay adequate attention to these, members should also be rewarded for contributing to secondary foci that enhance the group's standing in the community, such as academic achievement, political leadership, and physical prowess.

To the extent that an individual's values correspond to his ways of acting overtly, high-status members should therefore be more likely than low-status members to hold values compatible with these organization-maintaining functions. Also, since the attainment of any status, high or low, depends on how a person is evaluated by significant others, just what personal traits are associated with differential prestige should depend on the dominant values of the conveyers of status, the other group members.

Elimination of Deviants

Attrition of membership comes about in a number of ways. Most important of these, for campus social organizations, is termination of members' university enrollment, either through graduation or through dropping out of school prior to graduation. Membership attrition may also reflect failure of the individual and group to maintain a mutually satisfying relationship. The group's dissatisfaction is typically expressed in low status assigned to the member; if this condition becomes extreme, he may leave under pressure. The individual member's dissatisfaction is typically expressed in a dislike for the group, either as individuals or as a collectivity. His disaffection will probably be manifest first in withdrawal from interpersonal contacts within the group and in shirking of his organizational responsibilities — attendance at meetings, participation in other house activities. Finally, he may disaffiliate if he sees other avenues of satisfaction outside.

Attrition that occurs in the absence of specific academic

reasons may be expected to reflect some sort of deviancy in the departing member, whether his departure is group- or self-instigated. The fact that a person finds fraternity or sorority life uncongenial probably means that his own orientations do not dispose him to gain satisfaction in the same ways that other members do. The fact that the group finds a particular member uncongenial probably means that he doesn't fit their notions of how a good member ought to behave. In the extreme, a deviant may pose a threat to group maintenance, and also to the conceptual systems of individual members, for in his deviancy he challenges the validity of their standards for appraising appropriate conduct. In self-defense they will try to exclude him, formally or informally.

To the extent that a deviant orientation stems from basic value differences between a member and his group, one would expect that those who drop out will tend to hold values that are divergent from those of the rest of the house. This should be especially true in organizations where personal values are explicitly emphasized in the group norms and where conformity to them is a requisite for acceptance.

Other organizational processes besides these might also be conducted. However, these five — recruitment, status differen-of personal values to the manner in which these processes are conducted. However, these five — recruitment, status differentiation, maintenance of member loyalties, socialization, and attrition — constituted the focus of the present study. Analyses in subsequent chapters are concerned chiefly with the ways in which values enter into the several organizational processes. It is clear that a large number of different values may be held by the various members. Many will be idiosyncratic and only tangentially — if at all — relevant to the group's functioning. Some values should be substantially emphasized in all fraternities and sororities, since they contribute to the maintenance of this type of organization — values stressing group loyalty, interpersonal skills, and consideration for one's friends. Others will tend to be emphasized in particular organizations because prestigious members think they are important — perhaps through their sensitivities to certain requirements for adaptation in the wider community. Hence one might expect inter-house differences in the value accorded to such traits as academic achievement, athletic skill, aesthetic appreciation, religious devotion, and so forth.

CONFLICT AND CONGRUENCE WITH
THE ACADEMIC COMMUNITY

It has been argued that functions of the academic and social aspects of campus life are quite different, the former dealing mainly with individual achievement, the latter primarily with group-endowed security. This divergence of functions alone does not necessarily give rise to "conflict of values" between the two segments. The same students, after all, participate in both, and they are generally able to find some mode of resolution for conflicting pressures. Moreover, both social and academic organizations exist in the context of a wider society from which members are recruited, and on which both are dependent for continued maintenance. Therefore the value norms of the two are unlikely to be diametrically opposed in most instances.

Nevertheless, there are occasions in the conduct of organizational processes when the welfare of the group appears to indicate one course of action, while the immediately surrounding community (meaning the university professors and administration) demands another. Both parties to the conflict can find value bases to rationalize their positions, and the nature of the resolution depends on which values prevail.

A striking example of this sort of "value conflict" has recently occurred on many campuses with respect to the organizations' recruitment practices. From the fraternities' and sororities' point of view, the aim of selection is to obtain new members who are compatible with existing group perspectives, to whom the old members can relate comfortably, and whose acceptance will not require an uncomfortable stretching of the usual bases for selecting friends. This means that applicants from minority races will generally be excluded, and this may even be a matter of explicit policy. University admission policies, on the other hand, stress the application of universalistic criteria whose relevance to the functioning of the institution is demonstrable. Moreover, explicit norms of the wider society are coming more and more to stress the unfairness and detrimental effects of racial segregation; hence it is difficult to justify such practices in a public institution. In this conflict, the values of the wider academic community are tending to prevail; this occurs, not through denial of the value of compatibility in social organizations, but rather through insistence that compatibility be judged more directly than by classifying people into irrelevant categories.

Other instances of normative conflict are more chronic: It can be expected, for instance, that the Greek organizations will make every effort to hang onto their valued members. Standards of friendship and ingroup loyalty demand unrestricted aid to a needy member. Certain kinds of aid, however, are proscribed in the individualistic, achievement-oriented university setting. Flagrant cheating on examinations is likely to result in dismissal from the university and the termination of membership. But the fraternity file of examinations, long a source of concern to some professors, has in many places become legitimized to the extent that the faculty routinely deposit their old exams in the library where Independents, too, can have convenient access to them.

Thus "value conflicts" are continually born and resolved in large universities. We have illustrated two that stem from a differential emphasis on universalistic achievement values, as opposed to particularistic friendship values, because this is the type of conflict that is most likely to be encountered in the context of fraternity and sorority living. But other value-relevant issues are constantly arising within each of the many activity complexes of the total campus. The student newspaper is likely to get embroiled in controversies over freedom of expression vs. editorial responsibility, the religious organizations in dilemmas involving the role of dogma in a rationalist culture, the athletic establishment in conflicts over scholarship vs. varsity spirit, the alumni organizations in the problem of maintaining a favorable public image vs. unrestricted inquiry and free expression of political views. And so on.

From one perspective, these represent social conflicts among different segments of the university community. From another perspective, however, they pose internal conflict for the participating individuals, for these people often profess the values of both sides to the dispute. An optimum resolution will be one that provides a redefinition of the circumstances so that both sets of values appear to be realized.

Students in this complex culture are thus confronted not only with different value emphases in the different segments of campus activity, but with complex individual sources of influence that appear to profess first one value, then another. It is hardly surprising, then, to find little in the way of uniform value impact on the total student body, if one conceives as impact only a unidirectional change in a particular value. What may happen in this complex culture is that some students will be influenced one way, some students another; some may shift back and forth, depending on how their predominant reference figures of the time seem to be going; others may show no marked change in the strength of any particular value, but instead may develop an increased awareness of the diverse values that can legitimately be professed; finally, a sizable number of students may remain substantially unaffected in the domain of personal values, because their would-be influencers are not sufficiently compelling in this particular way, or because the students already share essentially the major values to which they are being exposed.

SUMMARY

Of the many studies that have dealt with the impact of college life upon students, hardly a one has focused explicitly on fraternities and sororities as a source of influence. The few investigations that have found clear evidence of any effect on students' values seem to have been conducted within small residential colleges with a fairly homogeneous ideology, strong student loyalties to the institution, and a fairly concerted effort toward influencing new students in a direction different from their pre-existing values. In the typical large, complex university setting, residential fraternities and sororities may be expected to provide a focus for their members' orientations which takes the place of an orientation toward the entire university, and therefore may constitute a source of uniform value influence that is not found in the student body as a whole.

Yet these organizations are not exclusively, or even predominantly, socializing agencies. Perhaps their most important function is acting as screening and selecting agencies, aiming to admit members who already match the group's ideal of what a good member should be like. Therefore, any study of the role of values in campus fraternities and sororities must take into account the part that members' values play, not only as objects of group influence, but also as determiners of member participation — as bases for recruitment, group acceptance, and continuing orientation of the members toward their organizations.

College fraternities and sororities are far from autonomous institutions. Embedded in the wider campus culture, they are subject to academic controls in the selection, retention, and influence of their membership. The members themselves belong simultaneously to the larger campus community and are oriented significantly toward some aspect of it besides their own living group. Any conflicts between the academic and social aspects of campus life are therefore felt within the individual members. This dual, or multiple, affiliation of the membership undoubtedly serves to engender intra-individual strains, but it also should help to limit intra-campus cleavages. The values professed by one segment of the community are seldom diametrically opposed to those of another segment. They constitute rather, sources of differential emphasis among a wide range of culturally legitimate values.

It may be expected that the entering student who joins a fraternity or sorority will be strongly oriented at first toward this primary living group as a source of major interpersonal gratifications. But, as he encounters, and achieves secure status in, a wider segment of the total campus culture, the potential of these social organizations for influencing him may be progressively lessened. Insofar as the present study was concerned with value socialization within fraternities and sororities, it was focused mainly on influences that occurred during the first year of membership. But the role of personal values in other organizational processes — in selection, status differentiation, maintenance of member allegiance, and attrition — was studied at various levels of seniority within the groups.

CHAPTER 4

ASSESSMENT OF GROUP CHARACTERISTICS

The groups chosen for study were ten social organizations at the University of Colorado — six fraternities and four sororities. This university is fairly widely known for its active social life — an image the administration and faculty have been trying to alter in recent years. Though the Greek organizations by no means dominate campus life, from the student's point of view they represent a potent and prestigious part of it. Nearly one-half of the undergraduate women and nearly one-third of the undergraduate men belonged at the time of this study. On the average, their families are wealthy enough that dues and extra living costs impose no special hardship.[1]

At Colorado, as in many other universities, campus sentiment concerning the social organizations is sharply, sometimes bitterly, divided. With a few exceptions, the fraternities and sororities tend to espouse Republican politics, which are anathema to liberal groups such as the student newspaper. Faculty opinion of the organizations ranges from loyal partisanship through benign paternalism to denunciation of the "evil, undemocratic" fraternity system. When we first requested entry into these groups for research purposes, we occasionally encountered the not too subtle query, "Are you yourself a fraternity man?" suggesting an understandable concern over how the study might be slanted.

[1] Among 1961 graduating seniors the median 1960 income reported by parents on federal income tax forms was $16,100 for out-of-state students, $8,500 for residents.

The six fraternities were approached directly, following consultation with the fraternity advisor in the Dean of Men's office, who suggested that these particular organizations would provide a diversity of size, prestige, and orientation which would meet the aims of the study. Together, they contained about 30% of the membership of the 23 fraternities on campus. In all cases the fraternity presidents readily assented to the request, and obtained the necessary approval of their members. The sororities were approached at a meeting of the Panhellenic Association, where the aims of the study were explained in a general way and volunteers solicited. Initially, five sororities volunteered to participate, but one of these had to drop out under pressure from its regional alumnae advisor. The sorority had previously encountered unfavorable publicity as a result of research conducted within it, and the advisor wanted to make sure the experience was not repeated. The remaining four groups contained about one-quarter of the membership of all 17 campus sororities.

Very likely the aims of the study could have been better met with a larger number of groups, for generalizations across organizations from a sample of only ten are quite hazardous, especially when one encounters occasionally significant differences in relationships within fraternities and sororities. However, the number of subjects included in these ten, together with small comparison groups of freshmen who did not intend to pledge, already exceeded 900, which was about the upper limit possible given the budget and personnel for the study. Sub-sampling within groups would have been inappropriate, since the research design required complete sociometric assessment of all members. Such limitations pose a dilemma for social scientists who wish to use the group as their unit of analysis. In order to get a large enough sample of groups, it is often necessary to obtain measures on many hundreds of individuals, so that much time, effort, and money are extended in the sheer mechanics of data collection and quality control. Throughout the analysis, conventional standards of statistical significance were adhered to in hypothesis testing, so it is not likely that erroneous generalizations have been proposed. However, in cross-organizational comparisons with only ten groups, the probability of Type II errors is exceedingly high, so it is quite possible that many important relationships have been overlooked.

In individual conferences with the organization presidents, the aims of the study were explained fully and honestly, and the major variables were described in non-technical language. These leaders were requested, however, not to broadcast this information, for fear that it might affect some members' answers to the questions. The general design, involving two tests of the total organization separated by a one-year interval, was also described so that these officers would have some feeling of enduring commitment. (As it turned out, most of the newly elected officers contacted the following year for the second test had no knowledge whatsoever of the study's aims, but they cooperated readily at that time also.)

A preliminary draft of the questionnaire war also presented to the presidents at this time. This was done for two reasons: To meet any possible objections to its content and to enlist their help in phrasing questions so as to get the desired information. It had been anticipated that, since these organizations were presumably focused on the dominant goal of establishing and maintaining friendships, the sociometric section of the questionnaire might prove a bit delicate. So the presidents were asked if they thought anyone would object to rating everyone else, and being rated, on the several attributes listed. Actually, there were no objections in principle, but some of the officers felt that the active members were not yet well enough acquainted with their pledges to rate them accurately; for this reason, pretest sociometric ratings in all four sororities and one of the fraternities[2] were confined to actives only (though all current members rated everyone else on the posttest).

[2] In one sorority, pledges rated each other on the pretest, but they did not rate, nor were they rated by, the actives.

The second reason for checking the preliminary questionnaire with officers turned out to be well founded, for they were able to offer many helpful suggestions for clarifying the wording. From the time of initial contact, and throughout all subsequent relations with the subjects, it was stressed that all individual results would be kept anonymous and that even the groups' names would not be divulged to outsiders. However, feedback on group data pertinent to their own organizations was promised to the officers and members; some of these were provided in the form of "straight-run" distributions on certain variables several months after the pretest.

CHARACTERISTICS OF THE ORGANIZATIONS

No identifying features need be presented for the individual groups, but it may be noted that they varied widely in size, in local prestige, in quality of the dwelling, in mean attraction of members to the organization, in parents' incomes, and in patterns of personal values. Specifically, F tests among the houses showed that the fraternities differed significantly in the values of kindness, social skills, loyalty, religiousness, and self-control; the four sororities differed significantly only in the religious value, and this was entirely because of the one Jewish organization, which scored lower than all the rest on this scale. The appearance of relatively greater value similarity among the sororities than among the fraternities may reflect primarily the different ways in which the organizations were selected for inclusion in the study (see p. 108).

The original sizes of the ten groups may be seen in Table 8, which also shows the numbers of subjects actually assessed in both pre- and posttests. The initial response rates varied from 82% to 100% of the total membership (both pledges and actives), with an over-all rate of 89%. Ninety-two per cent of the pretest sample completed questionnaires a year later, with the retest rates varying between 88% and 95% for the several organizations. By the time of the posttest, many of the subjects had either graduated or left school, so they had to be reached by mail — some of them as far away as Paris and Rio de Janeiro. Considering both pretest and posttest status of the subjects, eight different categories were potentially distinguishable: actives and pledges, each separated into four sub-groups — still in organization, graduated, left school without graduating (including subjects who changed schools), and left the organization but remained in school. Actually, only one pretest pledge had graduated, and very few of the sorority actives had dropped the organization while remaining in school. Therefore, for subsequent analyses, the one graduating pledge was included with the pledges who left school, and the actives who had dropped the organization were combined with those who had left school without graduating.

It will be noted in Table 8 that both graduation and drop-out rates varied somewhat among the several groups. Sorority actives who remained in school rarely dropped their organization membership, but the proportion of them leaving school was higher than it was for fraternity actives, and the same as the drop-school rate for pledges. This high rate of attrition of sorority actives is largely attributable to marriage before graduation, but many of the drop-outs of both sexes left to attend other schools.

MEASURES OBTAINED

The pretest was administered separately to the various organizations in group sessions held within a three-week period in November 1957. Questionnaires from stray absentees were collected individually through January 1958. The posttests were administered to groups in November 1958, then mailed both to absentees and to pretest subjects who had left the organization (including graduates and drop-outs). Repeated requests were required in some cases, but the over-all high rate of posttest completions attests to the general cooperativeness of most subjects.

111

TABLE 8
CATEGORIES OF SUBJECTS ON PRETEST AND POSTTEST

Organization	Fraternities															Sororities										
	1		2		3		4		5		6		Total		1		2		3		4		Total	
	N^a	n^b	N	n	N	n	N	n	N	n	N	n	N	%	N	n	N	n	N	n	N	n	N	%
Pretest																								
Actives	82	72	59	53	39	27	37	31	38	29	19	19	274		75	66	43	43	53	48	23	22	194	
Pledges	35	30	37	36	43	40	39	37	34	30	14	14	202		46	40	64	60	34	30	37	33	181	
% of total org. in pretest	87%		93%		82%		90%		82%		100%			88%	88%		96%		90%		85%			91%
Posttest Actives																								
Still active	41	40	32	32	17	12	16	15	17	16	7	7	130	57%	28	28	20	20	18	17	9	9	75	42%
Graduated	14	13	7	7	5	5	8	8	4	4	4	4	45	19%	12	10	12	10	14	13	0	0	38	21%
Left org.[c]	8	6	6	5	3	3	2	2	4	4	1	1	24	10%	1	1	0	0	3	3	1	1	5	3%
Left school[e]	9	7	8	7	2	2	5	5	4	4	4	4	32	14%	25	21	11	10	13	12	12	12	61	34%
Total[a]	72	66	53	51	27	22	31	30	29	28	19	16	231	100%	66	60	43	40	48	45	22	22	179	100%

TABLE 8 (continued)

Organization	Fraternities 1 N^a	1 n^b	2 N	2 n	3 N	3 n	4 N	4 n	5 N	5 n	6 N	6 n	Total N	Total %	Sororities 1 N	1 n	2 N	2 n	3 N	3 n	4 N	4 n	Total N	Total %
Pledges																								
Went active	21	19	17	17	24	24	23	22	18	17	4	4	107	57%	27	26	21	21	15	15	17	17	80	49%
Graduated[d]	0	0	0	0	0	0	0	0	0	0	0	0	0		0	0	0	1	0	0	0	0	1	1%
Left org.	4	4	7	6	4	1	1	1	2	2	2	2	22	12%	4	3	14	13	8	8	0	0	26	16%
Left school[d]	5	4	12	9	10	10	13	10	8	8	8	7	58	31%	9	8	24	20	7	6	16	13	56	34%
Total[d]	30	27	36	33	40	38	37	33	30	27	14	13	187	100%	40	37	60	55	30	29	33	30	163	100%
% of total org. in posttest	79%		88%		73%		83%		76%		88%		81%		80%		89%		85%		80%		85%	
% of pretest sample in posttest	91%		94%		90%		93%		93%		88%		92%		92%		92%		95%		95%		93%	

[a] N, in the pretest, is the total number of organization members in a given category; in the posttest, N is the number of members in that category who had been assessed on the pretest.

[b] n, in both pretest and posttest, is the number of organization members from whom completed questionnaires were obtained.

[c] Actives who left the organization were combined with actives who left school for all subsequent analyses.

[d] The single pledge who graduated was included, in all analyses, with pledges who left school.

Included in questionnaires administered to current members on both pre- and posttests were measures of values, sociometric status, and attraction to the organization. For some of the pledge groups, pretest sociometrics were omitted (see p. 109), and subjects who left the organization were not given either sociometrics or measures of attraction to the group on the posttest.

Attrition

One important variable in this study could be assessed without asking subjects anything. That was the change in their membership statuses from pre- to posttest. Though graduation of actives and school drop-outs of pledges depend on circumstances largely outside the organizational processes, withdrawal of actives or of pledges who remain in school may reflect significant characteristics of the groups themselves.

At the individual level of analysis, one may compare the characteristics of disaffiliates with those of members who remain. At the group level of analysis, one can compare various organizations with respect to their total drop-out rate, without regard to who the disaffiliates are. Both kinds of analysis will be pursued in the following chapters.

Value Scales

The multiple-item value scales described in Chapter 1 were administered to all actives and pledges on both the pre- and posttests. This same instrument was also given to a random sample of the entire university student body (see p. 39), so the longitudinal sample can be compared with the random cross-section of fraternity and sorority members to see the degree to which members of the ten organizations studied here held values typical of all campus Greeks.

In the first two columns of Table 9 appear the mean value scores (expressed in standard deviation units) of Independents and Greeks within the representative sample of undergraduates.

TABLE 9

<small>Mean Value Scores (z) for Longitudinal Sample of
Greek Houses Compared with University Cross-section</small>

Value	(1) University Undergraduates Independents ($n = 108$)	(2) Greeks ($n = 64$)	(3) Longitudinal Pretest Greeks ($n = 760$)	Poor Match
Intellectualism	.07	−.13	−.31[b]	
Kindness	−.01	−.15	.02	
Social skills	−.14	.17[a]	.17[a]	
Loyalty	−.12	.21[a]	.71[b, e]	
Academic achievement	−.13	.09[c]	.23[b]	
Physical development	−.24	.18[b]	.06[b]	
Status	−.08	−.05	.08	
Honesty	.14	−.27[b]	.17[e]	x
Religiousness	−.04	−.06	.19[a, d]	x
Self-control	−.07	−.06	.06	
Creativity	.03	−.05	−.36[a, d]	x
Independence	.02	.00	−.30[a, d]	x

Note. — These are standard scores based on Ms and σs of a university random sample.
[a] Different from University Independents ($\alpha < .05$).
[b] Different from University Independents ($\alpha < .01$).
[c] Different from University Independents ($\alpha < .10$).
[d] Different from University Greeks ($\alpha < .05$).
[e] Different from University Greeks ($\alpha < .01$).

(Graduate students were eliminated for these analyses, to make the sample more comparable to the longitudinal groups in age and academic level.) The Greeks were significantly higher (at $\alpha < .05$) on the values of social skills, loyalty, and physical development, significantly lower on the value of honesty. Comparing pretest value scores of the ten organizations on these same values, it will be noted (Col. 3) that these groups were also significantly higher than the cross-section of Independents on social skills, loyalty, and physical development; and they were significantly higher on the value of academic achievement, where the difference in the cross-sectional sample reached the .10 level of significance. In these respects, then, the Greek organizations included in the longitudinal study seem to have represented the total campus Greek membership rather well. However, in other respects the match was not so good. The differences between Greeks and Independents on the values of intellectualism and loyalty tended to be exaggerated in the longitudinal sample, and there are four values — honesty, religiousness, creativity, and independence — on which the longitudinal sample differed significantly from the cross-section of Greeks in a way that is not a mere exaggeration of cross-sectional Greek-Independent differences.

The locus of similarities and differences can be better ascertained by looking at male and female subjects separately. From Table 10 it may be seen that campus sorority members differed from Independent women in several respects: They tended to

TABLE 10

Mean Value Scores (z) for Longitudinal Sample of Sororities Compared with University Cross-section Women

Value	(1) University Women Independents ($n = 31$)	(2) University Women Greeks ($n = 28$)	(3) Longitudinal Pretest Sororities ($n = 342$)	Poor Match
Intellectualism	.17	.14	−.02	
Kindness	.39	.13	.24	
Social skills	−.08	.26[c]	.33[a]	
Loyalty	−.18	.29[a]	.77[b, e]	
Academic achievement	−.42	.19[b]	.32[b]	
Physical development	−.42	.11[a]	.20[b]	
Status	−.35	.13[a]	.01[a]	
Honesty	−.07	−.34	.23[e]	x
Religiousness	.19	−.03	.40[d]	x
Self-control	−.01	.05	.25	
Creativity	−.10	−.11	−.08	
Independence	.09	−.35	−.44[b]	

Note. — These are standard scores based on Ms and σs of a university random sample.
[a] Different from University Independents ($\alpha < .05$).
[b] Different from University Independents ($\alpha < .01$).
[c] Different from University Independents ($\alpha < .10$).
[d] Different from University Greeks ($\alpha < .05$).
[e] Different from University Greeks ($\alpha < .01$).

value loyalty to the group, academic achievement (striving for good grades), physical development, and status (prestige through leadership) *more,* and independence *less,* than did unaffiliated women. In all of these respects the sororities in the longitudinal study showed the same pattern of differences from the cross-section of Independent women (though on the value of loyalty the difference was exaggerated). On only two of the values, honesty and religiousness, were the longitudinal female subjects distinctly atypical of Greek women on campus. The over-all similarity of value patterns between the four sororities in the study and all campus sororities may be represented by a coefficient of correlation over the twelve pairs of mean z scores in the second and third columns of Table 10. This yields an r of .61 $(\alpha < .05)$.

Quite a different picture appears in the male sample (Table 11). First of all, there are fewer significant differences between Greeks and Independents in the university cross-section; the fraternity members do not display the values that make up the prevailing stereotype of Greek social organizations so markedly as do the sorority girls. There are some marked differences, however, between the six fraternities and both the campus Independents and the random sample of Greek males. The six fraternities were especially low on the values of intellectualism, creativity, and independence, especially high on loyalty to the group, and higher than the random sample of Greek males on status and honesty values. Altogether, the fraternities included in the longitudinal study provided a poor match with the cross-sectional sample of fraternity members on six out of the twelve values — a poor match in the sense that the mean values showed distinct patterns of differences in relation to Independent males. The correlation over the paired mean z scores in Columns 2 and 3 of Table 11 is only .27 — not significantly different from zero.

The upshot of these analyses is that the two different ways of soliciting fraternities and sororities for the longitudinal study yielded quite different types of organizations as far as value

TABLE 11
MEAN VALUE SCORES (z) FOR LONGITUDINAL SAMPLE OF FRATERNITIES
COMPARED WITH UNIVERSITY CROSS-SECTION MEN

	(1) University Men	(2)	(3) Longitudinal	
			Pretest	Poor
	Independents	Greeks	Fraternities	Match
Value	(n = 77)	(n = 36)	(n = 418)	
Intellectualism	.03	−.32[c]	−.55[b]	
Kindness	−.20	−.37	−.16	
Social skills	−.16	.09	.04	
Loyalty	−.10	.14	.66[b, e]	x
Academic achievement	.00	.03	.15	
Physical development	−.17	.24[a]	−.06	x
Status	.02	−.19	.13[d]	x
Honesty	.22	−.21[a]	.13[d]	x
Religiousness	−.14	−.09	.03	
Self-control	−.09	−.15	−.09	
Creativity	.07	.00	−.59[b, e]	x
Independence	−.02	.27	−.18[d]	x

Note. — These are standard scores based on Ms and σs of a university random sample.
[a] Different from University Independents ($\alpha < .05$).
[b] Different from University Independents ($\alpha < .01$).
[c] Different from University Independents ($\alpha < .10$).
[d] Different from University Greeks ($\alpha < .05$).
[e] Different from University Greeks ($\alpha < .01$).

similarity to all campus fraternities and sororities is concerned. In the fraternity sample, where a deliberate attempt had been made, through consultation with the Dean's Office advisor, to select a "representative" sample of distinctive organizations, the distinctiveness goal was achieved (i.e., F tests among value means for the several houses showed a number of significant differences), but the goal of representativeness was not well met. In the sorority sample, by contrast, where voluntary participants were solicited from attendants at a Panhellenic Council meeting, the inter-organizational differences among values were much less marked, while comparability with the total sorority population was considerably better.

There is no way of knowing for certain whether atypicality

in values affected any of the organizational processes studied here. The assumption to be followed is that the findings reported in subsequent chapters — insofar as they refer to relationships found within all groups — would be replicated essentially in other houses as well. In some of the analyses, however, inter-house differences in mean scores constitute a critical variable, so the exaggeration of these differences obtained in the fraternity sample may have artificially magnified the cross-organization relationships. On the other hand, the differences among these ten fraternities and sororities are not nearly so great as might be found among other types of organizations and institutions in the wider society. It seems reasonable to expect that where inter-group differences in values are more pronounced than in the present study, the cross-organization relationships might be even more marked. Thus, there is a seemingly legitimate temptation to extrapolate certain findings from the present study to organizations with more distinctive value patterns than were encountered here.

Sociometrics

An organizational process central to this investigation is the differential allocation of status within a group. It was assumed that differential status could be adequately measured by a socio-metric instrument in which every member rated every other on a seven-point scale indicating how much he liked him (see Appendix C). Use of this "friendship" sociometric as a measure of status depends on the assumption that the dominant function of social organizations such as these is the establishment and mainte-nance of friendships. In some other type of organization, with a different central function, the appropriate measure of status may be quite different. For instance, in a business enterprise oriented toward the production of goods or services for some external social system, a more useful measure of status might be obtained from sociometric ratings of the degree of relevant expertise possessed by each member. This is because expertise would pre-sumably be a more important basis of status than the ability to maintain friendships — though the latter certainly could not be discounted altogether.

Since a major focus of the study was on the bases for friendship choice within houses, certain other rating scales were included in the sociometric instrument (Appendix C). Out of all the possible traits on which members might evaluate one another, three were chosen which seemed most intimately related to certain subsidiary functions of the houses, and for which appropriate value measures were available in the instrument discussed in Chapter 1. The three additional ratings were on the attributes of academic orientation ("how seriously they take their schoolwork"), organization orientation ("their contribution to house activities"), and social orientation ("their ability to get along with other people"). These three rating scales were intended to parallel, respectively, the values of academic achievement, loyalty, and social skills. The third one, social orientation, and the friendship rating scale, the basic criterion for intra-house status, may

TABLE 12
FRIENDSHIP SOCIOMATRIX (PARTIAL) FROM FRATERNITY 6

Subject				Object				Mean Rating
	A	B	C	D	E	F	G	Given
A		2	2	7	4	1	1	2.83
B	1		3	1	3	3	3	2.33
C	2	4		3	4	2	1	2.67
D	2	4	3		4	3	2	3.00
E	2	2	4	5		1	1	2.50
F	2	2	1	2	1		1	1.50
G	1	1	1	3	1	1		1.33
Mean Rating Received	1.67	2.50	2.33	3.50	2.83	1.83	1.50	2.31

Note. — The meanings of the numbers designated on the rating instructions were as follows:
   1. Outstanding — one of the few top people in the group
   2. Very high — but not quite tops
   3. Quite high — better than average
   4. About average for the group
   5. Somewhat below average
   6. Rather low — but not at the bottom
   7. Very low — in the bottom of the group
The attribute reported here was designated on the questionnaire as "How much you like them."

appear to be almost redundant. Indeed, these ratings were virtually synonymous within many of the houses. But the degree of redundancy probably depends heavily on the dominant orientation of the organization; there are undoubtedly some groups in which friendship choices would not parallel so closely the perceived skill of others in social interaction. Therefore, one reason for including the sociometric rating on social orientation was that it permitted an indirect test of a major assumption concerning the dominant function of these groups.

Additional sociometric ratings might have been useful — on such traits as intellectualism, physical development, religiousness, and so on — but the rating task gets boring for subjects after the first couple of times through the entire house membership, so some limitation had to be imposed. These other traits were excluded either because it was suspected that the members could not clearly discriminate one another on them or because it was assumed that, in comparison with the included traits, the excluded ones were less important as differential bases for friendship choice within the several houses.

Analysis of Rating Matrices. For each organization, and for each of the traits rated, a sociomatrix could be constructed, as shown in Tables 12 and 13. (These are actually abbreviated matrices from the pretest, including only those actives who were

TABLE 13

SCHOOLWORK SOCIOMATRIX (PARTIAL) FROM FRATERNITY 6

Subject	Object							Mean Rating
	A	B	C	D	E	F	G	Given
A		1	1	4	7	3	2	3.00
B	3		1	4	6	3	1	3.00
C	4	1		3	6	4	3	3.50
D	3	1	2		4	4	3	2.83
E	2	1	1	2		3	1	1.67
F	5	1	1	2	5		2	2.67
G	3	1	1	3	7	3		3.00
Mean Rating Received	3.33	1.00	1.17	3.00	5.83	3.33	2.00	2.81

Note. — See footnote to Table 12. The attribute represented here was designated on the questionnaire, "How seriously they take their schoolwork."

still in Fraternity 6 by the time of the posttest.) In each row are reported the ratings given by a particular subject to his fellow members (the diagonal cells are blank, since Ss did not rate themselves), and the mean of these ratings is shown at the extreme right. At the bottom of each column is the mean of all ratings received by a particular person from his colleagues.

It will be noted, either from comparison of the column means or from examination of the table entries, that there was more consensus within the organization on how the various members stood on "devotion to schoolwork" (Table 13) than there was on their likableness. (Table 12). The "liking" ratings, on the other hand, showed considerably greater tendencies toward mutuality than did the "schoolwork" ratings. That is, subject A's rating of how much he liked B could be predicted fairly well from B's corresponding rating of A; but A's rating of B's studiousness could be better predicted from the mean rating B received from other members; and so on for all pairs of subjects.

Rating matrices such as these can be anaylzed into three major components that are important for describing the rating process within a group (see Appendix D). The first component, variance due to differential rater *bias*, reflects differences among the row means. The second component, variance in *status* on the trait, is derived from differences among column means. The third components, *mutuality*, depends on the similarities of ratings within each pair of subjects (or on the differences among pair means). These bias, status, and mutuality components are not independent, for the more one of them contributes to the total variance among ratings, the less the others can contribute. If there were high agreement on the likableness of all subjects, there would be little mutuality; conversely, with high mutuality, there is little room for consensus among raters.

The mutuality component is itself divisible into two principal elements, status-bias concordance and differential mutuality. The first of these represents the degree to which mean ratings given to others are correlated with mean ratings received from others. A high status-bias concordance in a friendship matrix would imply that people who liked others well, on the average, were themselves well liked by most, while people who disliked others were themselves disliked. Differential mutuality reflects the degree to which variations around the mean ratings given and around the mean ratings received are correlated; in a friendship matrix high differential mutuality would show that people whom *A* liked best tended to like him better than other people did, and so on for all subjects.

The magnitudes of each of these components may be represented by correlation coefficients, which range (maximally) between +1.00 and −1.00. For measuring bias, status, and status-bias concordance, the coefficient of intra-class correlation (see Haggard, 1958) is the appropriate index, since it represents the degree of agreement on ratings. Differential mutuality is appropriately measured by the more familiar product-moment correlation coefficient, which disregards differences in means or variances of the two variables being related. A correlation between ratings given and ratings received is computed for each subject, and these measures are averaged over all subjects to yield an over-all index of differential mutuality for the group.[3]

Table 14 reports each of these four correlations for all-ten organizations. The mean intra-class correlation for friendship status is .15. Though significantly different from zero, it is nevertheless of rather small magnitude, being significantly smaller (at $\alpha < .01$) than the mean correlations for status on the other attributes. There was evidently less agreement in these houses concerning who was most and least likable than there was concerning who was most and least oriented to studies, to the organization, and to interpersonal relations. This finding immediately raises questions concerning interpretation of the mean friendship

---

[3] Actually, $r_{diff\ mut}$ is computed directly from the sums of squares and cross-products; it equals a weighted mean r, in which the r for each subject is weighted by the geometric mean of the variance of his standings and the variance of his ratings.

TABLE 14

STATUS, BIAS, AND MUTUALITY INDICES FOR THE RATING MATRICES
(Pretest Actives Who Remained in Organization for Posttest)

Attribute: Component: Organization	Friendship				Schoolwork				House Activities				Getting Along			
	Status	Bias	Stat-bias	Diff mut	Status	Bias	Stat-bias	Diff mut	Status	Bias	Stat-bias	Diff mut	Status	Bias	Stat-bias	Diff mut
Fraternity 1	.20	.21	.20	.28	.38	.11	-.10	.03	.33	.17	-.18	.00	.25	.17	.10	.15
Fraternity 2	.10	.25	-.12	.25	.46	.12	-.40	-.14	.46	.11	-.15	-.04	.14	.18	-.23	.10
Fraternity 3	.13	.32	.50	.40	.28	.24	-.32	.41	.26	.16	-.09	.02	.21	.30	.44	.37
Fraternity 4	.04	.40	.14	.32	.42	.03	-.33	-.07	.50	.05	-.42	-.09	.13	.20	.15	.30
Fraternity 5	.13	.19	.04	.29	.57	-.01	-.41	-.19	.44	.06	-.21	-.01	.23	.10	-.23	-.07
Fraternity 6	.08	.04	.64	.25	.78	-.09	-.55	-.14	.13	.39	-.69	-.06	-.04	.17	.45	-.14
Sorority 1	.14	.20	.49	.41	.39	.16	-.04	.07	.51	.07	-.12	-.01	.15	.23	.15	.22
Sorority 2	.22	.07	.05	.39	.28	.08	-.18	-.08	.44	.05	-.13	.06	.34	.12	-.10	.03
Sorority 3	.15	.26	.37	.37	.27	.08	.10	.14	.44	.08	-.12	-.01	.18	.24	.34	.24
Sorority 4	.34	.05	.04	.35	.38	.14	-.14	.09	.51	.00	-.43	-.21	.54	-.06	-.39	-.07
Mean (via z transformation)	.15	.20	.25	.33	.44	.09	-.25	.01	.41	.12	-.27	-.04	.22	.17	.07	.11

Note.— Indices for status, bias, and status-bias concordance are intra-class correlation coefficients; index for differential mutuality is a (weighted) mean product-moment correlation coefficient.

score received by a person as an index of his over-all status within the house. How well he was liked depended considerably on which of his colleagues was rating him. The mean correlation of .33 as a measure of differential mutuality indicates that how well one person liked another depended on how much he was liked by that other in return.

Individual differences in rating bias are not especially pronounced for the friendship variable. Though significantly larger than in ratings of schoolwork, they are not significantly different from bias in ratings of house activities or of ability to get along with others.

The mean status-bias correlation of .25 indicates that the more a member liked his colleagues, the better he was liked by them, on the average. It was not often that subjects admitted to actual dislike of a fellow member; ratings larger than 4 on the 7-point scale (see footnote on Table 12) were infrequent. This status-bias concordance in the friendship ratings contrasts sharply with concordance on the other attributes. The rating matrices on schoolwork and house activities for nearly all the organizations showed negative status-bias concordance: A person with high status on these attributes tended to rate others lower, on the average, than did a person with low status. Results for the ratings on ability to get along with others were intermediate between these two extremes: status-bias concordance was significantly lower than in liking ratings, but higher than in ratings on schoolwork and house activties ($\alpha < .05$).

One might infer from these results that the average level at which one rates other people on an "objective" attribute ("objective" in that there is reasonably high status consensus) is inversely correlated with one's own status on that attribute; rating is done, in part, by contrast with oneself. On a "subjective" attribute, however, where there are marked individual differences in judgment of the same stimulus, these judgments are much more likely to reflect mutual sentiments; if one person rates another high or low, that rating is likely to be reciprocated.

Non-constant Rating Group. Though it would have been desirable to obtain knowledgeable ratings from all members on each other for all four attributes, this ideal was only approximated in practice. Not all the subjects in a given house knew everyone else well enough to rate him. They were therefore permitted to leave unknown names blank. Though all objects (ratees) were rated by a substantial group of others, in some groups these differed somewhat from one object to another. The instructions for the sociometric instrument encouraged some sort of rating even in cases of uncertainty. This was intended to minimize the number of objects on whom status scores could not be computed; but it undoubtedly led to considerable randomness of ratings as well, which would tend to muddy any precise functional relationships.

In analyzing change in sociometric status from pre- to posttest, certain additional complications stemmed from the fact that raters were not usually the same on both occasions. Many pretest raters had left by the time of the posttest, and some who did not know a particular member on the pretest had become acquainted with him a year later. This led to an arbitrary decision, namely, that in all analyses of change in sociometric status, a matched sample of subjects (Ss) and objects (Os) would be used: Only those Ss who had had an opportunity to rate a given person (O) both times would be used in computing O's change in status. This matched-Ss-and-Os procedure was employed in the change analyses to make sure that a changing population of raters did not contribute spuriously to any changes in sociometric status.

Attraction to the Organization

In addition to the development of somewhat selective attractions among individual members, one of the significant organizational processes is the establishment and maintenance of allegiance to the organization as a whole. Though the sum of a member's attractions toward his colleagues may be an important component of his total attraction to the group, the two concepts are by no means identical, for a great many other considerations may mediate group loyalty. In spite of strong dislike for certain of its members, one may nevertheless feel a general positive attitude toward the group as a whole, either for the more salient friendships found within it or for other reasons, such as the fact that the group and its activities serve other important goals for him. In one sense, attraction to the organization may function as a more inclusive attitude than feelings about individual members; in another sense, it may represent something quite different, as when one feels that the organization is fine, except for the people in it, or that here are otherwise nice people involved in a ridiculous organization.

An attempt was made to get at members' over-all feelings about the group by constructing a multiple-item index of attraction to it (see Appendix E). This included questions such as, "How important is membership in this organization to you?" "If you moved to another university, would you join the same organization immediately, or would you wait to see what it was like first?" The index was administered on both pre- and posttest to all pledges and actives currently in the house. After an item analysis, six of the original nine items were retained for the final index, which had an average inter-item correlation of .31 and a reliability coefficient (Cronbach, 1951) of .73.

Some indication of the validity of the index is offered in Table 15, which shows pretest mean attraction scores within subgroups of Ss for each of the organizations separately, and for all of them combined. Though these scores represent feelings about the organization at the time of the pretest, the sub-groups are formed on the basis of the members' fates one year later, i.e., whether or not they were still in the house and, if not, for what reason. It may be noted that pledges as a group scored higher than actives, but among actives, those who left the organization by the time of the posttest showed a significantly lower mean attraction score than those who remained in the house. Also, the mean scores of seniors (actives on the pretest who had graduated a year later) were significantly lower than those of the younger

127

TABLE 15
PRETEST ATTRACTION TO THE ORGANIZATION AMONG VARIOUS MEMBERSHIP GROUPS

| | Organization | | | | | | | | | | |
| | Fraternities | | | | | | Sororities | | | | Mean |
Sub-group[a]	1	2	3	4	5	6	1	2	3	4	
Actives											
(a) Still	3.4	3.2	3.7	3.3	4.3	5.3	3.9	3.8	3.6	3.6	3.7
(b) Graduated	3.4	2.9	1.8	3.1	1.5	3.4	2.3	2.3	4.2	b	3.0
(c) Left	3.1	2.9	1.2	2.9	4.1	3.2	2.9	2.9	3.1	3.5	3.0
(d) Total actives	3.3	3.1	2.9	3.2	3.9	4.1	3.2	3.1	3.6	3.5	3.3
Pledges											
(e) Went active	3.7	3.4	3.3	4.0	3.3	4.3	4.3	4.0	3.4	3.8	3.7
(f) Left org.	4.5	2.9	3.8	4.0	3.5	5.0	4.3	2.4	3.8	b	3.4
(g) Left school	4.8	3.0	3.4	4.2	3.7	4.4	4.3	3.3	3.7	2.7	3.6
(h) Total pledges	4.0	3.1	3.4	4.0	3.4	4.4	4.3	3.3	3.6	3.3	3.6

t tests of differences between means of sub-groups (all organizations combined):

(a) vs. (b): $t = 3.03$; $\alpha < .01$.   (e) vs. (f): (NS)

(a) vs. (c): $t = 3.23$; $\alpha < .01$.   (e) vs. (g): (NS)

                                        (d) vs. (h): $t = 2.04$; $\alpha < .05$.

[a] See description of sub-groups in Table 8.
[b] No Ss in this sub-group.

128

actives; this accords with the common observation that seniors frequently become disenchanted with the fraternity as their time in it draws to a close.

Background Characteristics

In addition to the foregoing variables, which provided major foci for the study, certain other information about members was obtained on the pretest — the size of their home community, their own and their parents' political preferences, their own and their parents' rated degree of religiousness, and their approximate family income. These measures were taken to determine whether any of them related significantly to pretest values and, if so, whether the magnitudes of such relationships would diminish from pre- to posttest.

INDIVIDUAL AND GROUP VARIABLES

Though this chapter is concerned mainly with the measurement of organizational characteristics, this was both a study of individuals and of groups. In fact, measurement of most of the designated characteristics of organizations depended on responses of individuals. This was true of such properties as group cohesiveness, dominant house values, consensus on sociometric status, and attrition rates. In what sense, then, do these attributes constitute "group characteristics," as distinct from individual characteristics?

The answer entails both conceptual and methodological considerations. From one point of view, a group property is no less "real" than an individual property — which is also to say that the latter is no more "real" than the former. Individuals are complex, changing entities, and any assessment procedure captures only an aspect of the total person, often just a fleeting aspect. From behavior emitted by an individual one is tempted to infer certain personal qualities as causal antecedents. But these qualities — be they values or other personalty traits — are mostly hypothetical contructs, rather than empirical observables. To the extent that different response-eliciting stimuli, such as the several items in a test, produce behaviors that correspond less than perfectly, a single determining attribute cannot legitimately be inferred. To the extent that the same stimulus administered at different times elicits different responses, one cannot infer that the organism has remained constant in the relevant respect. Since "personality" is a construct that refers to individual consistencies in response over time and over different modes of assessment, and since different measures typically yield only moderately correlated results, the enduring reality of personality characteristics (Campbell, 1958, has called this "entitativity") must be regarded as quite incomplete.

Thus it is with group properties and, hence, with the entire concept of a "group." Perhaps measures of these constructs show even less correspondence among one another, and from one time to another, than do measures of personality attributes. But both kinds of attributes must be inferred or postulated from their measures; they do not exist apart from these, hence one is, a priori, no more "real" than the other.

Just what domain of construct is to be inferred does not depend wholly on the source of data about it. Ultimately, measures of all kinds of events — from climatic conditions to chemical processes — are obtained via humans. Just because an individual human is used as a source of data is no reason that the data must describe his own characteristics, rather than characteristics of some external system to which he is (deliberately or unintentionally) responding. Thus, there is no reason, in principle, why data obtained from individual subjects cannot be used to infer properties of their groups just as well as to infer properties of them as individuals. This may even be true regardless of the person's own intent as to the object of his report.

One is led, then, to assert that whether a group or an individual property is to be inferred from a set of measures depends initially on the intention of the researcher, and that the legitimacy of his inference can be checked tentatively by the degree of correspondence among several measures aimed at the same attribute. Such a check, however, serves only the function of a reliability or homogeneity analysis and does not establish the theoretical meaningfulness or empirical usefulness of the inference. These can only be determined through the demonstration of lawful relations that involve the construct and its measures. If these appear, and the results cannot reasonably be interpreted on any more obvious basis,[4] then the inference may, at least tentatively, be considered a "valid" one — or, what is indistinguishable from this, a pragmatically useful one.

SUMMARY

The organizations selected for longitudinal study were six fraternities and four sororities at the University of Colorado. Their participation was solicited after a purposive selection among the available fraternities, and by requesting volunteers among the sororities. Pretest questionnaires were administered in the fall of 1957 to about 90% of the total membership (actives and pledges) of the ten organizations, and over 90% of this entire group completed posttests approximately one year later. These questionnairies included measures of personal values, attitudes toward the organization, sociometric ratings on four different attributes, and certain background characteristics. Responses to them, together with data on attrition, provided measures of the individual and group variables included in this longitudinal study. By the time of the posttest, about half of the original members had either graduated or left school or dropped the organization; their posttest questionnaires did not assess sociometrics or attitudes toward the organization.

The values of members within the four sororities tended to

---

[4] What is "more obvious" will, of course, depend on the state of previous knowledge and on the preferred thought patterns of the researcher and his colleagues.

correspond fairly well with the values of all sorority members on campus. Their mean scores were higher than those of Independent women on the values of social skills, loyalty, academic achievement, physical development, and status; lower on the value of independence. The six fraternities, on the other hand, showed mutually distinctive value patterns but, as a total group, they did not correspond well with the values of all fraternity members on campus. It cannot be known for certain whether this atypicality would vitiate the generalizability of findings from the longitudinal study; but since the analyses deal only with relations among variables, rather than with their central tendencies, it is assumed that this non-representativeness is not critical to the study's conclusions.

Interpersonal rating scales (sociometric measures) were included in the questionnaire to determine for each member how well he was liked by others, and how much he was perceived as oriented toward schoolwork, toward house activities, and toward interpersonal relations. Each of the four subject-by-object rating matrices derived from these instruments was anaylzed into components of variance due to rater bias, to status of ratee, and to mutuality of ratings. While members' statuses on a particular attribute were of major concern for subsequent analyses, the mutuality component was sufficiently pronounced in the "liking" matrices to cast some doubt on the meaningfullness of an over-all status score. Individual differences in raters' perceptions must be taken into account in understanding the ratings they give to others.

A member who liked his colleagues tended to be well liked by them in return, but the higher a person was rated by others on the attributes of academic orientation and orientation toward the house, the lower he tended to rate his colleagues on these attributes. Thus, mutuality of ratings tended to be positive for the "subjective" attribute (liking) and negative for the "objective" attributes (devotion to schoolwork and devotion to house activities).

Attraction of members to their organization was measured by a multiple-item scale aimed at tapping over-all feelings of devotion to their particular group. In the pretest, pledges tended to score higher than actives on this measure. Also, actives who subsequently dropped out of the organization (while remaining in school), as well as members in their senior year, showed lower attraction to the group than did those who were still in the house at the time of the posttest.

CHAPTER 5

RECRUITMENT

The assignment of individuals to social organizations takes place through that mutually challenging practice known as "rush week." This is the time when aspiring members, or the curious who are "just looking," visit various houses in which they have expressed an interest, to decide which (if any) they wish to join. This is the time when the old members of each organization look over the visitors and try to decide whom they would prefer to accept as members. It is, to varying degrees, a stressful experience for both parties. In addition to assessing their own preferences, the rushees are trying to guess what their prospects for acceptance are at each prestige level of organization they encounter, perhaps adjusting their levels of aspiration to their own self-concepts and to the apparent stiffness of competition for membership. The organizations, for their part, are evaluating rushees as best they can and also trying to guess what proportion of each quality grade will choose to join their group, so that they can determine the number of acceptances and the cut-off point on their quality scale.

Information that each side has about the other is not based solely on the house visits, however. The Greek organizations may have provided descriptive material even before the freshmen reached the university, and their reputations may be more or less known through their alumni. From their alumni the fraternities and sororities themselves have received letters of support for would-be pledges.

At the close of rush week, each rushee ranks his favored organizations in order of preference, and each organization lists the candidates acceptable to it. These mutual preferences are first fed into a mechanical analysis so as to fill as many of the rushees' first choices as possible; then their second and third choices are used, as necessary. In a typical year at Colorado, about 2% to 4% of the rushees find no acceptable match at all, others drop rushing prior to the final selection.

Much attention has been focused on the inevitable disappointment that confronts some freshmen who fail to gain admittance to their favored — or, indeed, to any — house. A balanced view of the process should also note the concomitant disappointment of many of the less prestigious houses, which fail in their attempt to attract the most desirable rushees — or, indeed, enough new pledges to keep the organization going. Less heed has been paid to the delayed, and only gradually realized, disappointments on both sides over failure to achieve an adequate match between individual and group. Many proposals have been made, and many campuses have adopted procedures, aimed at assuring a more rational choice based on better information. Mostly these entail delayed pledging — after one semester or even a whole year on campus. The logical relevance of this plan to improved long-term matching is obvious; it may also be seen as a device for avoiding some of the immediate disappointment among rushees as well, for after a period in the community they may be expected to develop other social ties which would help soften the blow of rejection; also, they may become more realistic about the possibilities of acceptance by a favored group.

At the time of this study, however, rushing took place at the beginning of the freshman year, and the shift in date proposed then was toward earlier, rather than later, rushing — i.e., during the week or two preceding fall registration. A surprising thing about the entire process is that any kind of satisfactory match can be made at all. One would hardly expect, from brief encounters between individual and organization, the degree of intra-group value similarity that resulted within the ten houses in this study.

In many respects, the process of organizational recruitment seen here is comparable to that found in other institutions, such as businesses, churches, and social clubs. The choices, both for individuals and groups, are critical, uncertain, and lasting in their consequences. Critical, because the individual's self-concept depends heavily on the prestige and intrinsic reward value of the group to which he is attached, and the organization's "corporate image" depends on the continuing quality of its members. Uncertain, because predictions about compatibility have to be made by both sides on the basis of rather scanty and unreliable evidence. Lasting in their consequences, because so many things impede a dissolution of the individual-group relationship once established: Both sides are loath to recognize a mismatch; sheer lethargy may keep either from doing anything about it; direct remedial action is embarrassing to one party and insulting to the other.

The rushing practice has, however, certain features that distinguish it from processes of recruitment in other institutions. In the first place, it tends to highlight the selection process by focusing exclusively on this aspect of the organization's activity for a two- or three-week period each year. Second, by the formalized attention to recruitment, it probably encourages more explicit and concentrated consideration by applicants of the alternatives available to them.

Third, it gives more easily to potential members the alternative of not joining *any* organization than do many recruitment processes. A freshman can choose not to rush more easily than an employable male can choose not to work anywhere, probably more easily than an eligible woman can choose not to get married. Of course, the climate on some campuses may be such that choosing not to rush is tantamount to "choosing" not to get married, in its consequences for exclusion from culturally valued activities. But this degree of Greek domination does not obtain at the University of Colorado.

Thus, from the standpoint of the individual student, there is an explicit two-step process in his path toward social affiliation: First, the decision whether or not to go Greek; second, if Greek, which of the available houses to join. In the first of these steps, the organizations, for the most part, exert only an indirect and long-term influence through their collective alumni and through other forms of "public relations." It is the individual, finally, who declares whether he shall go Greek or Independent (though this decision can hardly be considered a wholly autonomous one). It is in the second step that both organizational and individual forces come directly to play on the ultimate outcome. The strategy of analysis in this chapter is to treat these two steps separately, by first considering what distinguishes all pledges from a comparison group of non-pledging freshmen and, second, considering differences among pledges in the several organizations studied.

PLEDGES COMPARED WITH NON-PLEDGING FRESHMEN

In order to study the recruitment process optimally, it would have been desirable to follow entering freshmen from their pre-university period through their deliberation and choice among houses to their final admittance to pledge status. For various practical reasons, such an extended longitudinal study was not feasible — because rush time is so busy and the rushees are so dispersed that it is difficult to get them settled down together for testing; because, in order to get even a few organizations *in toto*, this strategy would have required assessment of the entire group of entering freshmen, for no one knows where they are going to end up until all selections have been made. So we started with the organizations in October, after they knew who their pledges were. This made the groups to be studied identifiable and facilitated group testing.

To obtain a comparison group of non-pledging freshmen, a men's and women's freshman dormitory were visited, and participation in the study was solicited among students who had decided not to pledge any Greek organization. Though 103 men and 79 women complied, there is no way of knowing how many of the "decisions" not to pledge resulted from rejection by organizations in the preceding rush period. As it turned out, 13% of these men and 20% of the women actually did join some fraternity or sorority on campus (not necessarily one of the ten in the present study) by the time of the posttest one year later.

Certain demographic differences between the initial pledge and non-pledge groups bear out commonly accepted notions: For both male and female subjects the family incomes of pledges tended to be higher. Except for the single Jewish organization, both male and female pledges were more likely than non-pledges

TABLE 16

MEAN PRETEST VALUES OF MALE PLEDGES AND OF NON-PLEDGING FRESHMAN MALES

COMPARED WITH MEAN PRETEST VALUES OF MALE ACTIVES

Value	(1) Non-pledging Freshmen (n = 103)		(2) Pledges (n = 187)	(3) Actives (n = 231)
Intellectualism	−.39	*	−.59	−.52
Kindness	−.20		−.16	−.17
Social skills	−.32	**	−.13	−.04
Loyalty	.27	**	.79	.55
Academic achievement	.20		.30	.03
Physical development	.06		.04	−.13
Status	−.01		.22	.07
Honesty	.35		.18	.09
Religiousness	.10		.14	−.05
Self-control	−.05		−.13	−.06
Creativity	−.26	**	−.63	−.56
Independence	.02	*	−.25	−.12

Note. — These are standard scores based on Ms and σs of a university random sample.
*Difference between pledges and non-pledging freshmen significant at $\alpha <$ .05.
**Difference between pledges and non-pledging freshmen significant at $\alpha <$ .01.

138

to have come from Republican families. Among both male and female freshmen, the pledges were more likely to have been raised in urban, rather than rural, areas than were the non-pledges. (This trend also appeared to a significant degree in the male group considered alone, but not in the female group.) Among the male pledges there was a preponderance of Protestants — 83% as compared with 68% in the non-pledge sample — but the female groups showed no significant religious differences when the single Jewish house was excluded from the pledge sample.

Though none of these demographic variables was correlated with values in the present sample to a significant degree, somehow the initial recruitment process served to segregate the pledging from non-pledging freshmen on certain relevant values. In the first two columns of Table 16 appears a comparison of value means of these two groups for male subjects, and in Table 17 the

TABLE 17

MEAN PRETEST VALUES OF FEMALE PLEDGES AND OF NON-PLEDGING FRESHMAN FEMALES COMPARED WITH MEAN PRETEST VALUES OF FEMALE ACTIVES

Value	(1) Non-pledging Freshmen (n = 79)		(2) Pledges (n = 163)	(3) Actives (n = 179)
Intellectualism	−.11		−.16	.10
Kindness	.54	**	.17	.31
Social skills	−.02	**	.36	.31
Loyalty	.10	**	.78	.77
Academic achievement	−.02	*	.20	.44
Physical development	.08		.18	.22
Status	−.22	*	.02	.01
Honesty	.40		.25	.21
Religiousness	.37		.44	.37
Self-control	.30		.18	.33
Creativity	−.24		−.15	.00
Independence	−.18	**	−.53	−.36

Note. — These are standard scores based on Ms and σs of a university random sample.
*Difference between pledges and non-pledging freshmen significant at $\alpha <$ .05.
**Difference between pledges and non-pledging freshmen significant at $\alpha <$ .01.

same data appear for the females. Male pledges tended to score higher than their comparison group on the values of social skills and loyalty, lower on the values of intellectualism, creativity, and independence. Female pledges, somewhat similarly, were higher than non-pledges with respect to the values of social skills, loyalty, academic achievement, and status, and lower on the values of kindness and independence.

To what extent did the values of pledges reflect — or rather, anticipate — the values of the Greek organizations they were joining? Was each group of freshmen — pledge and non-pledge — pre-socialized into a pattern of values appropriate to the "culture" that it was to adopt? One way of answering these questions is to compare the pledge values with the values of actives. Column 3 of Tables 16 and 17 present such a comparison. It may be noted that, for each sex, in every case where the pledges differed significantly from the non-pledging freshmen, it was always in the direction of the actives' values. Considering the total pattern at once, one may compute a correlation over the twelve values between the means for pledges and the means for actives. This is .96 for male subjects and .94 for females (in both cases $\alpha <$ .001). By contrast, the corresponding correlations between actives and non-pledging freshmen are .74 and .49 — both significantly smaller (at $\alpha <$ .05) than the correlations for pledges of the same sex.

In some instances — especially for the males — there was even a tendency for the pledge group to "overshoot" the active mean by scoring more extremely in that direction than the actives themselves. This is most apparent for the values of social skills, loyalty, and independence among male subjects, and for the value of independence among female subjects. It is tempting to interpret this tendency toward extreme value scores as a manifestation of excessive anticipatory socialization among the pledge groups: They may have tended to adopt, opportunistically and to an extreme degree, those values which they perceived as distinctively characterizing the groups to which they aspired.

140

One may also compare the value differences between pledging and non-pledging freshmen with the value differences previously reported between Greeks and Independents for the campus as a whole. Such a comparison will help to determine whether entering freshmen had already adopted, at the time of the pretest, certain distinguishing values of "Greek" and "Independent cultures." For women this seems to have been true: The value differences between pledges and non-pledges (Cols. 1 and 2 of Table 17) correspond quite closely with the value differences between all campus Greeks and Independents (Cols. 1 and 2 of Table 10, p. 116). The correlation between difference scores, over the twelve values, is .78 ($\alpha <$ .01). Among men, however, there is no substantial correspondence between freshman differences and campus-wide differences. The correlation over the two sets of difference scores (Table 16 and Table 11) is only .36 — not significantly different from zero.

It will be recalled, however, that the six fraternities included in this longitudinal study were somewhat atypical of all campus fraternities (see pp. 117-118), while the four sororities provided a much closer value match with all sororities on campus. Thus, one may conclude that, at this university, there is a fairly distinctive value culture in the sororities, and that entering pledges tend to be pre-socialized for it. There is probably no such distinct value culture that characterizes all fraternities (see Table 11); but pledges in the six organizations studied here did tend to hold values like those of actives in the same six houses.

The results thus provide evidence concerning the relevance of personal values for the first phase of the recruitment process — in which the individual decides whether or not to join *some* organization. Since contact of the pledges with the houses had been slight up to the time of the pretest, whatever causal relation existed between organization membership and values was probably in the direction of values' having influenced the freshman's intent either to join or not to join. Of course, having decided to join, the rushee may then, in anticipation, have emulated those valued characteristics that he deemed appropriate to the status of member; indirectly, therefore, the organizations may have influenced certain values of aspiring members by presenting an image for emulation, thus contributing to the observed difference between pledges and non-pledges. But a more direct interpretation of these results is simply that a freshman's decision either to pledge or not to pledge was a function of the values he held and of the way he saw these organizations in relation to his values.

One consequence of this first stage of recruitment was to bring into the Greek community a new membership whose total value structure was similar to that of the old members. "Similar" only to a degree, of course, for absolute identity could hardly be achieved even though both parties to the selection were maximally perspicacious. Actives and rushees rarely ask one another directly about their values; they simply don't have time, let alone the proper measuring instruments. But the organizations have presumably been emitting relevant cues since long before rush week, and the house visits are arranged to permit actives to observe relevant cues in rushees' behavior, with the result that some sort of better-than-chance matching on values is achieved. The pledges to these ten organizations initially maintained a total set of values which was more like those of actives (of the same sex) than were the values of the non-pledging freshmen with which they were compared. Recruitment of these students as pledges tended to keep the over-all value pattern of the ten fraternities and sororities more constant than it would have been had the non-pledges been selected instead.

SIMILARITIES WITHIN HOUSES

So much for recruitment of freshmen into the total population of students available as pledges. How about differential recruitment by the several houses according to the distinctive value patterns of each? That is, within the total group of pledges, was there a distribution of recruits over the houses such that those who actually joined any one of them tended to match their own organization's values better than a random sample of pledges from the total group would have?

The degree of active-pledge value matching within a single organization was represented by a correlation between actives and pledges over their respective means for the twelve values. These means were first expressed as standard scores based on the mean and standard deviation of all pretest subjects of the same sex. It was appropriate to compute standard scores for the two sexes separately, because men and women differed on some of the values, and failure to take these differences into account would have spuriously inflated the predicted correlation over values; the result might demonstrate only that fraternities tended to pledge men and sororities tended to pledge women. Also, standard scores were computed separately for pledges and for actives within each sex, because their means also differed on some of the values, and it seemed appropriate to compare standings of a particular sub-group relative to all members of that class, either actives or pledges. One would expect that the fraternity highest on the honesty value, for example, would tend to select pledges who were the highest on honesty *relative to the group of available male pledges.* An added advantage of computing standard scores for the actives and pledges separately was that this procedure yielded an expected value of zero, under the null hypothesis, for the mean within-house correlation between actives' and pledges' values.

The correlations within each of the ten houses over the mean standard scores of actives and pledges for the twelve values are presented in Column 1 of Table 18. They are arranged in order of magnitude, with the houses identified by the numbers used in Table 8 (pp. 112-113). Eight of the ten within-house correlations are positive ($\alpha = .055$, by sign test), and their average size can be represented by the mean z (from Fisher, 1941) of .29. Estimating the error variance from the actual distribution of zs over the ten groups yields a t ratio of 3.05, significant beyond the .01 level.

TABLE 18
SIMILARITIES BETWEEN PRETEST VALUES OF ACTIVES AND PLEDGES IN
EACH ORGANIZATION AND SUBSEQUENT
ATTRITION RATES OF PLEDGES

Organization	(1) Active-Pledge Value Similarity[a]	(2) Per Cent of Pledges Who: Left Org.	(3) Left School	Total Pledge n
Fraternity 4	.887	3%	35%	37
Fraternity 2	.510	19%	33%	36
Sorority 4	.424	0	48%	33
Sorority 1	.377	10%	23%	40
Fraternity 1	.377	13%	17%	30
Fraternity 6	.234	14%	57%	14
Sorority 2	.182	23%	40%	60
Fraternity 5	.110	7%	33%	30
Sorority 3	−.030	27%	23%	30
Fraternity 3	−.172	15%	25%	40
Mean	.290			

[a] These similarity scores are z transformations of product-moment correlations between active and pledge means over the twelve values, after each sub-group mean had been expressed as a standard deviate of the entire active or pledge group of that sex (see accompanying text).

On the average, then, these several houses did tend to recruit from the total pledge population those pledges whose value patterns were similar to their own and this similarity between value patterns was greater than it would have been had the pledges been randomly selected. The degree to which this end result reflects the actives' capacities for assessing candidates and the degree to which it reflects the pledges' appraisals of the organizations (and, perhaps, "anticipatory socialization" in accord with their image) cannot be established from these data. But the remarkable fact is that some differential matching of values did occur in this second stage of the recruitment process.

CONSEQUENCES OF SUCCESSFUL AND
UNSUCCESSFUL MATCHING

Though it might be argued that, in some respects at least, the induction of new members with values divergent from the pre-established norm could benefit the groups, it is unlikely that diversity in these kinds of values is purposely sought. Some organizations may desire pledge groups with heterogeneous talents and interests to broaden the public image of the group and to extend its sphere of influence over a wider range of campus activities. But it would be hard to maintain organizational cohesiveness and stability if the basic values of pledges which are relevant to the organization's functioning were to diverge too much from the current norm. Therefore, it seems reasonable to maintain that organizations obtaining pledges with values like their own have had a more successful recruitment than organizations whose pledges turn out to have rather different values. From the pledges' standpoint, too, the outcome could be deemed more successful, for they would find themselves in a new group that would be more likely to appreciate their own dominant orientations than to challenge their validity. Though diversity in some respects may be functional for the long-range adaptation of an institution to its environment, short-run member satisfaction and intra-organizational harmony are probably better facilitated by homogeneity of values.

The attrition rates for pledges in the several organizations bear out this interpretation. There were two classes of drop-outs among the pledges: Those who left school and those who left the organization but remained in school. The former type probably represents "exogenous attrition"; that is, it is less likely to be under the control of the organizations, for it is made up largely of students who do not make the minimum grades required by the university. Pledges who leave the organization but remain in school are more likely to represent "endogenous attrition"— the disaffected proportion of the membership plus those whom the organization chooses to drop during the pledge period. Drop-out rates of both types are indicated in the second and third columns of Table 18.

Dividing the organizations at the median similarity score, the over-all drop-out rates of the high-similarity organizations averaged 9% of the pledges leaving the house and 31% leaving school; for the low-similarity organizations, the corresponding rates were 18% and 34%. (These are weighted averages that take into account the varying sizes of the pledge groups.) The differences between high- and low-value–similarity groups in the proportions of pledges who left the organization (while remaining in school) is significant at the .05 level.[1] Thus, it may be inferred that the more successful these social organizations were in recruiting new members with value patterns similar to their own norms, the lower was the subsequent rate of endogenous attrition, i.e., attrition due to intra-organizational causes.

The difference between high- and low-similarity organizations in the proportions of pledges who dropped school is not significant. This fact provides one indication that the preceding result is not due to some unknown, extraneous factor. But certain specific explanations may be rejected directly. First, the difference is not attributable to the small differential in drop-out rates between fraternities and sororities, for houses of both sexes are pretty well scattered along the range of value-similarity. Second, it is not due to differing sizes of the pledge groups, for their sizes are fairly constant over groups and, again, not correlated with the degree of active-pledge similarity in values.

Finally, the possibility was examined that the results reflected differing levels of prestige among the several organizations — that high-prestige houses were capable of attracting "ideal" pledges (according to their particular value criteria) and were also less likely to lose them subsequently, because their pledges valued their membership more than did those in low-prestige houses. It was easy, from the physical quality of their buildings, to divide the ten organizations into two levels of prestige — the high groups being Fraternities 1, 2, 3, and 4 and

[1] The standard error of the difference between proportions was computed from the formula for clustered samples (see Scott & Wertheimer, 1962, p. 231); if simple random sampling had been assumed, the significance level would have been .01.

Sororities 1 and 3. It may be seen from Table 18 that these six high-status organizations *did* have quite low exogenous attrition rates (represented in Col. 3), but their rates of endogenous attrition (Col. 2) were about average. This result would seem to indicate that prestigious fraternities and sororities were relatively successful in screening out rushees who would fail to make their grades, but not rushees who would subsequently drop membership for non-academic reasons. Successful recruitment in the latter sense evidently depended more on value compatibility than on house prestige.

SUMMARY

From the would-be member's perspective, the process of recruitment to these organizations consists of two steps — coming into the population of member-aspirants (rushees), and being admitted to a particular organization as a pledge. It is likely that predisposing member characteristics largely determine selection at the first stage, while characteristics of both aspirants and old organization members jointly affect the outcome of the second stage. In this study the total pledge sample was found to differ from a non-pledge comparison group with respect to certain values which may be considered central to organization processes: Male pledges as a whole tended to place more emphasis on social skills and loyalty, less emphasis on intellectualism, creativity, and independence, than did non-pledging freshman males. In the female samples, pledges tended to score higher on the values of social skills, loyalty, academic achievement, and status, lower on the values of kindness and independence, than did non-pledging freshmen. For each sex, these are precisely the directions of differences that distinguished the total pretest actives from the non-pledging freshmen.

In some instances the pledges tended to "overshoot" the actives' mean values, away from the positions of non-pledges, thereby adopting a degree of emphasis in excess of what was required for conformity to the actives' norms. Nevertheless, the resulting over-all pattern of pledges' values was more similar to that of actives than was the over-all pattern of the non-pledges' values.

Besides segregating the total pledge group from non-pledges on the basis of relevant values, the recruitment process also resulted in a significant tendency to distribute the pledge sample itself among houses in such a way that similarity to actives' values was enhanced. The ten organizations differed in the degree of success attained in this process of value-matching between actives and pledges. In groups where it was most successful, the subsequent endogenous attrition rates of pledges tended to be lower than in houses with less successful value-matching.

CHAPTER 6

STATUS DIFFERENTIATION

In most social systems one may find some sort of mechanism for allocating differential prestige among the membership. The mechanism may consist of formal rank-grading, as in the military and other forms of bureaucracy, or of pay differentials, or election to office by the membership, or the awarding and withholding of privileges. Status differentials established in any of these ways are generally assumed to reflect, in part, the differing contributions that members make to the organization's functioning. In fact, status differentiation may be regarded as serving to maintain the social system, since it orients the membership toward collective goals by rewarding those who contribute most to them.

Fraternities and sororities may allocate prestige formally by electing some members to office and excluding undesirables from the organization. But such formal recognitions are not widely conferred; they provide status distinctions only among a select few of the membership. Perhaps attempts at more refined discrimination among members of informal groups can be only partially fruitful, because who is allocated what status depends largely on who does the allocating. It is an oversimplification to speak of any member's status as if it were uniquely definable, for he can be regarded as having multiple statuses, depending on who is appraising him and what method of appraisal is being used.

In spite of the imprecise conceptual meaning of "status" for most individuals, the present study used a single, simplified operational definition, consisting of the mean rating given a member by all others rating him on the attribute "how much you like him." The rationale for using this friendship-rating measure of status has been presented in Chapter 4 (p. 119). It has the additional advantage of providing a status score for every member of the organization, so long as he is rated by enough others to yield a stable mean.

The value bases of the friendship rating can be investigated from three different perspectives: That of the subject (rater), that of the object (ratee), and that of the dyad (subject-pair) within which mutual attraction or repulsion may be found. From the first perspective one would seek to discover what values in the subject account for the way in which he rates his colleagues. From the second perspective one would ask what values in the members (as objects of rating) account for their being liked or disliked by others. From the third perspective one would wish to know about the relative degrees of value similarity in those pairs of subjects who mutually like, or mutually dislike, each other.

VALUES AND SOCIOMETRIC RATINGS

From the standpoint of the members as raters, the value bases for their judgments may be inferred, in part, from the manner in which their friendship ratings correlated with their ratings of the same people on the other three attributes — orientation to studies, orientation to the house, and orientation to interpersonal relations. The first three columns of Table 19 present these correlations averaged for members within each of the ten houses. For each subject, a product-moment correlation was computed, over the objects that he rated, between his friendship rating and his rating on each of the other three attributes. These correlation coefficients were averaged within a house, as the arithmetic mean of the computed rs from all subjects. At the bottom of each column in Table 19 appears the mean correlation across all ten houses, computed by weighting each mean intra-house correlation (transformed to Fisher's z) by ($n-3$), where n is the number of Ss included in the rating matrix for that house. The figures reported here are from the *pretest* ratings of actives who were still in the organization (and filled out questionnaires) at the time of the posttest. Results very similar to these appeared as well when either the entire pretest group of raters or the entire posttest group of raters was considered.

The mean correlations in the first three columns are all significantly different from zero and from each other (at $\alpha < .01$). Hence, it may be concluded that the "average" rater tended to regard people whom he liked as more studious, more helpful to the group, and more socially adept than people whom he disliked. Moreover, the association with liking tended, on the average, to be strongest for the social skills rating and weakest for the academic rating.

Quite comparable results appear when one considers the correlations of members' liking status with their status on these

TABLE 19
MEAN CORRELATIONS BETWEEN FRIENDSHIP RATING
AND OTHER RATINGS;
CORRELATIONS BETWEEN FRIENDSHIP STATUS AND OTHER STATUSES
(Pretest of Actives Who Remained in Organization)

Organization	n	Mean r Between Friendship Rating and Rating on:			r Between Friendship Status and Status on:		
		School-work (1)	House Activities (2)	Getting Along (3)	School-work (4)	House Activities (5)	Getting Along (6)
Fraternity 1	40	.19	.40	.61	.05	.75	.94
Fraternity 2	32	.15	.26	.57	−.07	.56	.92
Fraternity 3	12	.14	.29	.63	.20	.41	.98
Fraternity 4	15	.24	.35	.49	.48	.70	.90
Fraternity 5	16	.19	.37	.60	.28	.64	.82
Fraternity 6	7	−.03	.43	.48	.08	.03	.75
Sorority 1	28	.29	.42	.60	.45	.70	.89
Sorority 2	20	.27	.48	.70	.59	.62	.96
Sorority 3	17	.30	.32	.61	.34	.37	.92
Sorority 4	9	.15	.43	.71	.04	.64	.94
Mean r (via weighted z)		.21	.37	.61	.24	.63	.93

three attributes. The highest correlate of liking status was "ability to get along with others," next highest was "contribution to house activities," and lowest (though still significantly positive) was "how seriously they take their schoolwork." The ordering of magnitudes of these various correlations (among Cols. 1, 2, 3, and among Cols. 4, 5, 6) was, with a single minor exception, identical in all ten houses, so the average relative importance of these three attributes to friendship choices may be considered a fairly stable characteristic of these organizations.

These results have at least two possible sources. On the one hand, it may be that the most popular people were, in fact, those most able to get along with others (and so on, for the other attributes in relative ordering of importance). On the other hand, these correlations might reflect the raters' subjective conceptions about qualities of people whom they liked or disliked. Additional analyses, to be reported presently, on the values of subjects and objects will help clarify these two interpretations. In either case, it is apparent that ability (perceived or actual) to get along with one's fellows was the major concomitant of high friendship status within all of these houses, and that contribution to the house and attention to studies were less important, in that order. When *changes* in members' friendship status from pre- to posttest were correlated with their *changes* in status on the other three rated attributes, the same order of magnitudes appeared: The mean rs were .82 with change in "getting along" status, .53 with change in "house activities" status, and .35 with change in "schoolwork" status.

Individual Differences in Values

The ordering of mean correlations between friendship ratings and ratings on the other three attributes may be interpreted as reflecting value priorities most commonly found in these organizations — that it is good to study hard, even better to work for the benefit of the house, and best of all to get along with one's fellow members. This inference concerning the value bases of sociometric ratings can be better substantiated at the individual level of analysis, since direct measures of value strength are available for all members. It is reasonable to suppose that, where individual differences in certain of the values occur, they will be reflected in different patterns of correlation among the sociometric ratings; a particular member who strongly values academic achievement, for example, should show a higher correlation between his friendship ratings and schoolwork ratings than some other member who does not admire academic achievement so much.

The relevant data are presented in Table 20, which shows the posttest correlation between (1) the strength of each value and (2) the magnitude of the coefficient of correlation between subjects' liking for others and their ratings of these others on the three remaining sociometric traits. (These *r*s were arrived at by averaging the correlations, via *z* transformations, for active and pledge groups within all ten houses. Averaging the within-houses correlations is preferable to pooling all subjects into a single matrix, because it eliminates from the result any possible contaminating effect due to inter-house differences in mean values or in mean correlation between ratings.) The total posttest sociometric ratings were used for this analysis because they were obtained from the maximum number of subjects at a time when they knew one another fairly well.

The italicized figures in Table 20 are the correlations that were predicted on the basis of a priori assumptions about the meanings of the sociometric rating scales in relation to the values. It was assumed in designing the instrument that orientation toward schoolwork would correspond to the value of academic achievement, orientation toward house activities would correspond to the value of loyalty, and ability to get along with people would correspond to the social skills value. Therefore, it was expected that the more a rater valued one of these traits, the more he would tend to perceive his favored persons as possessing it to a higher degree than persons whom he did not like.

TABLE 20
CORRELATIONS BETWEEN VALUES OF RATERS AND
SOCIOMETRIC RATING CORRESPONDENCES[a]
(Posttest Actives and Pledges; $n = 378$)

| Value | Rating Correspondence Between Liking and: | | |
	Schoolwork	House Activities	Getting Along
Intellectualism	.17**	.00	.06
Honesty	.15**	.05	.10
Academic achievement[b]	*.11**	.11*	.06
Religiousness	.10	.09	.10
Kindness	.09	.04	.06
Self-control	.08	.02	.10
Loyalty[b]	−.12*	*.24***	.12*
Social skills[b]	−.04	.08	*.11**
Status	−.14*	.10	.23**
Physical development	−.16**	.06	.08
Creativity	−.01	−.08	−.02
Independence	−.07	−.16**	−.10
Mean non-predicted r	.01	.03	.07
Predicted r exceeds non-predicted rs	9	11	9

[a] Table entries are mean within-house correlations (averaged by z transformation) between value strength and magnitude of each S's r between friendship ratings and other ratings over the Os whom he rated.
[b] Italicized figures represent rs between the sociometric rating correspondences and values to which they were, a priori, deemed relevant. These constitute the "predicted correlations."
* $\alpha < .05$.
** $\alpha < .01$.

(The direction of the effect might, of course, be the reverse: Ss tend to like Os in whom they perceive valued traits.) All of these three correlations (italicized figures) are significantly different from zero (at $\alpha < .05$). They are also larger than at least nine of the other correlations with values for which there was no a priori prediction; this result would occur by chance less than four times in a hundred if there were actually no difference between the predicted and the mean non-predicted correlations. Thus, these three values — academic achievement, loyalty, and social skills — were differentially relevant for sociometric ratings given to others. This result supports an interpretation offered earlier (p. 152), that the high correlation between status on the friendship sociometric and status on the "getting along" sociometric reflects the pre-eminent relevance of the social skills value to intra-group status differentiation in this fraternity culture.

Some of the other significant correlations in Table 20 help to clarify further the value bases for sociometric ratings. A relatively high correspondence between friendship ratings and schoolwork ratings was likely to be given by members who valued intellectualism and honesty, and a relatively low correspondence between these two sets of ratings tended to come from members who valued loyalty, status, or physical development. People *low* on the value of independence tended to associate friendship ratings with ratings on "contribution to house activities." And a high correlation between friendship ratings and ratings on "ability to get along with others" was most likely to occur among Ss who scored high on the values of loyalty and status (as well as social skills).

It may be concluded, then, that the friendship ratings given in these social organizations, and the way they related to ratings on the other attributes, reflected, to some extent, the values of the raters. A member was likely to choose as friends those colleagues who seemed to embody traits that he admired. Thus, an individual's friendship status within a house presumably depended, in part, on the values of the total house membership, or of the particular sub-group that was rating him. The value placed on social skill was so universally prominent in friendship ratings that a member's status was closely tied to his perceived skill, almost regardless of who rated him (see Table 19). The attribute of perceived contribution to house activities was of less universal relevance, and studiousness was least relevant of the three for the organizations as a whole.

Whether or not judgments of studiousness correlated substantially and positively with friendship choices depended on how much the particular raters valued such qualities as intellectualism, academic achievement, and honesty, on the one hand, as opposed to the qualities of loyalty, status, and physical development on the other.

VALUES AND SOCIOMETRIC STATUS

So much for the influence of raters' values on their ratings of others. How about the relevance of one's values for his own sociometric standing? In general, the only significant correlate of friendship status for the total posttest sample was the value of loyalty; members high on this value tended to be liked better than others, though the mean within-houses correlation ($r = .14$) was not large. For posttest actives considered alone (i.e., those who had been active at the time of the pretest and were still in the organization at the time of the posttest), there were significant correlations between friendship status and the values of loyalty, social skills, status, and intellectualism (see Table 21, Col. 1). If one interprets these four values as among the most relevant to the organization's functioning (as opposed, say, to honesty, religiousness, and independence), then the proposition might be advanced that, for members who have been in the group longest (the old actives), their own intra-group status will tend to reflect the degree to which they espouse values relevant to the organization's functioning. (The interpretation would seem apt for the values of loyalty, social skills, and status, but the correlation between status and the intellectualism value is not readily explained on this basis.)

It is also interesting to note that, when all values except independence are considered as a total set, and the average correlation between values and friendship status is computed, this correlation turns out to be relatively higher within the six high-prestige organizations. (See p. 146 for a designation of these houses.) The explanation of this result must remain speculative, but an appealing possibility is that the high-prestige organizations were able to attract a kind of membership which reinforced manifestations of these culturally "good" (i.e., society-maintaining) values, whereas the membership of low-prestige organizations, though espousing the values overtly, did not genuinely admire them enough to accord exceptional status to an exemplar. This is to say that one difference between the high- and low-status organizations may have been that, in the former, "virtue" was more likely to be rewarded.

Table 21 suggests some of the value bases for ratings received on the other sociometric attributes. The significant correlations in this table could be interpreted in either of two ways: (1) As indicating the values of people who actually possess the rated traits, or (2) as indicating the characteristics that provide relevant cues for raters when they are required to assess people on the several traits. It is evident, for example, that members' statuses on "how seriously they take their schoolwork" were positively correlated with their own value of intellectualism, and

TABLE 21

CORRELATIONS BETWEEN VALUES AND SOCIOMETRIC STANDINGS
(Posttest Actives; $n = 197$)

	Sociometric Standing on:			
Value	*Friendship* (1)	*Schoolwork* (2)	*House Activities* (3)	*Getting Along* (4)
Intellectualism	.16*	.23**	−.05	.16*
Kindness	.06	.12	.07	.10
Social skills	.17*	.00	.15*	.19*
Loyalty	.17*	−.13	.27**	.17*
Academic achievement	.10	−.04	.07	.16*
Physical development	.04	−.15*	.02	.06
Status	.15*	−.10	.09	.19*
Honesty	.04	.12	.04	.01
Religiousness	.02	−.03	.05	.05
Self-control	.03	.08	.00	.06
Creativity	.08	.01	−.04	.08
Independence	−.05	.08	−.05	−.06

Note. — Table entries represent mean within-house correlations (averaged via z transformation).
* $\alpha < .05$.
** $\alpha < .01$.

negatively with their value of physical development, but not significantly with the degree to which they valued academic achievement (as defined by the present scale). One may infer from these results either (1) that those members who were actually studious tended to admire intellectual things, but not sports and body-building activities, or (2) that a person's admiration for intellectual activities and disdain for sports tended to be manifest in ways that his colleagues interpreted as evidencing a scholarly orientation.

Similarly, from the positive associations between status on "contribution to house activities" and the values of social skills and loyalty, one may infer either that these values characterized the organization-oriented members or that behavioral manifestations of these values provided cues by which members judged one another on the attribute. Several different values were significantly related to perceived ability to get along with others; these are essentially the same values that were related to friendship status within the organization. It will be recalled (see Table 19, Col. 6) that being liked and being seen as able to get along with others were almost synonymous traits within these houses; so the correlations between values and perceived orientation to people actually provide no new information beyond that contained in the first column of Table 21.

A comparison of the second and third columns will show that the value correlates of perceived studiousness and of perceived contribution to the house were quite different from one another. (The correlation across the twelve values, between these two sets of correlations is $-.56$; $\alpha = .06$). This implies either (or a combination) of two things: (1) Studious members tended to hold a pattern of values opposite to that of organization-oriented members, or (2) the value-based behavioral cues from which raters inferred studiousness were, in many ways, the obverse of those from which they inferred devotion to the group. Either of these interpretations says something about the culture of these fraternities and sororities, namely that, for the majority of members, values associated with an academic orientation (perceived or actual) were quite different from the values associated with an orientation toward group maintenance.

VALUES OF ORGANIZATION PRESIDENTS

The president of a fraternity or sorority fills a special position of status within the organization. On the one hand, the post is prestigious, in that the incumbent represents his group in many campus affairs and is thereby recognized as a person of responsibility. On the other hand, duties of the office are extremely time-consuming, and thus constitute a burden which may seem onerous to many. Since this is an elective office, the president must at least be someone acceptable to the group and, at best, he may be someone who represents the organization's highest ideals. Whether the organization presidents were characterized by particular patterns of values was a question of special interest.

Data were available from two sets of presidents — those who held office at the time of the pretest and those who held office at the time of the posttest. Considering the pretest leaders as a group, it was found that, in eight of the ten organizations, the presidents' scores on the honesty value exceeded the mean for actives of their sex and also the mean for actives in their particular house. In addition, eight presidents' mean scores on the values of physical development and independence were lower than the means for all actives of their sex, and also lower than the means for actives within their own houses. The chance probability of each of these occurrences is about .11 (by two-tail binominal test), so the analysis was repeated on the following year's presidents. On none of these three values did the leaders' scores differ from their group means. Therefore, it was concluded that presidents, as a group, did not profess any of the values measured here to an extreme degree.

From another perspective, one might expect presidents to

embody the dominant values of their own houses, whatever these values might be. To test this hypothesis, correlations were computed, over the twelve values, between the pretest president's score and the mean score of all actives in his house. These correlations were found to be no higher, on the average, than the corresponding correlations between presidents' values and the mean values for all actives of their sex combined. Consequently, there is no evidence that these formally designated organization leaders held values that matched their distinctive house norms.

These results pose a challenge to the interpretation offered earlier that high-status members of the organization tend to profess a pattern of values that are especially functional to group maintenance. It therefore seemed appropriate to test the implicit assumption that the presidents were, indeed, members of exceptionally high status within their groups. Using the mean friendship rating received from others as a measure of status, it was found that, among pretest presidents, nine out of the ten were liked better than the average (median) for their houses. However, in only six of the houses did they fall within the top 20% of the friendship status scores. Among posttest presidents, only seven of the ten were ranked above the median for their house, and only four in the top 20%. It is clear, then, that by no means all of these presidents were exceptionally well liked by their colleagues.

Looking at the other sociometric statuses, it was found that the only trait that distinguished both pre- and posttest presidents from the other members was the mean rating received on "contribution to house activities." In all ten houses, presidents were ranked well above the medians for their groups; nine of the pretest presidents and eight of the posttest presidents were ranked first in their houses on this attribute. It is interesting to note, however, that the people who were to become presidents by the time of the posttest were not, on the pretest, rated exceptionally high on any of the four sociometric traits, including "contribution to house activities."

Though these results were hardly anticipated from the beginning, they can be interpreted, after the fact, in the light of Etzioni's (1961) analysis of "normative organizations" with predominantly "expressive" (i.e., group-integrative) functions. According to Etzioni (1961, p. 92), expressive activities require moral involvement; hence they are best performed by elites having moral power over their members. By contrast, instrumental (adaptive) activities require "calculative" involvement, hence are best performed by elites having utilitarian (remunerative) power over subordinates. Officers are most likely to control instrumental activities, while informal leaders (those of high sociometric status) are most likely to control the expressive activities. "For the culture goals of normative organizations, it is functional that expressive elites dominate, since expressive elites initiate and direct goal activities" (Etzioni, 1961, p. 106).

The inference to be drawn from this interpretation and the present data is that many of these fraternity and sorority presidents were probably not the most potent informal leaders within their houses. Perhaps they were elected mainly because they were willing to devote the time and effort required by the office. Though there were undoubtedly a few exceptions among the ten houses studied, it is clear that the presidents, as a group, were not chosen because they were exceptionally well liked; nor did they, as a group, profess distinctively functional (i.e., group-maintaining) values to an outstanding degree. It would be interesting to study the actual processes of influence in such organizations, where the officers do not enjoy exceptional prestige or embody the cherished group ideals.

VALUES AND MUTUAL FRIENDSHIP

Some of the variance in friendship ratings is associated with the values of the rater, and some of it is associated with the values of the person being rated. Generally, members tend to perceive in friends traits that they admire and, for the or-

161

ganization as a whole, well-liked people tend to profess, and be seen as manifesting, values that are widely shared. A good part of the rater's judgment is undoubtedly autistic, serving to maintain his own cognitive balance (Heider, 1946). This would help explain the high correlation between status and perceived social skills (Table 19, Col. 6), for example, which contrasts with the relatively small correlation between status and the value of social skills professed by the person rated (Table 21). It is also true, of course, that professed values may not correspond well with actual or perceived behaviors.

But a rater's judgment of others should reflect *their* actual traits as well as *his* own autistic distortions. To the extent that he judges their values accurately, he can use this information in establishing his likes and dislikes. Not all people would use this information in the same way, but it might be expected that value similarity would generally be more comfortable than value disparity; so, over-all, pairs of friends should have more values in common than pairs of non-friends. A number of studies (e.g., Byrne, 1961; Fiedler, 1963; Izard, 1960, 1963; Newcomb, 1961) have found greater than chance similarities between mutual friends on a variety of attitudes and personality traits. However, the reported relationships are generally of rather small magnitude, and occasional exceptions to the similarity-propinquity hypothesis have been encountered (see Izard, 1963).

In the present study the hypothesis was tested on both pre- and posttest, for two classes of mutual pairs: Those involving actives only, and pairs in which one or both members were pledges. The reason for making this distinction was to gain some control over degree of acquaintance. Presumably the actives knew each other fairly well at the time of the pretest, whereas they did not know most of the pledges well, nor did the pledges generally know each other. In order for value similarity to play a role in friendship choice, the members would need to have established some fair degree of acquaintance.

The mutual pairs of friends and non-friends were identified

from the friendship ratings ("how much you like them"). The ratings chosen to represent high and low degrees of friendship took into account the extremely skewed distribution of the ratings. When two members rated each other "1," they were identified as mutual friends. However, almost no ratings of "7" were given, and not very many were below the scale mid-point, "4." Therefore a non-friend pair was designated whenever one member rated the other between "5" and "7" (the "dislike" end of the scale) and was rated in return between "4" and "7." Though these cutoff points probably diluted the category of mutually unfriendly pairs somewhat, any more extreme division would have resulted in no such pairs in some houses. Either strong enmities were very rare, or subjects were loath to admit them.

Each subject was considered in turn, and his twelve value scores tabulated against the value scores of every other person (if any) involved in a mutual pair with him. Some Ss were involved in no mutual friendships, and some in no mutual non-friendships. If two or more other persons were involved in a given S's mutual pairs, his own value scores were tabulated with each of these — as many times as there were other people. An intra-class correlation coefficient (Haggard, 1958) was then computed on the entire array of mutual pairs in which that S was involved. (This amounted to a weighted mean intra-class ρ over his pairs.) The number of different others included in the calculation ranged from one to eighteen, but each S received only one value-similarity score, representing his (weighted) average agreement with all others who shared his friendship. An identical procedure was followed in computing a mean value-similarity score for each subject involved in one or more non-friend pairs.

The purpose of this averaging within subjects was to give equal weight to all Ss, regardless of how many mutual choices they made, and to yield independent scores (mean intra-subject ρs) for statistical analysis. Complete independence was not achieved, however, since any given correlation between subject

A's and subject B's values entered twice into the computations for the group — once as a component of A's mean intra-class ρ and again as a component of B's mean intra-class ρ. There was no simple way of obtaining completely independent scores, so it should be recognized that the sampling error formulas (which assume simple random sampling of scores) may under-estimate the probability of Type I errors.

Since the intra-class correlations were computed over raw value scores, they were inflated somewhat, as a result of differences in scale means among the twelve values. However, the focus of interest here was not on the magnitudes of the correlations themselves, but on the difference in mean correlations of friendly and unfriendly pairs. It was expected that mutual friends would show greater value similarity, on the average, than mutual non-friends. Though there were wide differences among subjects and among houses, this expectation was generally borne out when the results from all subjects were combined.

Table 22 presents the mean value-similarity scores for friendly and unfriendly pairs, on both pre- and posttest, and distinguishes "well acquainted" from "poorly acquainted" pairs on the basis of members' pretest status as active or pledge. The same population of subjects is represented on both pre- and posttests; members who had left their organizations by the time of the posttest are not included in the pretest tabulations. (Also excluded are a few subjects who failed to rate other members on the pretest — presumably because of insufficient acquaintance.) However, any single subject from this population may have been in a mutual pair (either liked or disliked) at one time but not at the other time; hence the ns differ between pre- and posttest.

If it is assumed that the scores from friendly pairs and unfriendly pairs are independent, the means are found to differ significantly in the predicted direction for all cases where the pairs are well acquainted. That is, on the pretest, the values of mutually friendly actives were more similar (on the average) than the values of mutually unfriendly actives. On the posttest, the values of all mutually friendly pairs tended to be more similar than those of mutually unfriendly pairs. The only exception to this general tendency occurs among subjects who were presumably not very well acquainted, i.e., within those pairs involving pledges on the pretest.

Since some of the same subjects appeared in both friendly and unfriendly pairs, however, the scores are not really independent. Considering only members who were involved in *both* mutual likes *and* mutual dislikes, and computing significance tests that take this correlation into account, essentially the same results appeared: Except for pretest pairs involving pledges, subjects tended to show greater value similarity to persons with whom there were mutual positive feelings than to those with whom there were mutual negative feelings.

These results corroborate those obtained by Newcomb

TABLE 22

VALUE SIMILARITIES OF MUTUAL FRIENDS AND
MUTUAL NON-FRIENDS[a]

Pretest mutual acquaintance:[b]		High		Low	
		Friends	Non-friends	Friends	Non-friends
Pretest similarity:	M	.235 **	.142	.231	.206
	σ_M	.023	.026	.033	.038
	n	118	99	84	65
Posttest similarity:	M	.211 *	.131	.273 **	.105
	σ_M	.022	.032	.036	.042
	n	125	113	87	101

[a]A similarity score was computed for each subject, as the (weighted) average intra-class correlation between his value scores and the value scores of every other person involved in a mutual pair with him. These intra-class ρs were averaged over all Ss (via z transformation), and the resulting means are tabled here.

[b]Scores included under "high pretest mutual acquaintance" are based only on pairs of subjects both of whom were actives at that time. Pairs involving one or two pledges (at the time of the pretest) are included under "low pretest mutual acquaintance."

*Difference between adjacent means significant at $\alpha < .05$ (The significance test assumed independence of the two groups — see text.)

**Difference between adjacent means significant at $\alpha < .01$.

(1961) in his study of a college men's dormitory. However, the mean differences in value congruence between friendly and unfriendly pairs were quite small in the present study, and there was no evidence that they become more pronounced after a one-year acquaintance.

It is quite likely, of course, that the values of all subjects within any particular organization were more similar than in Newcomb's house, for fraternity and sorority members are apparently selected and retained on the basis of value compatibility (see Chapter 5). They would thus be less apt to encounter within the group persons whose values were widely discrepant from their own, and the range of potentially compatible friendships was therefore broader than it might have been in an unselected dormitory.

Regardless of the population studied, however, the degree of value similarity within friendship pairs may be lessened as a consequence of certain psychological processes. The first of these is the tendency toward cognitive balance. To the extent that one is disposed to maintain a balanced perception of his interpersonal world, he will attribute to liked persons traits that he admires, even if these persons do not possess them. In the present study, people who valued academic achievement were more likely than others to rate their friends high on studiousness; members who valued loyalty tended to rate their friends higher than average on contribution to the house; and persons who placed a high value on social skills tended to rate their friends higher than their non-friends on this attribute (Table 20). These ratings may have been accurate, in part, but they were probably also distorted so as to enhance cognitive balance. Thus, any mutual likings that arose for non-value reasons might have persisted simply through failure of the persons to perceive actual disparities in their values.

The other psychological process that might reduce the degree of value similarity within pairs is a tolerance for diversity or, expressed more positively, a desire to find friends with values different from one's own. Though extreme differences were probably not easy to find in these houses, the moderate diversities available might have been intriguing to some members who would rather be shocked but stimulated than feel self-righteous but bored.

SUMMARY

It has been shown that personal values play a role both in contributing to, and in detracting from, the degree of inter-member status differentiation in a social organization. Members tend to like others whose values approximate their own. The more they admire a particular trait, the more they tend to see their friends as embodying that trait. To the extent that values and the attendant interpersonal perceptions vary from one member to another, their friendship choices will differ, and any given person's status — measured as the average degree to which he is liked — will be correspondingly ambiguous.

In spite of individual differences in bases for liking, however, there was some degree of intra-group consensus concerning the likableness of the various members. Differences in friendship status correlated somewhat with the professed values of the members, and substantially with their perceived status on attributes that were relevant to the groups' functioning. On the posttest, older members who placed a high value on loyalty, social skills, status, and intellectualism were slightly better liked than others. Members who were regarded by others as studious were somewhat better liked than the (perceived) non-studious. But the highest correlates of friendship status were perceived ability to get along with others and perceived contribution to the group (in that order). Thus, it appears that these two characteristics figured prominently in the value norms of the fraternities and sororities.

The elected presidents of these organizations did not, as a group, hold any of the twelve values to an outstanding degree; nor did they tend especially to profess patterns of values that were distinctively characteristic of their respective houses. It seems doubtful, therefore, that the values of the presidents played much of a part in their being elected to office. It is even questionable whether the presidency could be regarded as a particularly prestigious role in some of these organizations, for it was often awarded to members who had not enjoyed high status before assuming the office, and whose popularity even afterward was only moderate. These findings at least indicate that the "status" associated with elective offices in the organizations is a quality different from "status" as defined by the present sociometric instruments.

CHAPTER 7

MAINTENANCE OF MEMBER ALLEGIANCE

The maintenance of members' loyalties is one of the main functions that needs to be performed within a viable organization. Though members of voluntary groups are presumably motivated to belong at the time they join, their continued devotion cannot be taken for granted. In the fraternities and sororities of this study, the highest degree of attraction to the group was generally found among the newer members, and the lowest degree among the seniors (Table 15, p. 128). Though there are numerous exceptions to this general trend, there seem to be certain pressures toward progressive disidentification with the Greek organizations the longer a person stays in them.

The attraction that a member feels for other persons in the group contributes to his sentiment toward the organization as a whole, but there are other important ingredients of this global sentiment. People may value a group for the experiences it gives them, for the status they gain from membership, for the opportunity it provides them to do other things of interest, and for a variety of reasons that are only indirectly dependent on their relations with other group members. The index of group attraction (pp. 126-128 and Appendix E) was intended to assess global feelings of devotion to the organization. There was a small positive correlation on the posttest ($r = .14$; $\alpha < .02$) between expressed level of attraction and average liking for other members. But clearly, over-all attraction to the group did not depend substantially on average liking for all the members in it. When the mean posttest intra-house attraction to the organization was correlated, across houses, with the mean intra-house liking of all members for each other, the resulting cross-organization correlation was not significantly different from zero. Thus, it would be improper to consider the average member's attraction to others and the average member's global attraction to the organization as comparable measures of "group cohesiveness."

A much more important correlate of members' attitudes toward the organization was the value they placed on group loyalty. The average within-organization correlation between the loyalty value and attraction to the group was .41 ($\alpha <$ .001) on the posttest and approximately the same on the pretest. The posttest correlation across organizations between the mean intra-house loyalty value and the mean intra-house score on attraction to the group was .90 ($\alpha <$ .001). These two measures, then, might properly be regarded as equivalent indices of "group cohesiveness." The important inference suggested by these results is that devotion to one's fraternity or sorority is more probably a reflection of the basic value of loyalty to one's primary group than it is a reflection of one's average feelings about the other house members.[1] One might therefore suspect that people would tend to be either devoted or indifferent organization members, regardless of the particular group to which they belong, depending on the degree to which they value the trait of loyalty in general.

Other value correlates of attraction to the organization may be seen in Table 23, which presents, for fraternities and sororities separately, the correlation obtained on the posttest between group attraction and each of the twelve values. (These correlations are essentially similar in pattern to those obtained on the pretest,

---

[1] The possibility should not be overlooked that the difference in correlations reflects differences in the instruments used to assess these variables. It might be maintained that the form of the values instrument is more similar than the "liking" sociometric to the form of the measure of group attraction, hence the correlation of .41 may depend both on content and instrument factors. However, the relative similarities of instrument forms are hard to compare by just looking at them; anyway, these are unlikely to have been predominantly responsible for the rather sizable difference in obtained correlations.

though somewhat more consistent from one organization to another.)

None of the other values is so consistently or substantially correlated with attraction to the group as is the value of loyalty. However, certain of them bear significant relations on the average, though with considerable variation from group to group. Within fraternities the values of kindness, social skills, academic achievement, and religiousness all show significantly positive relations with attitude toward the organization, while the value of independence shows a significant negative relationship. Within sororities, social skills and status values are positively related, and intellectualism and independence are negatively related, to attitudes toward the organization. Generally, those values included in the "other-directed" cluster (see Table 2 for a description of the cluster) tended to show higher correlations with attraction to the organization than did the "inner-directed" values — intellectualism, creativity, and independence. (The difference in correlations

TABLE 23

CORRELATIONS BETWEEN VALUES AND ATTRACTION
TO THE ORGANIZATION
(Posttest of Members Still in House)

Value	*Fraternities* (n = 225)	*Sororities* (n = 153)
Intellectualism	.02	−.24**
Kindness	.15*	.13
Social skills	.16*	.23**
Loyalty	.39**	.46**
Academic achievement	.16*	.13
Physical development	.05	.14
Status	.10	.23**
Honesty	.05	−.06
Religiousness	.23**	.16
Self-control	.06	.14
Creativity	−.14*	.04
Independence	−.22**	−.27**

* $\alpha < .05$.
**$\alpha < .01$.

between inner- and other-directed values was more pronounced on the posttest than on the pretest, indicating, perhaps, some tendency among members to integrate, over time, their attitudes toward the organization with their relevant values.)

These results are quite consistent with the value differences previously reported (Tables 16 and 17) between pledges and non-pledging freshman controls. The main differences between these groups, it will be recalled, were that both male and female pledges tended to score higher on the values of social skills and loyalty, lower on the value of independence, than did the non-pledging freshmen. The directions of other value differences also tended to correspond with the magnitudes of the correlations reported in Table 23. When the differences between pledges and controls were correlated with the magnitudes of the rs in Table 23, over the twelve values, the resulting correlations were .88 for males and .75 for females ($\alpha < .01$ in both cases). Thus, it is apparent that values associated with intent either to pledge or not to pledge a Greek organization were, on the average, the same values that correlated with attraction to the organization among people who had actually joined.

Moreover, when *changes* in attraction to the group, over the one-year interval between pre- and posttest, were correlated with changes in the values, similar findings emerged: Increasingly favorable attitudes tended to appear among fraternity members whose values of social skills, loyalty, and academic achievement increased, and whose value of independence decreased. In sororities, increasing attraction to the organization was associated with increasing emphasis on the values of social skills, loyalty, academic achievement, and status. The correspondence between mean posttest correlations (Table 23) and mean correlations of change scores may be represented by the correlation between *them* of .80 in the fraternities and .65 in the sororities.

The import of these findings would appear to be that certain values are likely to be compatible with Greek organization membership and other values are likely to be incompatible. The relatively compatible values are those which have been called "other-

172

directed," and the relatively incompatible values are the "inner-directed" (as identified in Table 2, and as measured by the present instrument). Students who admire loyalty, social skills, academic achievement, and status are more apt to find fraternity and sorority membership congenial than are students who admire independence. It cannot, of course, be taken for granted that the sole direction of influence is from values to attitudes. Values may change, too, and a student who, for one reason or another, develops an increasingly positive or negative attitude toward a social organization might undergo changes in his values to bring them into better correspondence with his attitude. Though it is suspected that values of the kinds assessed here are likely to be more enduring and more determinant than specific attitudes (including attitudes toward one's fraternity), this interpretation has not been definitely established with the present data.

The attractions that members feel toward their organizations come to be reflected in their colleagues' impressions of them. On the pretest, there was a correlation among actives of .24 ($\alpha <$ .01) between attitude toward the house and status on "contribution to house activities," as rated by other members (see p. 120 for a description of the rating instruments). By the time of the posttest, this correlation for actives still in the organization has risen to .44. Posttest attitude toward the organization also correlated .29 with status (i.e., mean rating received from colleagues) on "ability to get along with others" and .30 with friendship status (mean rating received on "how much you like them") — in both cases $\alpha <$ .01 — but not significantly with status on "how seriously they take their schoolwork." The corresponding correlations for pledges were all non-significant, and significantly less than those for actives. Moreover, there had been a significant increase among actives (but not pledges) in all three of these correlations (excluding "schoolwork" status) from pre- to posttest.

Actives' *increases,* from pre- to posttest, in favorableness of attitude toward the organization correlated positively with *increases* in sociometric status as follows: Contribution to house activities, .30 ($\alpha <$ .01); ability to get along with others, .24 ($\alpha <$ .01); and friendship, .18 ($\alpha <$ .05); there was no significant correlation between change in attraction to the group and change in "schoolwork" status. Thus, it seems reasonable to infer that the degree of devotion to the group that a member feels affects his degree of leadership and participation in group activities; this contribution comes to be recognized by other group members, who tend to like or dislike the person accordingly.

It will be recalled (Table 20) that the magnitude of the correlation between friendship ratings and "house activities" ratings depends on the degree to which the person doing the rating himself admires loyalty. So the value of loyalty would appear to play a dual role in determining a member's status within the house: First, it may affect the way the member himself feels about his group and the degree to which he works for its benefit. Second, it affects the way his colleagues evaluate his group-oriented activity — the degree to which they like him better because of it. In the presence of other members who value loyalty highly, the group-oriented person will be perceived as such and liked for it; but his devotion to the organization is less likely to be appreciated by those who do not themselves value loyalty. Precisely this result appeared in a cross-organizational analysis of inter-house differences in the correlation between attraction to the group and friendship status. The magnitude of this correlation was itself correlated .69 ($\alpha <$ .05) with the within-house mean value of loyalty: The greater the average value placed on loyalty within a house, the more was any given member's feeling of attraction to the organization likely to be accompanied by high friendship status for himself.

SUMMARY

The scale of over-all attraction to the organization tapped an attitude that was different from the members' average liking for their colleagues. The mean within-houses correlation between these two variables was quite small, and there was no significant cross-houses correlation between them. Attraction to the organization, on the other hand, correlated substantially with the value of loyalty, both within and across houses. Also, members with the most favorable attitudes toward the groups tended to score *higher* than others on the values of social skills, academic achievement, status, and religiousness, *lower* on the value of independence. This pattern of results is very similar to the pattern of differences found between the values of pledges and non-pledging freshmen. In other words, the values that predisposed incoming freshmen to join (or to be accepted by) Greek organizations in the first place tended also to contribute to members' continuing allegiance to the groups after they had been admitted.

Members with the most favorable attitudes toward the organization tended to be seen by their colleagues as contributing more to house activities than did members with less favorable attitudes. By the time of the posttest (though not on the pretest), they were also liked better, on the average, and rated higher on ability to get along with others. The higher the mean intra-house value of loyalty, the higher was the intra-house correlation between a member's attraction to the organization and the degree to which he was liked by others. This result implies that a person's expressions of devotion to the organization will be appreciated by his colleagues to the extent that they admire group loyalty as a human virtue.

CHAPTER 8

ATTRITION

The membership of campus social organizations is subject to fairly constant turnover. Most of this is directly due to the environment in which the organizations exist — an academic community with a limited period of involvement for any one member, and with minimum standards of scholastic performance demanded for continuance in the community. These external circumstances greatly restrict the freedom of the groups to select and retain the members they wish. About one-fifth of the pretest actives in the present sample left their groups because they graduated from the university. (See Table 8.) Another one-third of the active women and one-seventh of the active men left school without graduating. About a third of the pledges of both sexes were no longer in school a year later, most of them presumably having failed to maintain minimal grade requirements.

The kind of endogenous organizational attrition directly relevant to this study is a severance of membership at the instigation of either the organization or the individual member, without pressure from the external community. Therefore, graduating members are not considered among the subjects treated in this chapter. Just which of the other drop-outs should be considered is not completely clear. On the posttest, members who had dropped were not asked their reasons for doing so, because it was felt that such a potentially threatening question might disrupt rapport, and because it was suspected that subjects would be reluctant to admit that they had left under pressure.

Actives who left their houses while remaining in school are

likely to have done so either at their own or at the organization's instigation, but this category included only 21 men and 5 women for all ten organizations together — far too few to treat as a separate group within each house. Actives who left school had not necessarily flunked out; some of them had transferred to other universities. Among the reasons for their departures may have been dissatisfaction with life in the social organizations. So this group of 84 subjects was combined with the other 26 in the category of endogenous attrition.

Pledges who failed to go active but remained in school were also classified under endogenous attrition even though it was suspected that a sizable number of these may have been on academic probation, hence prevented by university regulations from going active. Pledges who dropped school were not treated as instances of endogenous attrition, since it was considered likely that most of these drop-outs occurred for academic reasons.

Such crude classifications are bound to obscure many individual differences in reasons for disaffiliating, but the grade-point averages of these four sub-groups attest to the general reasonableness of the assumptions: 47% of the pledges who dropped school had averages below 1.5 (on a 4-point scale), while only 17% of the pledges who dropped their organizations, but remained in school, were this low. Among the disaffiliating actives, only 12% of those who left the university, and none of those who remained, had grade-point averages below 1.5.

DIFFERENCES BETWEEN MEAN PRETEST VALUES
OF DROP-OUT PLEDGES AND REMAINING PLEDGES

The principal question to be asked here is whether pledges' disaffiliation from the organization can be attributed to their values. This analysis requires a comparison between pretest values of pledges who remained and values of pledges who dropped out. (A comparison of posttest values would confuse the interpretation by including value changes following drop-out along with the predisposing value differences.) Are pledges who left the organization characteristically different from pledges who went active? Specifically, do the former hold values more deviant from actives' than the latter?

Table 24 reports, for fraternities and sororities separately, the mean pretest values of pledges who left the house but remained in school, compared with mean pretest values of pledges who went active. Only the value of independence within the sororities showed a significant trend — in the direction of higher scores for pledges who dropped their organizations. Among fraternity pledges no significant differences appeared for all houses combined. Only one organization — Sorority 1 — showed significant discrepancies across several values. Thus one is led to infer that pledges who dropped their organizations did not tend to hold a common set of values substantially different from those who re-

TABLE 24

PRETEST VALUE MEANS (z-SCORES) OF PLEDGES WHO DROPPED THE
ORGANIZATION (BUT REMAINED IN SCHOOL) COMPARED WITH
PRETEST VALUE MEANS OF PLEDGES WHO WENT ACTIVE

| | Fraternities | | Sororities | | |
Value	Dropped (n = 22)	Went Active (n = 107)	Dropped (n = 26)		Went Active (n = 80)
Intellectualism	−.60	−.61	.02		−.29
Kindness	−.06	−.13	.31		.15
Social skills	.28	.17	.26		.29
Loyalty	.80	.79	.45		.75
Academic achievement	.23	.38	.31		.23
Physical development	.23	−.03	−.06		.14
Status	.10	.26	−.15		−.02
Honesty	.38	.17	.24		.34
Religiousness	.16	.17	.17		.50
Self-control	.01	−.11	.30		.10
Creativity	−.70	−.51	.13		−.26
Independence	−.34	−.26	.06	*	−.75

Note. — These are standard scores based on Ms and σs of a university random sample.
*Difference between adjacent means significant at $\alpha < .05$.

mained; certainly no one particular value tended uniformly to distinguish the drop-outs from their fellow pledges.

The total pattern of values may be treated by converting each pledge group's mean value to a standard score based on the mean and standard deviation of the total pretest actives of the same sex. The absolute magnitudes of these standard scores were, on the average, no different for one group of pretest pledges than for the other. Therefore, the pattern of value means for pledges who disaffiliated was not more discrepant from the total active pattern than was the pattern of value means for pledges who maintained membership.

The two groups of pretest pledges may also be compared with two groups of pretest non-pledging control subjects. By the time of the posttest, some of these controls had pledged a Greek organization, while others had remained Independent; still others had left school. If values are significant determinants of pledge attrition, one would expect that pledges who dropped their organizations would show a pretest value pattern similar to that of controls who remained Independent, and different both from controls who subsequently pledged and from pretest pledges who went active. The reverse should be true of pledges who went active: Their pretest value pattern should be similar to that of controls who pledged and different from the value pattern of controls who remained Independent. Table 25 reports relevant data for the two sexes separately. These are product-moment correlations over the twelve value means, when these means are computed as standard scores based on total pretest actives of the same sex.

Among female members the expectations are borne out to some extent: The pretest value pattern of pledges who dropped the organization was significantly similar to that of freshman women who remained Independent, and significantly different from the value pattern of sorority pledges who went active. That is to say, the posttest status (Greek or Independent) of a freshman girl could be predicted, to some extent, from her

TABLE 25
CORRELATIONS BETWEEN PRETEST VALUE MEANS OF
VARIOUS FRESHMAN GROUPS

	Males		Females	
	n	r	n	r
Pledges Who Dropped Organization	22		26	
Correlated with:				
Controls, Remained Independent	54	−.59*	30	.77**
Controls, Pledged	13	−.24	16	.01
Pledges, Became Actives	107	.68*	80	−.56*
Pledges Who Became Actives	107		80	
Correlated with:				
Controls, Remained Independent	54	−.42	30	.27
Controls, Pledged	13	.02	16	.33
Controls, Remained Independent	54		30	
Correlated with:				
Controls, Pledged	13	.69**	16	.37

Note. — Each mean value score for a given sub-group was converted to a standard score based on the mean and σ of total pretest actives of the same sex. This procedure was used to reduce the artificially high rs that would have been obtained by correlating raw-score means, owing to the differences in scales for the several values.
*Significantly different from zero, at $\alpha < .05$. The significance test is based on a z transformation of r, where $\sigma_z = \sqrt{1/(n-3)}$, and $n = 12$ (since there are twelve mean value scores for each group).
** $\alpha < .01$.

pretest values. Among the men, however, quite the opposite was true. Pledges who dropped their organizations showed a pattern of values significantly similar to that of pledges who remained, and significantly different from that of freshman males who remained Independent. In other words, the pretest value patterns of males were more closely associated with their pretest than with their posttest status. Since neither kind of relationship held consistently within both sexes, it would be risky to draw any definite conclusions from these data concerning the relevance of personal values for attrition of pledges within the Greek organizations. It is perhaps prudent at this point to consider the apparently significant, but discrepant, results within the separate male and female groups as unexplained — perhaps because of sampling error or unusual characteristics of these particular groups of subjects.

DIFFERENCES BETWEEN MEAN PRETEST VALUES
OF DROP-OUT ACTIVES AND REMAINING ACTIVES

Similarly, one may inquire whether attrition of active members was a function of their pretest values. The data presented in Table 26 show a somewhat consistent pattern: Within all fraternities combined, and within all sororities combined, the actives who subsequently left their organizations without graduating tended to score lower on the loyalty value than did actives who remained as members. Within fraternities they also tended toward higher scores on the independence value. (The difference is not

TABLE 26
PRETEST VALUE MEANS (z-SCORES) OF ACTIVES WHO DROPPED THE ORGANIZATION (OR DROPPED SCHOOL) COMPARED WITH PRETEST VALUE MEANS OF ACTIVES WHO REMAINED

Value	Fraternities			Sororities		
	Dropped (n = 56)		Remained (n = 130)	Dropped (n = 66)		Remained (n = 75)
Intellectualism	−.61		−.44	.16		.04
Kindness	−.28		−.02	.30		.39
Social skills	−.16		.10	.30		.33
Loyalty	.34	*	.68	.70	*	.98
Academic achievement	.12		.13	.57		.44
Physical development	−.20		.01	.22		.25
Status	−.01		.19	.04		.08
Honesty	.29		.00	.24		.15
Religiousness	−.12		.04	.38		.28
Self-control	−.22		.02	.34		.32
Creativity	−.52		−.47	.00		.04
Independence	.02	*	−.28	−.29		−.49

Note. — These are standard scores based on Ms and σs of a university random sample.
*Difference between adjacent means significant at $\alpha < .05$.

significant for sororities alone but when both fraternity and sorority members are combined, the total difference is significant at the .05 level.) It is important to note, however, that on both these values the same directions of difference distinguished actives who graduated from actives who remained in the organizations. In other words, disaffiliates tended, more than the remaining members, to approximate the values of (presumably) high-status seniors — toward lower valuation of loyalty and higher valuation of independence. From these comparisons, one would infer that dropping out by an active occurred largely at the individual's own initiative, rather than as a result of direct exclusion by the organization; he simply was likely to be oriented more toward individual self-sufficiency and less toward group maintenance than were his colleagues who stayed in.

OTHER PRETEST DIFFERENCES BETWEEN DROP-OUTS AND CONTINUING MEMBERS

On none of the demographic variables assessed — religious affiliation, professed degree of religiousness, income, own or parents' political preference — did pledges who left the organization differ consistently from those who remained. However, on some specifically group-relevant variables, meaningful differences appeared, which may help clarify the significance of disaffiliation. These are the pretest statuses of pledges on the sociometric attributes. In only five of the organizations (all of them fraternities) were actives able to rate pledges on the pretest (see p. 109); hence, the present analysis is restricted to these five fraternities. Table 27 shows the statuses of pledges (i.e., the mean ratings received from actives) on each of the four sociometric variables,[1] together with pledges' scores on the scale of attraction to the organization.

---

[1] Mean ratings that pledges received from other pledges showed essentially the same pattern of differences, though generally somewhat smaller — presumably because, at the time of the pretest, pledges were better known by the actives (who had selected them) than they were by their fellow pledges.

TABLE 27

PRETEST SOCIOMETRIC STATUS AND ATTRACTION TO THE
ORGANIZATION OF PLEDGES IN FIVE FRATERNITIES

| | Posttest Classification | |
	Went Active (n = 82)	Left Organization (n = 19)
Sociometric Statuses[a]		
(based on ratings received from actives)		
Friendship	2.9 *	3.3
Schoolwork	3.2	3.4
House activities	3.3	3.5
Getting along	3.0 *	3.4
Attraction to organization[b]	3.5	3.0

[a]In the sociometric ratings, scores ranged from 1 ("outstanding — one of the few top people in the house") to 7 ("very low — in the bottom group of the house"); therefore, low numbers indicate *high* status on the attribute.
[b]In the scale of attraction to the organization, the range of scores was from 0 to 6, with high numbers indicating high attraction.
*Difference significant at $\alpha < .01$.

It is apparent that fraternity pledges who dropped the organization, but remained in school, were less well liked by actives in the pretest than were pledges who stayed on, and they were rated as less able to get along with others. The pledges' own attitudes toward their organizations did not differ significantly between subjects who dropped out and those who remained. Thus, one would infer from these results that attrition of pledges in the five fraternities was more a function of the actives' attitudes toward them than it was a function of their own attitudes toward the organization. Those who left within the year were less well liked by others to begin with, even though they may themselves have felt favorably disposed toward the group.

A somewhat different basis of attrition would be inferred for pretest actives. As Table 28 shows, actives who left the organization without graduating were liked no less well than those who remained, but they themselves tended to show less positive feelings toward the organization. They were also rated significantly lower than remaining actives on contribution to

183

house activities and on devotion to schoolwork. Since the departed actives included both members who left school and members who left the organization while remaining in school, it is likely that non-studious orientations characterized some of them, while disaffection from the organization characterized others. Though the data in Table 28 come from only the five fraternities in which pledges were also rated on the pretest, essentially identical results (at better significance levels) appear when all actives are combined, including those from sororities. Therefore the bases for actives' departures — disaffection from the organization and lack of attention to schoolwork, but *not* rejection by other members — appear to have been similar for both fraternities and sororities; the five organizations reported in Table 28 were not atypical in this regard.

TABLE 28

PRETEST SOCIOMETRIC STATUS AND ATTRACTION TO THE
ORGANIZATION OF ACTIVES IN FIVE FRATERNITIES

	Posttest Classification	
	Still Active (n = 114)	Left Organization or Left School (n = 49)
Sociometric Statuses[a]		
(based on ratings received from actives)		
Friendship	2.9	3.1
Schoolwork	3.1 **	3.6
House activities	3.5 **	4.0
Getting along	3.2	3.3
Attraction to organization[b]	3.6 *	3.0

[a]In the sociometric ratings, scores ranged from 1 ("outstanding — one of the few top people in the house") to 7 ("very low — in the bottom group of the house"); therefore, low numbers indicate *high* status on the attribute.
[b]In the scale of attraction to the organization, the range of scores was from 0 to 6, with high numbers indicating high attraction.
*Difference significant at $\alpha < .05$.
**Difference significant at $\alpha < .01$.

INCREASING GROUP HOMOGENEITY
THROUGH ATTRITION

Up to this point, we have sought mean value differences between drop-outs and remaining members which appeared consistently in all organizations, in order to determine if there was a particular pattern of values that tended to be incompatible with the total fraternity-sorority culture. However, each of the organizations may also be considered as a separate group that provides a somewhat distinct value culture for its members. From this view, one might expect that disaffiliating members would be those whose patterns of values deviated from whatever modal pattern was provided by their particular organizations, regardless of their relation to the mode of the wider fraternity-sorority culture.

A direct way of measuring the degree of deviancy is to compute the variance among pretest scores on a particular value for groups that differ in degree of inclusiveness. If, for instance, the total pretest organization showed a fairly wide dispersion of scores on the intellectualism value, but when only members who remained in the group were considered, the dispersion was substantially reduced, then one would infer that drop-outs tended to maintain levels of the intellectualism value which were rather deviant from the organization mean — either excessively high or excessively low. This kind of analysis was performed over all twelve values, and the average variance of the more inclusive group was compared with the average variance of the less inclusive group, with the expectation that the larger pretest group (which included subsequent drop-outs) would be more variable than the "purified" pretest group (which included only members who remained in the organization throughout the year).

Since this was intended as an analysis of endogenous attrition (due to intra-organizational causes), the relevant groups for comparison on the pretest were (1) the smaller group of actives and pledges who were to remain as members and (2) the larger group, including the group just noted plus subjects who were

TABLE 29
MEAN VARIANCES OF PRETEST VALUE SCORES FOR VARIOUS COMBINATIONS OF SUBJECTS

	(1) Actives, stay + Pledges, stay + Actives, drop + Pledges, drop + organization	(2) Actives, stay + Pledges, stay	(3) Actives, stay + Actives, drop	(4) Actives, stay	(5) Pledges, stay + Pledges, drop + organization	(6) Pledges, stay
Fraternity 1	1.80	1.71	1.82	1.70	1.75	1.76
Fraternity 2	1.75	1.69	1.80	1.69	1.68	1.64
Fraternity 3	1.82	1.83	2.12	2.13	1.59	1.61
Fraternity 4	1.79	1.84	1.71	1.79	1.90	1.91
Fraternity 5	1.91	1.75	2.05	1.53	1.99	2.02
Fraternity 6	2.08	1.82	2.17	1.88	2.11	1.37
Sorority 1	1.66	1.63	1.73	1.74	1.50	1.52
Sorority 2	1.64	1.54	1.64	1.54	1.63	1.55
Sorority 3	1.49	1.33	1.37	1.35	1.65	1.35
Sorority 4	1.55	1.43	1.66	1.46	1.76[a]	1.76
Mean	1.75 **	1.66	1.81 *	1.68	1.76	1.65

Note – Population variances were estimated as $s^2 = \dfrac{\Sigma (X-M)^2}{n-1}$.

[a]No pledges dropped this organization while remaining in school.

*Difference between adjacent columns significant at $\alpha < .05$.

**Difference between adjacent columns significant at $\alpha < .02$.

destined to drop out for reasons other than graduation or failure to make grades. Additional subjects to be considered in the larger pretest group are (1) actives who left the organization or left school without graduating and (2) pledges who left the organization but remained in school. These, then, are the more, and the less, inclusive groups represented in Table 29. The first two columns report mean variances over all twelve values for actives and pledges combined, the next two for actives only, and the last two for pledges only.

A comparison of the first two columns shows that, on the average, homogeneity of pretest values was increased through attrition of members. The mean variances tend to be smaller when only those subjects who remained are considered than when these are combined with members who dropped out.[2] Since a comparison of these first two columns represents the effect of eliminating both active and pledge drop-outs, it is of interest to perform further analyses to determine whether the increased homogeneity is due mainly to the attrition of actives or to the attrition of pledges. From the remaining columns in the table (Col. 3 vs. Col 4, and Col. 5 vs. Col. 6) it may be seen that the departing actives tended to be deviant from the remaining actives, but that departing pledges were not significantly deviant from the remaining pledges. In other words, the increased intra-group homogeneity of values that resulted from attrition was mainly due to the fact that disaffiliating actives tended to hold values that differed (in one direction or the other) from the values of actives who remained in the group.

It will be recalled (see Table 26) that, in all organizations combined, the drop-out actives tended to score higher on the

[2] The variances computed here are actually unbiased estimates of population variance (see Note in Table 29). The reason for using this estimate, s^2, rather than the sample statistic, σ^2, is because σ^2 will tend to be smaller as n (the sample size) decreases; this effect would contribute spuriously to the predicted decrease in variance from eliminating drop-out subjects. Any decrease in s^2 (the unbiased estimate) would not be attributable to a mere reduction in sample size.

independence value and lower on the loyalty value than did actives who remained. This cross-organizational difference might therefore account for the intra-group reductions of variance reported in Table 29. To see if this were the case, the mean variances of value scores for the several groups were computed again, this time eliminating the values of loyalty and independence, and considering only the remaining ten values. Essentially the same results emerged: elimination of active drop-outs from the pretest sample resulted in increased homogeneity on the set of ten values other than loyalty and independence.

Thus one is led to conclude that, within the "average" social organization represented in this study, actives who dropped out before graduation tended to be those with relatively high independence values, relatively low loyalty values, and a pattern of other values which was somehow deviant from the modal values of actives who remained in their particular houses. Yet there are differences among the houses in the degree to which active drop-outs led to increased in-group homogeneity of values; in two of the houses (Fraternities 3 and 4), the effect did not appear. Perhaps one characteristic of an organization which would tend to yield such "value purification through attrition" is a rigid normative structure which requires value-conformity and, hence, would tend to alienate deviants. No direct measures of "normative rigidity" were obtained in this study. However, a reasonable expectation is that pressures toward norm-conformity would be highest in the houses that were most "cohesive." If the mean pretest attraction of actives to the organization may be treated as a measure of "group cohesiveness," then one would expect a positive correlation, over the ten houses, between mean attraction to the group and the degree of increase in value homogeneity which resulted from member attrition. The relevant data are presented in Table 30.

The correlation between pretest group cohesiveness (measured as the mean attraction to the organization of total active members) and the magnitude of increase in value homogeneity, through attrition of both actives and pledges, is .85 ($\alpha <$ .01). When only attrition of actives is considered, the corresponding correlation between pretest cohesiveness and increase in value homogeneity is .75 ($\alpha <$ .01).

TABLE 30

MEAN ATTRACTION TO ORGANIZATION OF TOTAL PRETEST ACTIVES
AND DECREASE IN MEAN PRETEST VALUE VARIANCE
RESULTING FROM ATTRITION

Organization	*Total Actives' Attraction to Organization* (1)	*Increase in Value Homogeneity Through Attrition:* Actives + Pledges (2)	Actives Only (3)
Fraternity 1	3.34	+.09	+.12
Fraternity 2	3.08	+.06	+.11
Fraternity 3	2.89	−.01	−.01
Fraternity 4	3.16	−.05	−.08
Fraternity 5	3.86	+.16	+.50
Fraternity 6	4.05	+.26	+.29
Sorority 1	3.22	+.03	−.01
Sorority 2	3.12	+.10	+.10
Sorority 3	3.60	+.16	+.02
Sorority 4	3.55	+.12	+.20

Col. (1) by Col. (2): $r = .88$ ($\alpha < .01$).
Col. (1) by Col. (3): $r = .75$ ($\alpha < .01$).

SUMMARY

Actives seem to have dropped out of the social organizations more or less at their own choice. They were not especially disliked by the other members, but they did tend to be less favorably disposed toward the house and its activities. These tendencies to reject the organization were accompanied by a heightened value of independence and a lowered value of group loyalty.

Pledges, on the other hand, did not seem to leave the group so much on their own initiative as they did because of rejection by the other members. They did not show, at the time of the pretest, significantly lower attraction to the organization, and there were no consistent value differences between pledges who left and those who remained.

Attrition of actives tended to leave the remaining group more homogeneous in values than it had been before the disaffiliates departed. This was especially true in the more "cohesive" houses. Thus, one may conclude that actives are most likely to disaffiliate when (1) they value independence, but not loyalty to the group, (2) they differ from house members on other values, and (3) there is a high group-oriented spirit within the house, which makes life uncomfortable for the deviant.

CHAPTER 9

SOCIALIZATION

An organization may influence its members in numerous ways — by exposing them to new experiences, by requiring certain uniform practices, by differential role assignments, by encouraging and rewarding the expression of preferred ideas. It was expected that values would be acquired and maintained by members of these social organizations in response to such influence processes. The principal reason for selecting fraternities and sororities as the organizations for study was that they appeared to provide better than most organizations of adults the essential features of primary groups: A high rate of face-to-fact interaction among members, strong motivations to belong, and clear distinctions between members and non-members. These features of a group are presumably essential if it is to have maximum impact on its members' moral ideals.

This longitudinal study has certain deficiencies for a clear identification of characteristic changes and, especially, for attributing these changes to the impact of group membership. There is the essential limitation that members were, to a large extent, self-selected. It was not possible to exercise controlled assignments of subjects to various conditions of membership and non-membership. It is doubtful if such a requirement for true experimental design could ever be met in natural organizations; if it were, the very nature of normal influence processes might be altered, for the groups would contain many unwilling members. Group influence processes occurring under such artificial conditions might well be quite different from those that would obtain in a natural setting; hence the experimental study would yield little information relevant to the intended circumstances.

The best that can be done, if the phenomenon under study is to be minimally disturbed, is to start with self-selected subjects in each group, and compare their naturally occurring changes. Just as the fraternity and sorority pledges were self-selected, so the longitudinal comparison groups of non-pledging male and female freshmen were self-selected. Pledges were clearly different from non-pledges to begin with, in values and in other ways as well. Moreover, the groups studied here were not even necessarily representative of all Greek organizations on campus or of all non-pledging freshmen. The necessity of working with organizations that were willing to be studied did not permit a truly random selection of subjects for assessment.

Within these limitations, however, we shall do our best to interpret realistically the value changes observed in pledges over the one-year interval between pre- and posttests. This will require comparing their movements with those of the non-pledge "control" groups. When the pretest value scores of these groups differ, it will be necessary to keep these differences in mind when interpreting patterns of change. Though conclusions about group impact on members will necessarily be tentative, and not based on rigorous experiment, they are probably about as reliable as one can expect under the circumstances.

NORM-SETTERS AND NORM-FOLLOWERS

Underlying the expectation of group influences was an assumption about the presence of group norms for values. A group norm for a value may be said to exist to the extent that members agree on the desirability of the relevant goal-state. But the concept "norm" implies something more than simply an abstraction, or summary, of many individuals' beliefs. If it were only this, the norm would change with every alternation in membership, and there would be little basis for normative continuity, little reason for conceptualizing a norm in extra-individual language. The essential theoretical significance of a norm is that it is regarded as existing, and exerting influence, independently of the beliefs of at least some members; beliefs espoused by one part of the membership can govern the behaviors of initial non-believers, and eventually come to be accepted by the latter.

The presence of status differentiation in the group would appear necessary for the operation of norms in a continuing, extra-individual way. A status distinction may be made between old and new members, between majority and minority, between leaders and followers, between high-prestige and low-prestige individuals; or it may rest on any other basis that gives some members more power (formal or informal) than others to enforce their own concepts of right and wrong. Implicit in the identification of a norm is the assumption that sanctions will be imposed on violators, and the administration of any sanction requires some sort of power over the offender — if only sufficient power to make him feel bad when he is ignored. To the extent that a group member desires the friendship of his colleagues, each of them has some degree of potential norm-enforcing power over him, but this power will exert a consistent influence toward norm internalization only to the extent that a common norm is shared and, especially, to the extent that it is shared by high-status members.

As a way of identifying status differentiation relevant to norm enforcement, it was assumed that the active members of the organizations had more power than the pledges. Hence they were more likely to be in the position of norm-setting, while the pledges were more likely to be norm-adopters. Such an assumption is, of course, subject to all kinds of qualifications, but it seemed reasonable on the following bases: the actives were generally older than the pledges and of more advanced academic standing; they held prior membership in the organizations; and the pledges could only be admitted through the actives' consent.

Accordingly, for purposes of the analyses in this chapter, the "group norms" were assessed as the mean values of the actives, and it was expected that influence processes within the organization would be predominantly manifest in a movement of pledges' values toward those of the actives.

Not all of the initial pretest pledges were subject to influence by the organization throughout the entire year; a sizable number of them left the houses sometime before the posttest (see Table 8). Though their brief period of association may have resulted in some exposure to the actives' norms, this exposure was clearly less than it was for pledges who stayed with the group and had attained active status a year later. Therefore it is the value changes of pledges who remained in the organization that will be of concern in this chapter.

CHANGES OVER ALL ORGANIZATIONS

We are most interested in influences that go on in individual organizations. Therefore the focus of analysis will ultimately be on the changes in pledges' values within each house considered separately. However, in order to see what kinds of effects are common to all groups, and also to provide a baseline against which to compare distinctive intra-house movements, it will be useful first to look at changes that occurred among all pledges of a given sex. Table 31 reports these changes for the fraternities and sororities separately.

Among fraternity pledges there were significant mean decreases in the values of academic achievement and religiousness and a significant mean increase in the value of independence. Among sorority pledges there were significant mean increases in the values of intellectualism and independence and a significant mean decrease in the value of loyalty. Taken together, these results hardly support the interpretation that Greek organizations foster interpersonal values and suppress individual achievement values. Not one of the "other-directed" values (see Table 2) showed a significant mean increase over the one-year period,

TABLE 31
MEAN VALUES (STANDARD SCORES) OF COMBINED PLEDGE GROUPS

| | (1) | (2) | (3) | (4) | (5) | (6) |
| | Fraternities (n = 103) | | | Sororities (n = 79) | | |
Value	Pretest	Posttest	Change	Pretest	Posttest	Change
Intellectualism	−.61	−.51	+.10	−.29	+.11	+.40[c]
Kindness	−.13	−.31	−.18	+.15	+.20	+.05
Social skills	+.17	−.04	−.21[a]	+.29	+.39	+.10
Loyalty	+.79	+.59	−.20[b]	+.75	+.53	−.22[b]
Academic achievement	+.38	+.03	−.35[c]	+.23	+.27	+.04
Physical development	−.03	+.05	+.08	+.14	+.06	−.08
Status	+.26	+.04	−.22[a]	−.02	−.09	−.07
Honesty	+.17	.00	−.17	+.34	+.12	−.22[a]
Religiousness	+.17	−.07	−.24[c]	+.50	+.34	−.16[a]
Self-control	−.11	−.22	−.11	+.10	+.11	+.01
Creativity	−.51	−.46	+.06	−.26	−.23	+.03
Independence	−.26	−.06	+.20[b]	−.75	−.47	+.28[c]

Note. — Pretest and posttest columns (1, 2, 4 and 5) are standard (z) scores based on a representative sample of the university student body. In the change columns (3 and 6), a + indicates an increase in the mean standard score, and a − indicates a decrease, from pre- to posttest.
[a]Different from 0.00 at $\alpha < .10$.
[b]Different from 0.00 at $\alpha < .05$.
[c]Different from 0.00 at $\alpha < .01$.

and not one of the "inner-directed" values showed a significant mean decrease. If anything, there was a tendency toward increased emphasis on intellectualism and independence, and toward decreased emphasis on loyalty and religiousness.

Comparison with Pretest Active-Pledge Discrepancies

These unexpected directions of change become more intelligible when one considers the patterns of pretest differences between pledges and actives. Table 32 shows the pretest pledge means, repeated from the corresponding columns of Table 31. Also shown are the corresponding means for the entire group of pretest actives, including those destined to graduate or leave their organizations, as well as actives who were to remain the entire year. (It is assumed that the entire group of pretest actives

TABLE 32
PRETEST MEAN VALUES (STANDARD SCORES) OF TOTAL ACTIVES
AND PLEDGES WHO REMAINED IN ORGANIZATION

Value	(1) Pledges $(n = 103)$	(2) Actives $(n = 231)$	(3) Difference	(4) Pledges $(n = 79)$	(5) Actives $(n = 179)$	(6) Difference
		Fraternities			Sororities	
Intellectualism	− .61	− .52	+.09	− .29	+.10	+.39[c]
Kindness	− .13	− .17	− .04	+.15	+.31	+.16
Social skills	+.17	− .04	− .21[a]	+.29	+.31	+.02
Loyalty	+.79	+.55	− .24[b]	+.75	+.77	+.02
Academic achievement	+.38	+.03	− .35[c]	+.23	+.44	+.21[a]
Physical development	− .03	− .13	− .10	+.14	+.22	+.08
Status	+.26	+.07	− .19[a]	− .02	+.01	+.03
Honesty	+.17	+.09	− .08	+.34	+.21	− .13
Religiousness	+.17	− .05	− .22[b]	+.50	+.37	− .13
Self-control	− .11	− .06	+.05	+.10	+.33	+.23[a]
Creativity	− .51	− .56	− .05	− .26	.00	+.26[b]
Independence	− .26	− .12	+.14	− .75	− .36	+.39[c]

Note. — Pledge and active columns (1, 2, 4 and 5) are standard (z) scores based on a representative sample of the university student body. In the difference columns (3 and 6), a + indicates that the active mean score is higher than the pledge mean, and a − indicates that the pledge mean is higher than the actives'.
[a]Different from 0.00 at $\alpha <$ .10.
[b]Different from 0.00 at $\alpha <$ .05.
[c]Different from 0.00 at $\alpha <$ .01.

constituted the norm-setters from the point of view of the pledges.)

It may be noted that in the six fraternities the actives scored significantly lower than pledges on the values of loyalty, academic achievement, and religiousness; and in the four sororities actives were significantly higher than pledges on the values of intellectualism, creativity, and independence. These differences, again, are *not* what one would expect from the assumption that Greek organizations serve to socialize their new members toward "other-directed," and away from "inner-directed," values.

Nevertheless, the patterns of pretest differences seem to bear considerable correspondence to the changes in pledges' scores reported in Table 31.

Figure 1 portrays the pledge movements graphically in relation to the pretest active means. From this figure one may note that the values of pledges most often changed in the direction of the actives' pretest positions. Unfortunately for the sake of clear interpretation, there was often an "overshoot" in this movement, so that the pledges ended up further from some of the actives' means than they began. We shall return to this problem shortly.

Comparison with Changes Among Non-pledging Freshmen

The changes in pledges' values should also be compared with corresponding changes among the two groups of non-pledging freshmen (see p. 138). Only 54 males and 30 females remained in school and in Independent status at the time of the posttest. Their pretest values, posttest values, and change scores are presented in Table 33. There it may be noted that only one of the non-pledge changes is significantly different from zero, or significantly different from the corresponding change of pledges — namely, that for the independence value among female subjects. The female pledges appear to have shown a larger increase in this value than non-pledging freshman women.

But it will also be seen (compare Tables 31 and 33) that non-pledging women were higher on the independence value to begin with; therefore their mean score was less likely to increase simply as a result of regression. As an approximate control for the contaminating effects of differential regression between the two groups, an analysis of covariance was performed, partialling out of the difference between pledges and non-pledges the correlation between their pretest and change scores. This yielded an F ratio that had a probability of chance occurrence between .05 and .10. Therefore, the inference that

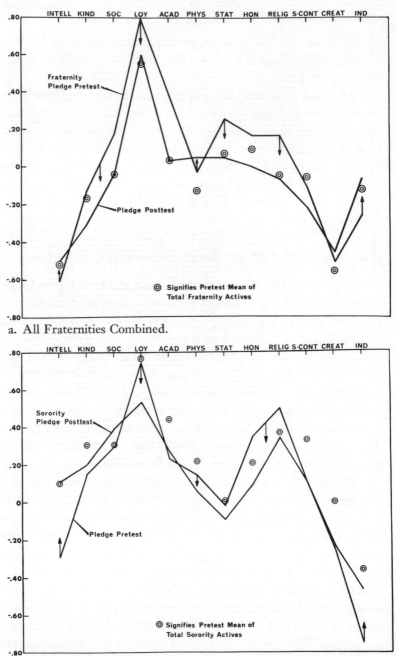

a. All Fraternities Combined.

b. All Sororities Combined.

Figure 1. Value Changes of Pledges in Relation to Pretest Means of Total Actives.

TABLE 33
MEAN VALUES (STANDARD SCORES) OF NON-PLEDGING
FRESHMEN WHO REMAINED INDEPENDENT

| | (1) | (2) | (3) | (4) | (5) | (6) |
| | Males (n = 54) | | | Females (n = 30) | | |
Value	Pretest	Posttest	Change	Pretest	Posttest	Change
Intellectualism	−.17	−.08	+.09	−.08	+.03	+.11
Kindness	−.17	−.09	+.08	+.34	+.24	−.10
Social skills	−.39	−.31	+.08	−.12	−.21	−.09
Loyalty	+.28	+.05	−.23	+.03	−.19	−.22
Academic achievement	+.27	+.13	−.14	−.16	−.42	−.26
Physical development	−.12	−.01	+.11	+.01	−.08	−.09
Status	+.13	+.04	−.09	−.36	−.45	−.09
Honesty	+.40	+.44	+.04	+.37	+.46	+.09
Religiousness	+.14	+.05	−.09	+.30	+.38	+.08
Self-control	+.08	+.06	−.02	+.18	−.10	−.28
Creativity	−.22	−.15	+.07	−.10	−.31	−.21
Independence	+.12	+.01	−.11	−.02	−.28	−.26*†

Note. — See corresponding note in Table 31.
*Different from 0.00 at $\alpha < .05$.
†Different from change in female pledges (+.28) at $\alpha < .01$. (See text for qualification.)

female pledge changes on the independence value differed from non-pledge changes, independently of initial score differences, is somewhat tenuous. Given the additional consideration that this is merely one borderline difference out of 24 comparisons, one cannot reasonably conclude that pledges changed on any particular value in a manner different from the corresponding change of non-pledging freshmen of the same sex.

Instead of treating each of the twelve values separately, it is possible to consider them as a set and look at the total pattern of value-changes among pledges, as compared with that for the "controls." This may be done in several ways. First, the correlation, over the twelve values, between change scores of pledges and non-pledges is +.22 for male subjects and −.17 for females. Neither of these correlations is significantly different from zero, so one cannot conclude that the pattern of pledge changes was either similar to or different from the pattern of changes among non-pledging freshmen. (This inconclusiveness still obtains when pretest scores of the two groups are equated through the partial correlation technique.)

Next, one may compare similarity of value patterns for pledges and for non-pledging controls, first on the pretest, then on the posttest, to see if there was either any convergence or any divergence over the one-year period. Among males the pretest correlation over the twelve value means was .51 and the posttest correlation was .23. Among females the corresponding figures were .28 and .16. Neither the difference for males nor that for females is significantly different from zero. So this analysis offers no ground for concluding either that freshman Greeks and freshman Independents became more alike in professed values or that they became more unlike during their first year in college.

A third comparison did show a small, but significant, difference in the movements of pledging and non-pledging freshmen when their total value-patterns were considered at once. Looking back at Figure 1, one may note an apparent tendency for the mean scores of pledges to have changed, from pretest to posttest, so that they came closer to the pretest active means. This observation seems especially applicable to the values of social skills, loyalty, academic achievement, and religiousness in the fraternities and to the values of intellectualism and independence in the sororities. The relevant comparative question here is: Did the pledges decrease their pretest differences from actives more than the non-pledging controls did? If so, then one might infer that pledges were responding distinctively to normative influences from the actives.

Table 34 presents the relevant data abstracted from the preceding three tables. Columns 1 and 4 indicate, for fraternities and sororities respectively, how much closer the pledges moved

TABLE 34
CHANGES IN DISTANCES FROM PRETEST ACTIVE MEANS OF
PLEDGES AND OF NON-PLEDGING FRESHMEN

	(1)	(2) Males Non-pledges	(3) Differ-ence	(4)	(5) Females Non-pledges	(6) Differ-ence
Value	*Pledges*			*Pledges*		
Intellectualism	+.08	−.09	+.17	+.38	+.09	+.29
Kindness	−.10	−.08	−.02	+.05	−.04	+.09
Social skills	+.21	+.08	+.13	−.06	−.09	+.03
Loyalty	+.20	−.23	+.43	−.22	−.22	.00
Academic achievement	+.35	+.14	+.21	+.04	−.26	+.30
Physical development	−.08	−.11	+.03	−.08	−.09	+.01
Status	+.16	+.03	+.13	−.07	−.09	+.02
Honesty	−.01	−.04	+.03	+.04	−.09	+.13
Religiousness	+.20	+.09	+.11	+.10	+.06	+.04
Self-control	−.11	+.02	−.13	+.01	−.28	+.29
Creativity	−.05	−.07	+.02	+.03	−.21	+.24
Independence	+.08	+.11	.03	+.28	+.26	+.02
Mean	+.08	−.01	+.09*	+.04	−.08	+.12**

Note. — In Cols. 1, 2, 4, and 5, a + indicates that the group mean came closer to the pretest active mean, from pre- to posttest; a − indicates that it moved farther away. In Cols. 3 and 6, a + indicates that pledges moved toward the pretest active mean more than did non-pledging freshmen; a − indicates the reverse.
* Different from zero at $\alpha < .05$.
**Different from zero at $\alpha < .01$.

to the actives' pretest positions on each of the twelve values. Columns 2 and 5 show the degree to which non-pledging freshmen decreased their pretest distances from actives. Column 3 is the difference between Columns 1 and 2; Column 6 is the difference between Columns 4 and 5. These show the degree to which pledges and controls moved in distinctive ways relative to the pretest actives' positions. The mean differences for both males and females are significantly greater than zero (at α less than .05 and .01, respectively). Therefore, we may conclude that pledges changed toward the active value pattern to a greater extent than did non-pledging freshmen of the same sex.[1]

In sum, these various analyses seem to indicate that the pattern of pledges' changes over the total set of twelve values was somewhat influenced by the actives. However, the differences between pledges' and non-pledges' movements was slight, and did not show up when each value was considered individually, nor did it appear to a significant degree when pledges' and non-pledges' movements were compared directly, instead of in relation to the actives' norms.

One is therefore led to conclude that the average impact of Greek membership on the values of these pledges was not a very distinctive one. Though the Greek organizations presented a somewhat distinct "value culture" (see pp. 138-141), it seems to have been transmitted primarily through processes of selection, rather than influence. Greek-Independent value differences were discernible from the early stages of recruitment, when pledges were found to differ from non-pledging freshmen in the direction of greater similarity to actives' values. The degree of similarity did not appear to increase substantially during their first year of membership in the organizations.

[1] This comparison of absolute discrepancies between mean value scores on the pretest and posttest is just one way of representing movements relative to the presumed norms. It leaves something to be desired as a measure of "normative influence," since it does not take into account the magnitude of the initial discrepancy. It could reasonably be argued that "normative pull" on pledges should be greater for those values which start out farthest from the actives. Therefore, when the pretest discrepancy is large, pledges should move the greatest distance toward the active norm; when the pretest discrepancy is small, the movement should be less, and might even be negative (away from the actives' position), since the "normative pull" is not strong. One can take the magnitude of pretest discrepancy into account by another index of norm-directed movement: viz., the intra-class correlation, over the twelve values, between the pretest discrepancy from actives and the change in pledges' mean from pre- to posttest. This index is substantially inflated by regression effects, but when appropriate controls for this are employed, the results turn out essentially as reported in Table 34, namely, that pledges' values moved toward the pretest active means significantly more than did the controls'.

DIFFERENTIAL CHANGES AMONG ORGANIZATIONS

If the Greek culture as a whole did not have a substantially distinctive impact on the values of pledges, it may simply have been because pledges were not generally exposed to the "total culture," but rather only to that portion of it which was represented in their individual houses. To the extent that the several organizations differed in value norms (see p. 110), one might expect their pledge classes to have been differentially influenced. Where actives emphasized a particular value, pledges should presumably have tended to increase their acceptance of it, while in another house, pledges might have decreased their scores on the same value in response to actives' de-emphasis of it. Such differential house effects could cancel each other out over the ten organizations, thus yielding no apparent normative impact on all pledges, considered together.

There were, in fact, substantial differences among the houses in the kinds of value changes that appeared among pledge groups. Figure 2 illustrates this point by reference to one fraternity and one sorority. In Fraternity 4, there was a large increase in the social skills value, but all the rest appear to have declined in strength; in Sorority 3, small increases appeared in intellectualism, social skills, and creativity. More important to the present question, however, is the degree to which these changes served to decrease the pretest difference from actives. In Fraternity 4, nearly all the movements were in the direction of the pretest actives' positions, and the over-all result was to increase the pledges' nearness to the actives. Quite a different outcome appeared in Sorority 3: Pledges moved toward the pretest active position on only four of the values, and the final positions were, on the average, farther away from the pretest active position than they had been to begin with.

The average results for all ten organizations are summarized in Table 35, which shows the degree to which pledges differed

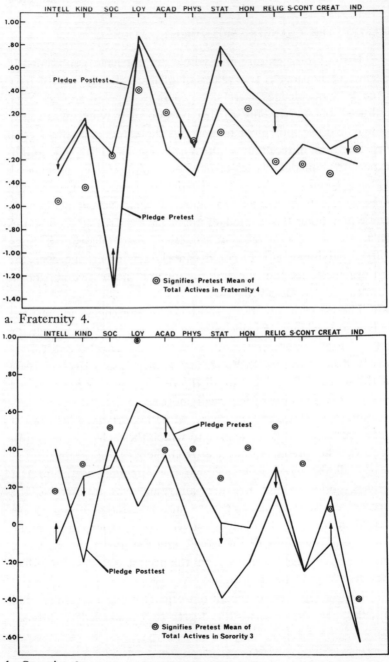

a. Fraternity 4.

b. Sorority 3.

Figure 2. Value Changes of Pledges in Two Organizations in Relation to Pretest Means of Their Own Actives.

TABLE 35

MEAN ABSOLUTE DIFFERENCES OF PRETEST PLEDGES AND
POSTTEST PLEDGES FROM TOTAL PRETEST ACTIVES
(Average for All Twelve Values)

Organization	Pretest	Posttest	Change[a]
Fraternity 1	.23	.27	+.04
Fraternity 2	.32	.40	+.08
Fraternity 3	.18	.22	+.04
Fraternity 4	.33	.27	−.06
Fraternity 5	.41	.24	−.17
Fraternity 6	.44	.43	−.01
Sorority 1	.24	.12	−.12
Sorority 2	.21	.15	−.06
Sorority 3	.26	.39	+.13
Sorority 4	.33	.31	−.02

Note. — The same subjects are included in both pretest and posttest pledge groups (only *S*s who stayed in their organizations throughout the year). The mean pretest value scores of all actives serve as the bases of comparison on both occasions.
[a] A + indicates that pledges increased their mean absolute difference from the pretest actives, a − indicates that they decreased their mean absolute difference, between pre- and posttest.

from the pretest actives, first on the pretest, then on the posttest. (These scores were obtained by summing over all twelve values the differences between active and pledge means, without regard to sign, and dividing this sum by twelve.) In six organizations, the average discrepancy decreased over time; in four organizations it increased. The third column of Table 35 reports the increases and decreases in mean absolute differences. It is apparent that no consistent normative effect appeared within all organizations. Pledges did *not*, in general, change their values so as to become more like the actives (or, rather, like what the actives had been on the pretest).[2]

Some of the actives remained in their groups for the posttest. It is therefore possible to see if, together, the remaining actives and pledges tended to move closer to one another throughout the

[2] An identical conclusion is reached when the magnitude of the pretest discrepancy is taken into account, by means of the intra-class correlation between pretest differences and change scores (see footnote 1, p. 202).

year. This analysis ignores the distinction between norm-setters and norm-followers (see p. 192), and simply inquires whether the values of actives and pledges became more alike with time. Table 36 shows that even this normative effect did not occur consis-

TABLE 36
MEAN ABSOLUTE DIFFERENCES IN VALUES OF ACTIVES
AND PLEDGES WHO REMAINED IN ORGANIZATION

Organization	Pretest	Posttest	Change[a]
Fraternity 1	.24	.24	.00
Fraternity 2	.28	.36	+.08
Fraternity 3	.23	.31	+.08
Fraternity 4	.27	.39	+.12
Fraternity 5	.36	.24	−.12
Fraternity 6	.59	.58	−.01
Sorority 1	.22	.16	−.06
Sorority 2	.34	.17	−.17
Sorority 3	.25	.30	+.05
Sorority 4	.44	.39	−.05

Note. — Includes only actives and pledges who remained in organization throughout the year. In contrast to Table 35, the changes reported here include movements of actives, as well as of pledges.
[a] A + indicates that actives and pledges increased their mean absolute difference, a − indicates that they decreased their mean absolute difference between pre- and posttest.

tently: In five organizations, actives and pledges tended to become more alike; in four organizations they became less alike; and in one there was no difference between the mean pretest and posttest discrepancies.

Looking at all members who remained in the organization throughout the year, without regard to their active or pledge status, one can ask whether the group as a whole became more homogeneous in values. Table 37 shows that this was not the case. Quite the contrary: Throughout the year, those members who were in the organization for both the pre- and posttest tended to increase their differences in values. In only one organization (Sorority 2) did members become more alike — and only by a trivial amount.

TABLE 37
MEAN VARIANCE IN VALUES OF ALL MEMBERS
(PLEDGES AND ACTIVES COMBINED)
WHO REMAINED IN ORGANIZATIONS

Organization	Pretest	Posttest	Change[a]
Fraternity 1	1.71	1.81	+.10
Fraternity 2	1.69	1.88	+.19
Fraternity 3	1.84	1.96	+.12
Fraternity 4	1.83	1.87	+.04
Fraternity 5	1.75	2.02	+.27
Fraternity 6	1.82	1.99	+.17
Sorority 1	1.63	1.69	+.06
Sorority 2	1.54	1.50	−.04
Sorority 3	1.33	1.72	+.39
Sorority 4	1.43	1.67	+.24

[a]A + indicates an increase in σ^2; a − indicates a decrease.

Thus, there is absolutely no evidence that these organizations exerted normative influences on the values of their incoming pledges. If anything, the members tended to become more different from one another, rather than more similar, with the passage of time. Clearly there was no general tendency within individual organizations to maintain distinctive value cultures through socialization of their new members. Such distinctiveness as was found depended on the initial recruitment processes (see Chapter 5), rather than on normative influences following recruitment.

NORMATIVE INFLUENCES ON DEVOTED PLEDGES

The analyses thus far have dealt with value changes among all pledges who remained in their organizations throughout the first year. These members were at least moderately motivated to belong, and as a group they tended to be more highly attracted to their organizations than the average active (see Table 15). Yet there were differences among the pledges themselves in degree of attraction to the organization, and it is possible that normative influences would operate most effectively on those with the highest levels of attraction. Numerous studies of communication processes in experimental groups (e.g., Back, 1951; Schachter, et al., 1951) have demonstrated that high attraction to the group makes a member more amenable to influence from his colleagues.

An exploration of this hypothesis was attempted with the present data. Pledges in each house were divided at the median score on the index of attraction to the organization (pp. 126 and 278) into "high" and "low" levels of attraction. Considering just the highly attracted half as the devoted pledges who might be most susceptible to normative influence from actives, an analysis of their value changes in relation to the pretest active norms was undertaken. The first three columns of Table 38 report the results for devoted pledges only, in a manner parallel to that used in Table 35 (which included the entire group of pledges who remained in the organization). In nine of the ten houses the devoted pledges showed a mean shift in their values in the direction of the pretest active positions (see Col. 3). Thus, we have tentative evidence that normative pressures may have operated within these houses to produce value change among that portion of the pledge class which was the most highly motivated toward membership.

TABLE 38

MEAN ABSOLUTE DIFFERENCES FROM PRETEST ACTIVES OF PLEDGES
HIGHLY ATTRACTED TO ORGANIZATION MEMBERSHIP

| | (1) | (2) | (3) | (4) | (5) | (6) |
| | Difference from Actives in Own Organization | | | Difference from Actives of Same Sex | | |
Organization	Pretest	Posttest	Change	Pretest	Posttest	Change
Fraternity 1	.30	.20	− .10	.37	.17	− .20
Fraternity 2	.47	.42	− .05	.34	.29	− .05
Fraternity 3	.31	.25	− .06	.30	.19	− .11
Fraternity 4	.42	.28	− .14	.41	.24	− .17
Fraternity 5	.62	.57	− .05	.59	.54	− .05
Fraternity 6	.58	.45	− .13	.47	.51	+ .04
Sorority 1	.37	.30	− .07	.35	.26	− .09
Sorority 2	.32	.26	− .06	.31	.29	− .02
Sorority 3	.20	.36	+ .16	.17	.33	+ .16
Sorority 4	.39	.33	− .06	.29	.29	.00
Mean change			− .06			− .05

However, a definite conclusion must be held in abeyance, since it cannot be known from these data whether pledge movements were toward their own specific house norms or toward some more pervasive norms for the Greek culture as a whole. In order to examine this alternative, we should make a similar comparison between pre- and posttest pledge discrepancies from the pretest active means for all houses of the same sex. This is done in the last three columns of Table 38, which show that values of highly attracted pledges also tended to change in the direction of all pretest actives of the same sex, regardless of house. The difference between the changes reported in Column 3 and those reported in Column 6 is not significant. In other words, whatever "normative impact" on the devoted pledges may have occurred, it did not necessarily emanate from their own houses. It may be that pledges highly attracted to their own organizations were also highly attracted to the entire Greek culture, and hence susceptible to pervasive influence from outside their own groups. It is also possible that the changes reported in Column 3 are attributable to regression effects: Highly attracted pledges may have started out with extreme scores on values such as loyalty and independence (see Table 23), and therefore have had more "room" for movement toward the actives' moderate positions than did less devoted pledges. Whatever the explanation, the present pattern of results leaves considerable doubt as to whether values of even the highly attracted pledges were influenced distinctively by the actives in their own houses.

CHANGES IN ACTIVES' VALUES

Insofar as the present study was concerned with processes of influence within Greek organizations, the focus of analysis was on changes in the values of pledges, rather than of actives. This choice of focus was based on the assumption that most of the group-induced changes in values would occur during the first year of membership. It was believed that the older members (the actives) would present a more or less stable norm for the pledges to move toward, and that these actives would not show very much systematic value change themselves.

This expectation was not borne out either. Actives who remained in the organization throughout the year changed their values about as much as pledges did, and in somewhat the same directions. Table 39 presents, for all fraternities combined and for all sororities combined, the pretest and posttest mean values of actives who were living in their houses on both pre- and posttests. Columns 3 and 6 show the changes in mean values, and can thus be compared with the corresponding columns in Table 31, which report the same data for pledges. It may be noted that, within the fraternities, actives showed significant mean decreases in the values of kindness, social skills, loyalty, religiousness, and self-control, while sorority actives decreased significantly only on the loyalty value.

TABLE 39
MEAN VALUES OF COMBINED ACTIVES WHO REMAINED
IN ORGANIZATION

| | (1) | (2) | (3) | (4) | (5) | (6) |
| | Fraternities (n = 122) | | | Sororities (n = 74) | | |
Value	Pretest	Posttest	Change	Pretest	Posttest	Change
Intellectualism	− .44	− .35	+.09	+.04	+.19	+.15
Kindness	− .02	− .22	− .20*	+.39	+.51	+.12
Social skills	+.10	− .07	− .17*	+.33	+.27	− .06
Loyalty	+.68	+.42	− .26**	+.98	+.52	− .46**
Academic achievement	+.13	− .03	− .16	+.44	+.25	− .19
Physical development	+.01	− .01	− .02	+.25	+.11	− .14
Status	+.19	+.12	− .07	− .08	− .01	− .09
Honesty	.00	+.03	+.03	+.15	+.15	.00
Religiousness	+.04	− .23	− .27**	+.28	+.31	+.03
Self-control	+.02	− .14	− .16*	+.32	+.09	− .23
Creativity	− .47	− .56	− .09	+.04	+.01	− .03
Independence	− .28	− .27	+.01	− .49	− .49	.00

Note. — See corresponding note in Table 31.
* Different from zero at $\alpha < .05$.
**Different from zero at $\alpha < .01$.

Considering the total pattern of mean changes on all twelve values simultaneously, the changes among fraternity actives correlated .63 with changes among fraternity pledges ($\alpha <$ .05). Within the sororities, actives' mean changes correlated .41 with pledges' mean changes ($\alpha <$ .10). Thus, far from providing a stable norm toward which to attract pledges, the actives were themselves moving — perhaps responding to some extra-organizational source of influence, which also may have accounted for the pledges' changes. Just what that source of value influence might have been, we are in no position to determine from the present study.

DISCUSSION

We have not found clear evidence for any substantial impact of these Greek organizations on the values of their new members — either when the several houses were treated separately or when all houses of the same sex were combined. A reasonable conclusion from these analyses is that there was not much distinctive impact. But the limitation of this conclusion should be made clear.

In the first place, of course, this was a study of changes in values, not of changes in all kinds of other traits which might result from fraternity living. Though the twelve values represented here span the spectrum of potentially relevant moral ideals reasonably well, they do not in any direct sense reflect overt behaviors in these domains — let alone in other domains, such as politics, sex, or drinking. We cannot know from the present study whether or not these Greek organizations had any distinctive impacts on such behaviors. A skeptical view might seem justified, however, since many reasonable expectations about their probable impact on values have not been borne out.

Also, we have been concerned here about the *distinctive* impact of Greek organizations on their membership — distinct, that is, from the impact of the wider campus culture, which impinges on Greek and Independent alike. If these organizations are indeed firmly embedded in the surrounding campus culture, perhaps all they can do is serve as mediators of that culture for their members. Thus, any influence that they may have on values would be contributory to, rather than distinctive from, the influence emanating from other sources — such as professors, chaplains, and the college newspaper. Since this study was not designed to investigate the value impact of the entire university, we have carefully avoided interpreting the data from this perspective. Some value changes, e.g., the decrease in religiousness, appeared to be common to all groups of subjects, Independents as well as Greeks, actives as well as pledges. But whether this was due to university-wide influences, or to some other concomitant of maturation, such as increasing sophistication or alienation from traditional institutions, cannot be guessed from the present results.

Finally, a specific limitation to the analysis of intra-organizational influences on values should be noted. We began by designating the entire group of actives as the "norm-setters" and the group of pledges who remained in the house as "norm-followers." It is possible that some other norm-setting group should have been considered; perhaps some sub-group within the total active membership *did* have a consistent influence on pledges. Or perhaps some sub-group within the total pledge membership was consistently influenced toward some definable norm. Of course, it is reasonable to expect that various groups of pledges would be differentially influenced by various groups of actives. But that is another research problem. The present study of value changes was limited to the question: Did the entire group of actives in each organization influence the values of all its pledges in a way different from other organizations? The answer seems to have been "no."

SUMMARY

Influences on pledges have been studied by noting the degree to which their values changed through the year so as to become more like the values that actives in their own organizations professed on the pretest. The analyses reported here indicate that the several houses made no distinctive impacts on their entire pledge groups. Also, there were probably no distinctive impacts even on those pledges who were most attracted to their organizations. In fact, the available evidence indicates that, within any single house, members' values were likely to become more heterogeneous, rather than more homogeneous, with time.

When all organizations of a given sex are combined, there is also little evidence of specific changes in pledges' values that were distinctively different from the corresponding changes in values of non-pledging freshmen. On no single value were pledges' changes significantly different from those of non-pledges. Only when the entire pattern of twelve values was considered as a totality could it be concluded that pledging and non-pledging freshmen moved in different directions throughout the year. Pledges tended to change toward a value pattern like the actives' more than did non-pledging freshmen.

CHAPTER 10

RECAPITULATION AND CRITIQUE

Findings from this study of values in campus fraternities and sororities have been presented in detail in the preceding six chapters. It now remains to consider their general significance for the broader questions, posed in Chapter 3, concerning the part that personal values play in various organizational processes. Though the investigation was limited to a particular kind of organization and to a particular set of potentially relevant values, these settings and measures were chosen with a view toward testing some general propositions that may be applicable to other groups, and to other values, as well.

PERSONAL VALUES

Within the formulation proposed in Chapter 1, a personal value (or moral ideal) is any individual's conception of an ideal relationship between people — a state of affairs that he considers ultimately, absolutely, and universally good. Though their hosts may treat them as absolutes, values are here conceptualized theoretically as standards of goodness held by individual humans, not as properties inherent in the nature of things or as necessary universals. A value is therefore identified, not by its content (i.e., the state of affairs which is regarded as ideal), but by the attitude of the person toward it. No matter what state a given individual regards as ultimately, absolutely, and universally good, that state constitutes, for him, a value. Since it appears subjectively as an absolute, the person will expect that other people should also value it, and he will be prone to condemn them as immoral if they do not.

By no means do all people hold values in this absolutistic sense. But preliminary samples of college students indicate that, even in this intellectually mature population, there are more "moral realists" (i.e., absolutists) than there are "moral relativists." Whether the relativists should be regarded as not holding values at all, or rather as holding non-absolutistic values, is a matter of definition. In either case, the present formulation has referred mainly to absolutistic moralities.

Since a value provides an internalized standard of right and wrong, the individual who holds it is in a position to reward himself (through feelings of self-righteousness) for acting in accord with it, and to punish himself (through guilt) for violating it. Given the opportunity, then, a person should tend to guide his behaviors in accordance with his conceptions of the ideal. The opportunity is not always present, however, if only because other significant people may disagree as to the absolute goodness of the valued state of affairs.

If one initially acts for non-evaluative reasons — e.g., because a friend asks him to, because it seems like fun, or because it is required by powerful figures — the act may not correspond to any pre-existing value in the person. (It may actually be antithetical to his values, but more likely it will simply be irrelevant.) However, if afterwards he wonders why he did it — and why he continues to do it — he poses a challenge to his self-concept as a rational being who acts for good and sufficient reason. Unless one can conveniently excuse the action as forced upon him, he is likely to develop — or rather, select from the many available in his culture — some reason that will justify it. The concept of an absolutely good state toward which the act was aimed provides sufficient reason for a subjectively rational person. Without a relevant value, the individual who has asked himself why he behaves in this way may be forced to give up the activity, to feel guilty, or to recognize the act as non-rational. Rationalization of the act by recourse to a value may prove more comfortable than these alternatives.

Moral ideals can thus play either a guiding or a rationalizing role in relation to behavior. Though external circumstances, as well as irrational wants, will constantly intervene to disrupt the equilibrium between values and behavior, there should be enduring pressures of personal consistency toward congruence between the two.

The first problem of the research was to develop measures of values which tapped some such psychological process as this. Though by no means all of the necessary properties have been established, there is some evidence that the present measures are tentatively appropriate. Twelve different values were measured by multiple-item scales, and the strength of each was inferred from the number of times the subject checked one of the behavior traits described (within a given scale) as something he "always admired."

The strength of each of the values measured in this way was highly correlated with the degree to which the subject regarded the trait as absolutely right, independent of his own preferences, and with the degree to which he thought that other people should admire the trait too. Moreover, there was some degree of correspondence between what the person claimed to admire and (1) his reports of his own overt behaviors, (2) his friends' ratings of his behaviors, and (3) his estimate of how bad he would feel if he were forced to violate the value. Though these measures are not recommended for purposes of individual diagnosis, they appeared to have adequate reliabilities for the intended research.

The twelve values were chosen to represent a range of presumed relevance to college life and to the functioning of campus fraternities and sororities. In a representative cross-section of the total student body, they tended to separate into two clusters. The "other-directed" cluster included the values of kindness, social skills, loyalty, physical development, status, religiousness, and self-control. The "inner-directed" cluster included the values of intellectualism, creativity, and independence. The value of honesty was not associated with either cluster, while the academic achievement value appeared in both.

VALUES AND ORGANIZATIONAL PROCESSES

In Chapter 3 a number of assertions were made concerning the alleged relevance of personal values for various processes of organization that go on within fraternities and sororities. These notions formed the basis for the research procedures and analyses undertaken in the present longitudinal study of ten campus social organizations. Some of the assertions were tested here; others provided a background of assumptions that guided the investigation. With respect to the propositions that *were* tested, it would seem appropriate to ask how well they were supported by the present results. In recapitulating the major findings from this study, therefore, we shall indicate how they bear on various beliefs about the role of values in organizations.

Two premises underlie many of the propositions: The first was that the kind of values that are emphasized in the various organizational processes depends on the functions that the organization performs for its membership and for its social surround. The second premise was that the principal function performed by these social organizations for their members was to facilitate the establishment and maintenance of friendships. These premises have the logical status of assumptions, rather than hypotheses, in the present study. So the evidence for them is quite indirect, and depends on the outcome with respect to other propositions that *were* directly tested. Therefore, we shall defer the basic question of group function until the specific organizational processes have been reviewed.

RECRUITMENT

Proposition 1. The initial values of freshmen help determine whether or not they will pledge a Greek organization. (Supported)

    a. *In the recruitment of pledges to Greek organizations, there is a general emphasis on interpersonal, organization-maintaining values.* (Supported)

This proposition recognizes that recruitment depends on the values of both parties to the process — the present members who select pledges from among the rushees, and the entering freshmen who decide whether or not to rush. It was expected that old members would seek pledges who showed some promise of furthering the dominant interpersonal function of these houses. If they were able to choose from a large pool of potential recruits, and if they were maximally perspicacious in their selection, they would succeed in pledging new members who placed high value on group loyalty, social skills, and mutual interdependence of members. Though the population of potential members from which fraternities and sororities recruit is by no means unlimited, each organization probably has more choice than does, say, a typical labor union or church or family. Therefore, the group has both the desire and the opportunity to pick new members with appropriate, group-maintaining values.

The selection is presumably aided by the recruits themselves, who must have some image of what is required for successful house membership, and who place sufficient value on the perceived requirements to make the initial choice to pledge some organization.

The main evidence for the proposition was this: When the entire sample of pledges (of a given sex) was compared with a "control" group of non-pledging freshmen, the former were generally found to value loyalty and social skills more than the latter, and to score lower on the value of independence (which is, in a way, antithetical to harmonious group functioning).

The evidence does not distinguish the relative contributions of the old and new members to functional recruitment: We cannot tell whether it was the desires of the rushees or the desires of the old members which were primarily responsible for the ultimate selection according to these values. Considering the fact that only a very small percentage of rushees fail to gain acceptance in any house at all, one would guess that, unless these are very atypical houses, it was mainly the pledges who were responsible for this value-matching.

There is the additional problem, since the pretest occurred around November, that pledges may have been subject to value influence during the preceding few weeks. Hence, what appeared to be a selection effect may actually have been due to rapid socialization. While this possibility cannot be eliminated altogether, it seems quite unlikely, given the limited contact between actives and pledges up to that time. More plausible, perhaps, is the objection that pledges may have "faked good" on the pretest, manifesting to an unreal degree the values they regarded as appropriate for members. If this kind of invalid self-presentation were widespread, then the differences found here between pledging and non-pledging freshmen could hardly reflect pre-existing value differences; rather, they would have been created, so to speak, by the circumstances of testing — in a fraternity house for the pledges and in a dormitory for the non-pledges.

Some tentative evidence against these interpretations is provided by a comparison of the pretest value scores of non-pledging freshmen who remained in Independent status with the scores of those who actually did pledge some house during the year following the pretest. The numbers of cases are small — only 13 men and 16 women in the control groups pledged — but the trend of results is as follows: Control subjects who subsequently pledged valued loyalty more, and independence less, than did controls who remained Independent. (The significance levels of these trends were .10 and .05, respectively.) When the entire pattern of mean pretest values was considered at once, the controls who subsequently pledged tended to show a pattern more like that of the pledges than did controls who remained Independent. (The significance levels of these trends were .05 for males and .10 for female subjects.)

Thus, it seems reasonable to conclude that the values of entering freshmen did help *predispose* them to join or not to join a Greek organization. It is almost as if some of the freshmen, though resolved to remain Independent, possessed a predisposing pattern of values, and so eventually joined a Greek organization, even though they had not initially intended to.

It is still necessary to face the fact that incoming pledges often scored more extremely than actives on certain of the values that were presumably relevant to the functioning of these organizations. Fraternity pledges tended to score higher on social skills ($\alpha <$ .10) and loyalty ($\alpha <$ .01); fraternity and sorority pledges together scored lower on independence ($\alpha <$ .02), than did the actives themselves. These results were interpreted as reflecting "anticipatory socialization," i.e., that new members entered the groups with some exaggerated expectations about their norms. The results could also mean, that, though the old members had themselves grown tired of group-maintenance values, when it came to selecting new members who were to embody the ideals of the organization, these values became temporarily salient. In any case, the findings suggest a rather paradoxical aspect of the recruitment process in these groups: New members are selected so as to reaffirm certain group-relevant values which the old members no longer espouse so strongly. We shall return to this problem later.

Proposition 2. Organizations tend to recruit new members with values similar to those of the old members. (Supported)

This proposition is intended to be distinct from Proposition 1. a., for it refers to a variety of values besides those which are of a general group-maintaining character. It says, in effect, that whatever traits are valued by the present membership will be sought in new recruits. Organizations that perform a common major function may still vary widely in ancillary emphases. Among campus fraternities and sororities there may be some houses stressing athletics, some stressing grades, yet others emphasizing intellectual endeavors. Regardless of how the particular focus came to be, it is likely to continue — both because current members tend to regard their own traits as desirable and, therefore, to seek them in others, and also because the house may have developed a reputation for its particular emphasis, so that rushees who value the quality will try to gain admittance.

Evidence for this proposition consists of the findings that, among the several houses of a given sex, those pledges who joined a particular organization tended to match the values of the actives in that organization better than a randomly selected group of (same-sex) pledges would have matched these same actives' values. In other words, though all pledges tended to value organization-maintaining qualities to an exceptional degree (Proposition 1. a.), they differed with respect to some other values; and they tended to sort themselves among the various houses in such a way as to find compatible values among the actives.

The foregoing propositions indicate that recruitment may function as a significant mechanism for maintaining normative continuity within fraternities and sororities. New members are pledged who (1) tend to share the values of the old members and (2) are committed to organization-maintaining values, so that they would presumably wish to perpetuate the group's value culture. We will now review some other mechanisms through which a value culture may be preserved.

SOCIALIZATION

Proposition 3. As a result of normative pressures within their houses, new members, over time, come more and more to adopt the values of the older members. (Not supported)

This proposition actually underwent a number of transformations in the course of data analysis. Its first statement, consistent with the view that friendship-maintenance is the essential function of fraternities and sororities, went like this: In response to normative pressures, pledges will come to place increasing emphasis on values relevant to group maintenance. However, it turned out that, at the time of recruitment, pledges already tended to emphasize some of the group-maintenance values more than actives did. Thus the hypothesis was internally inconsistent: Pledges could *either* increase their emphasis on these values *or* respond to normative pressures from actives, but not both.

A modified proposition was developed: The values of pledges will change, throughout the year, so as to become more like those of actives. This formulation referred to all values, not just those relevant to group maintenance. Thus the functional implication of the original proposition was discarded. It was simply hypothesized that pledges would come to emphasize whatever values the actives did; there was no specification of what those values might be.

In a way, some of the results were consistent with this modified proposition. Fraternity pledges decreased, over the year, with respect to the values of academic achievement and religiousness, and increased in the value placed on independence. Sorority pledges increased on the values of intellectualism and independence, and decreased their mean value of loyalty. These changes, for all organizations of a given sex combined, corresponded fairly well to the patterns of pretest differences between pledges and actives. When the actives were initially higher, the pledges' values tended to increase; when the actives were lower, the pledges tended to decrease.

However, implicit in this modified proposition was the assumption that pledge movements were due to normative pressure from the actives, and not to some extraneous factors, such as campus-wide influences or maturation. Several additional analyses failed to indicate that the value changes of pledges were substantially different from the changes that occurred in a control group of non-pledging freshmen. So even though pledges' values had moved toward the actives' positions, this movement could not be definitely attributed to any distinctive influence of actives on pledges.

Perhaps the most decisive evidence against Proposition 3 came from the analysis of intra-house changes in pledges' values. If normative pressures influence values, it is most reasonable to expect that they would operate within each house separately. Pledges, after all, are most exposed to their own actives' norms, not to the norms of other houses. In fact, the pledges did *not* move closer to their own actives' values. So there was little evidence for normative influence on the values of pledges throughout their first year of membership in the Greek organizations.

The lack of support for Proposition 3 raises a number of critical questions, relating both to the function of Greek organizations and to origins of personal values. Was the absence of influence simply a natural consequence of the selection process? Were pledges' and actives' values sufficiently similar to begin with to make further convergence unnecessary? This is a hard question to answer, since we do not know how similar is "sufficiently similar." There is probably a sense in which nearly all pledges — or even nearly all entering freshmen — are similar to actives, in comparison, say, with members of another culture, another social class, or another sex. Of more relevance is the fact that, of the ten organizations, there were seven in which the pledge mean for one or more values deviated from the active mean by as much as ½ σ; there were two organizations in which the pledge mean for a single value deviated from the active mean by 1 σ or more. These are σ-units based on the total university student body, so the frame of reference they provide is probably related to the viewpoints of the present subjects. And since these are differences in group means, it is clear that numerous pledges within the group deviated from the active mean by amounts that were considerably greater than that. Thus, one would suspect that, if actives had been sensitive to such deviations and disposed to do something about them, considerable convergence in value means could have taken place. Yet pledge-active mean value differences of over ½ σ remained in five of these seven houses on the posttest, and one more house had developed such a discrepancy by that time.

Is it possible that fraternities and sororities are not value-socializing agencies? Do the actives simply not care about value deviation among their pledges, once they have been admitted to membership? Throughout most of the analyses, we have treated the mean active value as a norm against which pledge movements were compared. Yet an average does not constitute a meaningful social norm unless there are group pressures to maintain it. It is quite possible that the active mean values were nothing more than that — simply arithmetical averages for the present members, in which no one had a strong enough vested interest to impose them on new recruits.

Might it be that, though individual actives cared very much about their own values and even attempted to develop converts among the pledges, the values they espoused varied so widely that pledges were confronted with several different "norms"? If the organization had no completely consensual value culture and no well-established status hierarchy, then incoming pledges might look to any number of different persons as sources of value influence. It could well be that the tendency toward fragmented (i.e., cliquish) sociometric structures in large primary groups limits their effectiveness in uniform indoctrination. This is not to suggest that value socialization does not occur, but that it occurs in units smaller than the entire house.

Though the sources of value influence have not been well identified in this study, it is nevertheless clear that new members did undergo value changes during their first year in the organization. The paradox, from the standpoint of a functional interpretation, is that the changes were not generally in the direction of increased emphasis on group-maintaining values. If anything, the "other-directed" values became weakened, while the "inner-directed" values were strengthened. Does this mean that the several values have been misidentified as to their functional or dysfunctional relevance for group maintenance? Are intellectualism and independence, after all, important for group maintenance, while loyalty and social skills are less so? Or do the results indicate that extra-organizational forces were operating to subvert the very values that would be maximally functional for the organization?

The latter interpretation would appear more plausible, i.e., that values of fraternity and sorority members tend to change throughout their college lives so as to become less compatible with their groups' major function. The fact that senior members were less attracted to their organizations than junior members may be cited as evidence for their alienation. Furthermore, the seniors tended to value loyalty less, and independence more, than the younger actives ($\alpha <$ .01); they were also less well liked ($\alpha <$ .05) by incoming pledges (though not by other actives). In various ways, then, the older members may have become maladapted to fraternity and sorority living: They tended to hold group-maintaining values less strongly than their younger colleagues; they found membership in the organization less rewarding; and they were not so highly regarded by the newest members.

Finally, the failure to find clear evidence of influence processes within these organizations leaves the whole question concerning the origins of personal values just where it has been. One of the major expectations that guided the study was something akin to Proposition 3, namely, that value development and change do continue beyond childhood, and that a major source of change is membership in primary groups. Though value changes did occur, they could not be attributed to distinctive normative pressures from within the living groups. Other interpretations concerning sources of influence remain speculative, so it cannot be said that the origins of personal values have been accounted for.

In hindsight, though, it may be recognized that groups cannot enhance values that new members hold to a pre-eminent degree already. Perhaps it is in the nature of voluntary groups to attract new members who already believe strongly in the essential values by which the groups function. This consideration would imply that voluntary groups such as these, in spite of all their *potential* for influence (due to valued membership, clear ingroup-outgroup distinctions, high rate of face-to-face interaction, and so forth) are unlikely to exert much *actual* influence toward *changing* their members' values. Perhaps value influence in natural settings is more apt to occur when a person unintentionally gets himself into a compelling (i.e., enjoyable or necessary) circumstance in which new values are being promulgated, and he has little choice but to attend, and insufficient social support to oppose them. Needless to say, this consideration suggests a strategy of investigation entirely different from that embodied in the present study.

MAINTENANCE OF MEMBER ALLEGIANCE

Proposition 4. The attractiveness of membership in voluntary organizations is higher in early stages than in late stages of affiliation. (Supported)

This proposition is based on the consideration that the effort required to gain entrance is sufficient to presuppose a considerable desire on the part of the recruit. Once in, he has an opportunity to become more acutely aware of the disadvantages of membership, which were probably not salient for him at the time he joined. But the embarrassment entailed in leaving the organization may be enough to keep many disaffected members from dropping out. Also, students most often join fraternities and sororities at a time when they have yet to establish other ties to the wider university community; hence their organization membership may appear more important to them in the beginning than it does later when other interests have developed.

Evidence in favor of this proposition consisted of the finding that the entire group of pledges in all ten organizations had a mean score on the index of attraction to their organizations higher than the mean for all actives combined. However, this difference was largely attributable to the low scores of senior actives. Seniors were significantly less attracted to their organizations than other actives, while the latter group was not, by itself, significantly different from pledges in this respect. Thus, one might infer that, though precursors of alienation appear earlier — in the form of a decline in group-relevant values — these do not generally affect one's explicit attachment to the organization until his last year. An alternative inference is that alienated members withdraw from the organization if they are still in their early or middle years of school; but if a member does not become alienated until his last year, there is not much point in withdrawing then, so he just sticks it out in relatively inactive fashion for the remaining time.

Proposition 5. Attractiveness of membership is correlated with the person's status within the organization. (Supported in modified form)

This proposition rests on two assumptions: First, that people will cherish their membership in a group to the extent that they derive the benefits of prestige from it; second, that members who are highly attracted to their groups will tend to act in ways that elicit favorable reactions from their colleagues, hence enhance their own status.

The evidence rests on the correlation between members' scores on the index of attraction to the organization and the average degree to which they were liked by their colleagues. The latter measure — friendship status — was taken as an index of status within the group. At the time of the pretest, there was no significant correlation, but on the posttest there was. It is likely that the absence of a relation between status and attraction to the organization on the pretest was due to the countervailing relationship described in Proposition 4 — namely, that the most devoted members are the newest ones, who have not yet been around long enough to acquire high status. Once the "newcomer" effect has worn off, the relation between attraction and prestige can begin to appear.

The highest sociometric correlate of attraction to the organization was the average degree to which the member was seen as contributing to house activities; this correlation was significantly larger than zero on the pretest, and by the time of the posttest it had become sizable. Thus, one might infer a chain of behavioral, perceptual, and evaluative processes as follows: Members who are highly attracted to their organizations tend to behave in ways that are quite early recognized as group-supporting, and subsequently provide a basis for favorable impressions by colleagues.

The highest correlations between friendship status and attraction to the organization were found in the houses with the highest mean value of loyalty among their total membership. This result suggests that a member's favorable orientation to his group is most likely to be recognized and appreciated by colleagues who place a high value on group loyalty. In combination, these results suggest that Proposition 5 should be modified somewhat as follows: *When differences due to length of membership (described in Proposition 4) are allowed for, one's degree of attraction to the organization and the level of prestige that one enjoys within it are positively correlated — especially in organizations whose members place a high value on group loyalty.*

Proposition 6. The degree to which a person is attracted to membership in any particular organization to which he belongs depends on the degree to which he values group loyalty in general. (Supported)

This proposition simply asserts that loyalty to one group is a special expression of general loyal sentiments; that people who admire group loyalty in the abstract will tend to make the most devoted members of whatever groups they belong to.

The evidence for this proposition rests on the sizable correlations that appeared, both within and across houses, between the index of attraction to the organization and the loyalty value scale. It should be cautioned, however, that the context of assessment may have induced a spuriously high correlation between these two measures. Moreover, we have measured the degree of attraction expressed only with respect to the particular fraternity or sorority, not with respect to other specific organizations, as implied in the proposition.

Proposition 7. The most satisfied members of an organization are those whose values are compatible with the dominant group functions. (Inferentially supported)

This proposition suggests that, although the loyalty value may be of crucial importance initially in orienting a member toward his organization, his degree of comfort within it will ultimately depend on his other values and on how well they fit in with the demands of group life. Just what these demands are will presumably vary, in part, with the functions performed by the organization. As we shall emphasize later, the allegedly characteristic functions of an organization are difficult to establish conclusively, difficult to translate unambiguously into requisite values. Therefore the proposition is a hard one to test directly. But we have postulated the primary function of fraternities and sororities as being the establishment and maintenance of friendships — essentially the preservation of harmonious interpersonal relationships — and have roughly identified the "other-directed" value cluster as generally supporting this function and the "inner-directed" value cluster as not supporting it. In particular, the values of loyalty and social skills seem most positively relevant to the proposed dominant function, and the value of independence seems most negatively relevant.

In addition to loyalty, the social skills and independence values figured as significant correlates of attraction to the organization (in positive and negative directions, respectively). Broadly speaking, the pattern of values that distinguished devoted from indifferent members was similar to the pattern of values that distinguished pledges from non-pledging freshmen. In other words, the very values that evidently disposed students to join Greek organizations in the first place seem to have affected their degree of satisfaction after they got in. Thus, two different operations for inferring "functional" values — those disposing people

to join and those disposing people to enjoy their membership —
have yielded highly similar results. Perhaps convergent analyses
such as these may help pin down empirically the meanings of
"function" and "functionally relevant."

*Proposition 8. The degree to which an organization influ-
ences the values of its new members depends on the new members' level of attraction to the organization.* (Not supported)

This proposition derives from the assumptions that the capacity to exert influence depends on the degree of reward-con-
trol exercised by the would-be influencer, and that the degree
of attraction to an organization reflects one's capacity to be rewarded by it. Pledges who value their membership highly, it was
argued, should be more ready than others to accept the kinds of
interpersonal cues that serve to guide behavior and shape values.

The relevant analysis focused on the value changes of pledges
who scored in the upper half of the index of attraction to the
organization. Although these subjects, in each organization separately, tended to move toward their own actives' values from
pre- to posttest, the devoted pledges' movements were equally
in the direction of the pretest value means of all actives of the
same sex. Therefore, there was no clear evidence that the highly
attracted pledges were being specifically influenced by their own
organization norms.

In the previous discussion of Proposition 3 were presented a
number of considerations that bear on the present outcome —
especially the central one that these groups may not function as
value-influencers at all, and hence devoted members would be
no more affected than the indifferent ones. In addition, attraction
to the organization may not be the most appropriate indicator of
readiness to be influenced *away* from one's current values. Instead, high attraction may be associated with the belief that one's
current position is supported by the group; thus evidence to the
contrary could result in lowered attraction rather than change in
values. If high attraction could somehow be maintained and a
clear value norm presented as an unambiguous standard, then

perhaps pledges would behave in accordance with Proposition 8. But it is not likely that such conditions ordinarily obtain in fraternities and sororities.

STATUS DIFFERENTIATION

Proposition 9. A member's status within an organization depends on the degree to which he is regarded as contributing to the organization's major functions. (Supported inferentially)

Status differentiation refers to the allocation of differing levels of prestige among the membership. In this study the measure of prestige used was the average degree to which a person was liked by his colleagues. It is assumed that the membership shares fairly widely the values that are relevant to the organization's functioning, and hence will tend to use them as standards for appraising each other, as well as new recruits (see Proposition 1). Idiosyncratic or less widely shared values may contribute to individual friendship choices, but they are unlikely to provide a basis for intra-group status, which depends on common appraisals.

In addition to rating all his colleagues on how well he liked them, each member rated them on three attributes, representing three values that were deemed differentially relevant to group functioning: Ability to get along with others (representing the social skills value), contribution to house activities (loyalty value), and studiousness (academic achievement value). The correlation of intra-group status (mean friendship rating received) with mean perceived ability to get along with others was .93; the correlation with judged contribution to house activities was .63; and the correlation with perceived studiousness was .25. All of these correlations were significantly different from each other (as well as from zero), so it may be inferred that manifestations of social skills are more important in determining status than are manifestations of group loyalty, and that both are more important than an orientation toward academic achievement. This ordering of correlates accords reasonably well with our assumptions concerning the relative importance of these three traits to the functioning of Greek organizations. Moreover, it agrees with the results concerning recruitment and maintenance of member loyalties (Propositions 1. a. and 7) in assigning greater significance to interpersonal values than to achievement values.

However, it is only by inference that the correlations between status and mean ratings on the three traits have been converted into conclusions about the directions of causality involved. In fact, it is likely that these correlations are due both to actual traits of the members being rated and also to judgmental biases of the raters, which reflect their own values. It is with these mediating processes that Propositions 10 and 12 are concerned.

Proposition 10. The status of a member depends on the degree to which he holds values compatible with the organization's functioning. (Weakly supported)

It may be assumed that part of the reason for high-status members' being perceived as interpersonally skilled and as contributors to group maintenance is that they *are*. In the absence of `objective behavioral data, it might be maintained that judgmental data from colleagues provide the best description of what a member is "really" like. However, these judgments are subject to some (unknown) degree of distortion in the service of "cognitive balance," so it is advisable to look for other indirect evidence concerning actual traits of the people whose status is being assessed. The values they profess may provide some indications (though quite imperfect), since these have been found to correlate with behaviors as reported by the subject himself.

On the pretest there was a significant (though small) correlation between members' statuses and the strength of their loyalty value. Among actives on the posttest, the average degree to which they were liked correlated with their values of social skills, loyalty, status, and intellectualism. The first three of these at least would seem relevant to the organization's functioning. It has previously been noted (Proposition 5) that intra-group status is also correlated with attraction to the organization on the posttest. Therefore, it seems reasonable to infer that an orientation toward organization maintenance, both in general values and in specific attitude, tends ultimately to be recognized and appreciated by one's colleagues, though there is considerable lag in this process and many instances in which professed values do not even ultimately correspond with intra-group status.

Proposition 11. Status differentiation within these social organizations is not very clear cut. (Empirical finding)

This means that members do not agree very well with one another concerning how much they like any given person in the group. There is, of course, no good absolute standard for determining whether the degree of status differentiation is high or low, so we have to compare it with some other indices computed in the study.

First, the extent of inter-rater agreement on degree of liking for a particular member was less than their agreement on any of the other three attributes they rated: Studiousness, contribution to house activities, and ability to get along with others. Second, of the total variance in friendship ratings, status differentiation accounted for no more than bias differentiation did, and less than the variance due to mutuality of ratings. This is to say that how much a person was liked by a particular colleague depended more on that colleague than on the person himself. "Likableness" is evidently not a very clearly defined attribute.

This result has important implications for Propositions 9 and 10, which refer to a "a member's status" as if it were a precisely ascertainable attribute, and go on to assert that this status will depend on certain perceived or professed characteristics of the member. Proposition 11 qualifies these by asserting that "status" is at best an imprecise average of all the varying ratings conferred by one's colleagues. It implies, moreover, that the rating given by any one of them may bear little relation to characteristics of the person being rated.

Proposition 12. The sociometric ratings that a person receives from others depend in part on the raters' own values. (Supported)

Whether or not one person likes another will presumably reflect the degree to which he sees the other as embodying traits that he values. A complementary cognitive process involves the attribution to liked persons of traits that one values and the attribution to disliked persons of distasteful traits. Both of these processes of interpersonal perception presumably act in the service of "cognitive balance," which is the essence of Proposition 12.

In the present study, it was found that the more a rater valued academic achievement, the higher was the correlation between his ratings of liking for others and his ratings of their studiousness; the more a rater valued loyalty, the higher was the correlation between his liking for others and his ratings of their contribution to house activities; the more a rater valued social skills, the higher was the correlation between his liking for others and his ratings of their ability to get along with people. Thus, the role played by the raters' values in contributing to a member's status within the group is indicated. It seems reasonable to expect that, if all a member's colleagues value a particular trait highly, their average liking for that member will correspond to their average rating of him on the trait; if they neither admire nor dislike a given trait, or if they disagree as to its desirability, their average liking for the member will show no constant correspondence with their modal rating of him on the trait.

Conversely, it may be inferred that, if there is a high correlation between the degree to which a member is liked and his average rating received on a particular trait, then all his colleagues must tend to place a uniformly high value on that trait. If there is little or no correlation between intra-group status and mean rating received on a particular trait, then one may infer either that the colleagues do not uniformly admire the trait or that they disagree concerning how people are to be rated on it. Applied to the results discussed under Proposition 9, the conclusions for the present study seem inescapable: Members of these Greek organizations quite uniformly admired interpersonal skills to a very high degree. Since there was substantial inter-rater agreement concerning how studious the various members were, one may also conclude that, on the average, studiousness was not greatly valued.

Proposition 13. The elected presidents of Greek organizations espouse to a greater-than-average degree those values which are functionally relevant for all houses, and also those values which are particularly emphasized within their own organizations. (Not supported)

Twenty different presidents served in these ten organizations over the two-year period of the study. On none of the twelve values did they score significantly different from the mean for all organizations of the same sex, or different from the means for their own respective houses. Thus, there is no evidence to indicate that these presidents professed group-maintenance values to an exceptional degree. Moreover, their values did not match their own house means any better than they matched the mean values of all subjects of the same sex. So there is no basis for concluding that these presidents were picked for their typicality with respect to values.

Of course, the sample of organizations is small, and certainly negative conclusions from just ten groups are exceedingly rash, because of the high probability of Type II errors of inference. One would certainly hesitate to deny that *any* fraternity or sorority president is selected for value-relevant reasons. However, within these ten organizations the basic assumption behind the proposition could be examined, and in this case was found unjustified. The assumption was that the presidents were among the few most prestigious people in the house. This was evidently not uniformly true — certainly not before their elections, and in some instances not afterward either. If they were not elected because of exceptional popularity, then there is less reason to expect them to have embodied the dominant organization values.

On what basis were they elected? Willingness to serve?

Recognition by the group that they possessed the relevant skills and interest for the position? We cannot tell from the present results. There should, of course, be no implication from these findings that the presidents were not successful in their offices. All of them were recognized as contributing a great deal to house activities. And it is certainly not necessary that a successful leader be exceptionally well liked. This condition had been expected in the present study, however, because of the predominant focus of these organizations on interpersonal relations.

Of course, these findings regarding house presidents might also be interpreted as challenging the definition of status employed for other members. If election to office, as one alleged mark of prestige, does not correlate well with popularity, as the other proposed criterion, which of the two is to be doubted? Tentatively, we choose to doubt (after the fact) the significance of election to presidency of these organizations as a clear sign of intra-house status. This is for two reasons: First, it is a measure that is inherently more subject to error than are the pooled ratings of all one's colleagues; too many other random and meaningful events besides status could influence the choice of president. Second, there are no other supporting results from the present study to lend confidence to the presidency measure, as there are for the measure based on colleagues' ratings (see Propositions 5, 9, and 10). In addition, of course, measures derived from colleagues' ratings have the practical advantage of being applicable as a continuously graded scale to the determination of all members' statuses, whereas measures based on discrete events, such as election to office, necessarily yield poor discriminations among most members.

MUTUAL FRIENDSHIPS

Proposition 14. Members who like one another are more likely to hold similar values than are members who dislike one another. (Supported)

Fundamental to Propositions 9 and 10, concerning status differentiation, is the assumption that members of a group judge one another on the basis of shared values: If the values they use are not widely shared, the behavioral and value correlates of status — perhaps even status differentiation itself — will not emerge. However, mutual friendships and cliques may emerge within the group to the extent that members base their judgment of one another on values that are not widely shared. That members of mutually friendly pairs will judge one another as embodying mutually valued traits is implicit in Proposition 12. Proposition 14 merely adds the assertion that these judgments will tend to be accurate more often than not.

In a way, this is a microcosmic equivalent of Proposition 2, which states that entire organizations tend to recruit new members whose values are similar to the group's pre-established norm. Within the group, value-based selection may continue at the individual level, so that sub-groups are formed with values more homogeneous than those in the total organization.

Evidence for this proposition comes from a comparison between the value similarities of mutually friendly pairs and the value similarities of mutually unfriendly pairs. On the average, the expected differences appeared. However, their small average magnitude, together with the fact of many exceptions, led to speculations concerning reasons for the relatively small difference between the value similarities of friends and non-friends. Among the reasons suggested were: (1) That these organizations were fairly homogeneous to begin with, so the value differences that occurred were not large enough to determine friendship patterns; (2) that processes of cognitive balance kept many members from becoming aware of actual value differences between themselves and their friends and of actual similarities between themselves and their enemies, hence some friendship patterns were artificially maintained; (3) that value similarity is not uniformly crucial for all friends, after all. Since there is independent evidence in this study concerning the degree of actual similarity among all members' values and concerning the operation of some pressures toward cognitive balancing, the first two explanations seem more compelling at the moment.

ATTRITION

Proposition 15. Departure of a member from a group is likely to reflect an incompatibility between his values and the group norms. (Partially supported)

It was noted that the main reasons for membership attrition in these organizations are academically determined: Graduation and suspension from school for failure to maintain grades. So our consideration of attrition was limited to loss of members who did not clearly fall within these two categories, but whose departure might more reasonably be attributed to intra-organizational processes. It was expected that, just as personal values are relevant to a member's considerations about joining a Greek organization, they should be relevant to his considerations about leaving; just as the organization is presumably sensitive to the values of its applicants in deciding whom to admit in the first place, so the values of accepted members may continue to affect the way they are appraised by others. Thus, attrition may result from value incompatibility that is recognized either by the individual member or by his colleagues.

Partial support for this proposition came from an analysis of the values of actives who left their organizations (or left school) without graduating. These drop-outs tended to value loyalty less and independence more than did the actives who remained in their organizations. Thus, it can be said that they were not generally disposed toward organization-maintaining values. More important, perhaps, they tended to hold patterns of values deviant from their own group's norms. Thus one may infer that value conformity or deviance was a consideration in the retention and elimination of old members.

238

However, the consideration evidently operated primarily in one direction — from the member toward his group, rather than the reverse. Though drop-outs among the actives tended to show a relatively low level of attraction to their organizations, they were liked no less well by their colleagues than were members who remained. A more refined interpretation of the attrition process would therefore suggest that established members who find themselves holding deviant values tend to leave at their own choice.

Analysis of attrition among pledges did not support the proposition. Pledges who dropped their organizations (while remaining in school) showed a pattern of mean values indistinguishable from that of pledges who remained to become actives, and their values were not especially deviant from the norms of their own particular houses. Moreover, their attitudes toward the organization were not significantly less favorable than the attitudes of pledges who stayed on. Instead, they tended to be less well liked by their colleagues and were rated as less able to get along with people.

It may be that another test of these pledges administered sometime during the middle of the year would have shown increased tendencies toward disaffection among the subsequent drop-outs. But the presumption from these data is that they left more "under pressure" than of their own accord (though there were undoubtedly wide individual differences in this regard). And there is no evidence that value deviancy was a factor leading to their rejection by other members. Thus Proposition 15 requires modification, perhaps to some such form as: *Established members who maintain (or develop) values that are deviant from the group norm tend to become alienated and leave the organization.*

Continuity of a group's value norms may thus be maintained through processes of attrition, as well as through processes of selection. When selection procedures have failed to keep out a potential dissident, and when attempts at socialization have no effect, the value deviant is likely to be unhappy in the group. Of course, he could remain in it and become an instrument of normative change. More likely, though, he will develop ties elsewhere and come to anticipate more gratification from leaving than from remaining.

Proposition 16. Attrition among value deviants is most pronounced in organizations with high group cohesiveness. (Supported)

The fact of deviancy itself is not sufficient cause for withdrawal from a group. The deviancy becomes uncomfortable only in the face of strong group pressures for conformity. Though some degree of conformity pressure may generally be expected — especially with regard to group-relevant values — the amount will vary considerably from one organization to another. It was expected that the greater the pressure toward consensus, the more likely it would be that value deviants would depart, either through their own choice or "under fire." There was little evidence that value deviancy was a cause for pledge attrition, so this proposition must be interpreted to refer primarily to voluntary departures of actives.

No direct measure of the magnitude of conformity pressures was available in this study. However, it was reasoned that such pressures would be strongest in highly cohesive groups; hence the statement of Proposition 16. The measure of cohesiveness consisted of the mean index of attraction to the organization among all actives in that house. This mean index for the house did, indeed, correlate with the extent to which intra-group value homogeneity was increased by the attrition of active members.

Proposition 17. Attrition among new members is highest in organizations where selection processes have resulted in the poorest value match with old members. (Supported)

This proposition reflects the view that recruitment and attrition are, in part, complementary processes for maintaining continuity of value norms within the groups. When new members already share the group's values to a substantial degree, they are likely to find a favorable reception and to be relatively content. However, widespread value deviance among new members could lead to a change in group norms, unless the deviance were corrected either by socialization or by attrition. It was discovered (see Proposition 3) that value socialization was not a very likely occurrence within these campus fraternities and sororities. Therefore, the burden of maintaining normative continuity would seem to rest on attrition processes.

It was found that the rates of pledge attrition were, indeed, highest in those organizations that had achieved the poorest matching between pledge and active mean values to begin with. So the proposition was supported in a way. However, this result must be considered in conjunction with those for Proposition 15. There it was discovered that pledges who dropped out of their organizations were no more likely to hold deviant values than were pledges who remained. So pledge attrition was apparently not serving the cause of continuity in value norms. This finding poses a dilemma and demands some alternative rationale for Proposition 17. Perhaps initial value deviancy among pledges reflects an inability of the organization to recruit new members who, in a variety of ways, would be found compatible with the old ones. Their incompatibilities — not necessarily with respect to values — are ultimately recognized, and they come to be disliked and to be regarded as unable to get along with others; this rejection by the old members results in their withdrawal. Or perhaps the actives, disappointed in a generally poor value-match with pledges, fail to treat the conformers and the non-conformers differentially, but instead treat all pledges in such a way that a large proportion of them are alienated. Examination of these, or other, explanations for Propostion 17 requires a larger number of organizations than was available in the present study, for the unit of analysis referred to here is clearly an entire group, rather than an individual member.

MAJOR FUNCTION OF CAMPUS SOCIAL ORGANIZATIONS

It was stated previously that the "principal function of campus fraternities and sororities is the establishment and maintenance of friendships." Although this assertion has more the status of an assumption than of a directly tested hypothesis, various outcomes of the analyses made it seem reasonable. For the most part, the values that played a distinctive role in the various organizational processes of selection, attrition, status differentiation, and maintenance of member allegiance were interpersonal values, like group loyalty and social skills, and their antithesis, the value of independence. One could then say that these various processes served to emphasize interpersonal values, and thus infer that this was a major function of the organizations.

However, this is rather indirect evidence for the inference, and requires some selective inattention to data. We have operationalized "group function" in terms of value differences between pledges and non-pledges, between liked and disliked members, between those who are highly attracted to their organizations and those who are not, between the drop-outs and the members who stay on. We have *not* used as an operational definition of "group function" the kind of impact that these organizations had on their new members; if we had, the results would have been much more ambiguous. Though there seemed to be good and sufficient reason for not expecting pledges to increase their stress on group loyalty, for example, in that they already stressed it more than actives at the time of admission, the problem nevertheless remains as to why they did so. Why did the senior members of an organization not profess those values which were presumably most functional for the group's maintenance? This poses a challenge to a functional interpretation of organizational processes.

Perhaps one might rationalize the present results in theoretical terms by distinguishing what is functional for group maintenance from what is functional for maintenance of the individual member. The older members, perhaps, no longer derive their principal sources of prestige and security from group membership; therefore they no longer need to profess inter-personal, group-maintenance values to the degree that they did as pledges. The burden of maintaining the group has passed on to the next generation of members, who derive their primary self-definition from it. Thus, socialization of group-relevant values does not occur within fraternities and sororities. Members are already "pre-socialized" to a sufficient degree for organizational maintenance, and the functional values are therefore manifest in other processes.

If this ad hoc reasoning is sound, it implies that college fra-ternities and sororities constitute a rather peculiar type of organ-ization — one that is maintained predominantly by junior, rather than senior, members. The seniors are not particularly oriented toward prestige from formal office — nor do the officeholders acquire exceptional prestige from their positions. In general, membership in the organization is less gratifying to the older members, hence they are not especially motivated to contribute to group maintenance. This is rather different from organizations focused upon occupational or political functions, where in-creasing gratification presumably comes with increasing seniority; in these, older members might be expected to espouse group-relevant values, and newcomers to acquire them more and more with time.

In any case, propositions concerning what is or is not func-tional for an organization will have to specify more carefully the precise ways in which the alleged functions are manifest, before they can be tested unambiguously. For the present, we may conclude that, given a selected definition of functionally relevant processes — related to recruitment, status differentiation, attraction to the organization, and attrition — the chief function of campus social organizations would appear to be the mainte-nance of friendly, interpersonal relationships, for this is the kind of value that enters most prominently into these processes.

LIMITATIONS

The conclusions reviewed in this chapter should be qualified in two ways. First, of course, they are based on a particular sample of social fraternities and sororities at a single university. Though the analyses stemmed from considerations that seemed relevant to most organizations with functions similar to these, there is only logical, rather than empirical, assurance that these results would be replicated in another sample of fraternities.

Even if the present results were replicated in other organizations like these, they would not account for all the different ways in which members are selected and treated by groups. The relationships reported here reflect the operation of only a small number of variables. Though their over-all average effects were statistically significant, not many of them were of large magnitude. So there was ample room for other considerations besides values to enter into the processes of selection, attrition, status differentiation, and so forth — and they undoubtedly did. Needless to say, the particular processes considered here do not represent everything important that goes on within these organizations; nor are the twelve personal values the only characteristics of members relevant to their group affiliations.

APPENDIX A

VALUE SCALES

Instructions

Please read over the following statements, and for each one indicate (by a check in the appropriate space) whether it is something you *always admire* in other people, or something you *always dislike*, or something that *depends on the situation* whether you admire it or not.

	Always Admire	*Depends on Situation*	*Always Dislike*	
1.	_____	_____	_____	Having a strong intellectual curiosity.
2.	_____	_____	_____	Creating beautiful things for the enjoyment of other people.

etc.

(The numbers beside the following items refer to their actual order in the questionnaire.)

Intellectualism

1. Having a strong intellectual curiosity.
19. Developing an appreciation of the fine arts — music, drama, literature, and ballet.
45. Having a keen interest in international, national, and local affairs.
50. Being an intellectual.
58. Having an active interest in all things scholarly.

Kindness

28. Being kind to people, even if they do things contrary to one's own beliefs.

37. Turning the other cheek, and forgiving others when they harm you.
46. Helping another person feel more secure, even if you don't like him.
51. Helping another achieve his goals, even if it might interfere with your own.

Social skills

3. Being able to get along with all kinds of people, whether or not they are worthwhile.
21. Being poised, gracious, and charming under all circumstances.
25. Being the person in the group who is the most popular with the opposite sex.
29. Being well mannered and behaving properly in social situations.
47. Dressing and acting in a way that is appropriate to the occasion.
52. Being able to get people to cooperate with you.

Loyalty

5. Defending the honor of one's group whenever it is unfairly criticized.
17. Helping organize group activities.
30. Treating an attack on one's group like an attack on oneself.
34. Concealing from outsiders most of one's dislikes and disagreements with fellow members of the group.
38. Doing all one can to build up the prestige of the group.
53. Working hard to improve the prestige and status of one's group.

Academic achievement

4. Studying constantly in order to become a well educated person.
13. Working hard to achieve academic honors.
39. Striving to get the top grade-point average in the group.
48. Studying hard to get good grades in school.

Physical development

14. Being good in some form of sport.
22. Developing physical strength and agility.
31. Taking good care of one's physical self, so that one is always healthy.
54. Developing an attractive body that others will admire.
56. Being graceful and well coordinated in physical movements.

Status

6. Being respected by people who are themselves worthwhile.
23. Having the ability to lead others.
32. Being in a position to direct and mold others' lives.
40. Showing great leadership qualities.
59. Gaining recognition for one's achievements.

Honesty

7. Always telling the truth, even though it may hurt oneself or others.
41. Never telling a lie, even though to do so would make the situation more comfortable.
49. Never cheating or having anything to do with cheating situations, even for a friend.
55. (reverse-scored) Helping a close friend get by a tight situation even though you may have to stretch the truth a bit to do it.

Religiousness

8. Being devout in one's religious faith.
15. Always attending religious services regularly and faithfully.
33. Always living one's religion in his daily life.
42. Encouraging others to attend services and lead religious lives.
57. Avoiding the physical pleasures that are prohibited in the Bible.

Self-control

9. Always being patient with people.
16. Never losing one's temper, no matter what the reason.
24. Practicing self-control.
43. Replying to anger with gentleness.
60. Not expressing anger, even when you have a reason for doing so.

Creativity

2. Creating beautiful things for the enjoyment of other people.
12. Constantly developing new ways of approaching life.
20. Inventing gadgets for the fun of it.
26. Devoting one's entire energy to the development of new theories.
35. Being able to create beautiful and artistic objects.
36. Developing new and different ways of doing things.

Independence

10. (reverse-scored) Conforming to the requirements of any situation and doing what is expected of one.

11. (reverse-scored) Working and living in harmony with other people.
18. Being outspoken and frank in expressing one's likes and dislikes.
27. Thinking and acting freely, without social restraints, and encouraging others to do likewise.
44. Being independent, original, non-conformist, different from other people.

TABLE A-1

MEANS AND STANDARD DEVIATIONS OF
ORIGINAL VALUE SCALES
OBTAINED FROM REPRESENTATIVE SAMPLE OF
STUDENT BODY AT UNIVERSITY OF COLORADO
($n = 218$)

Value	Mean	σ
Intellectualism	2.89	1.57
Kindness	1.80	1.27
Social skills	3.79	1.38
Loyalty	2.11	1.55
Academic achievement	1.80	1.27
Physical development	2.82	1.57
Status	3.06	1.19
Honesty	1.75	1.03
Religiousness	2.09	1.70
Self-control	2.57	1.42
Creativity	3.27	1.44
Independence	1.66	1.26

REVISED SCALES

Certain defects in the original scales have been noted — mainly (1) that they are too short to yield reliable measures and (2) that acquiescent response set may contribute heavily to their scores, since nearly all of the items are stated in a positive direction. Scales much longer than these would have been difficult to administer, together with all the other instruments, within the time available for assessment in the fraternity-sorority study. However, it is recognized that other researchers may wish to use some such value scales in their own investigations where time limitations are less pressing. For this reason, we have subsequently developed the following expanded scales, containing equal numbers of positively and negatively worded items.

Though subjects answer the items by checking in one of three categories ("Always Admire," "Depends on Situation," and "Always

Dislike"), it seems appropriate to the theoretical definition of a value (as an absolute "good" or "bad") to score the items dichotomously, with the "Depends" category always scored to indicate absence of an absolute value. Thus, on a direct-worded item, "Always Admire" would be scored 1, while "Always Dislike" and "Depends" would both be scored 0; on a reverse-worded item, "Always Dislike" would be scored 1, while "Always Admire" and "Depends" would be scored 0. It has been found that this "rational" method of scoring yields intra-scale homogeneities just as high as, and inter-scale correlations somewhat lower than, the alternative method of scoring, in which the three response categories are scored 3, 2, and 1 (for direct-worded items) or 1, 2, and 3 (for reverse-worded items).

The following scales were retained after an analysis of some 325 items in which each item was correlated with every other item in its own (intended) scale and with every other item in outside scales that correlated highly (.50 or more) with the item's own scale. Any item in the trial scale that had a mean intra-scale correlation less than .10, or which had a mean intra-scale correlation less than its mean correlation with the items in some other scale, was eliminated. This procedure was aimed at maximizing intra-scale homogeneities and minimizing inter-scale correlations. The extent to which these aims were met may be judged from Tables A-2 and A-3 (pp. 257 and 258), which report results obtained from a general psychology class ($n =$ 254) at the University of Colorado.

In actual presentation, the same instructions were used as appeared in the original scale (p. 245), and the following items were in mixed-up order.

Intellectualism

Direct-scored items

Having a keen interest in international, national, and local affairs.
Having a strong intellectual curiosity.
Developing an appreciation of the fine arts — music, drama, literature, and ballet.
Having an active interest in all things scholarly.
Having cultural interests.
Striving to gain new knowledge about the world.
Enjoying books, music, art, philosophy, and sciences.
Keeping abreast of current events.
Knowing what's going on in the world of politics.
Keeping up with world news through regular reading or by watching informative programs.

Reverse-scored items

Having restricted and narrow interests.

Having no knowledge of current events.

Being interested only in one's work.

Having no opinions about the world situation.

Knowing only one's specialty.

Having little interest in arts, theater, music, and other cultural activities.

Being uninterested in national and world affairs.

Showing little interest in the finer things of life.

Ignoring what goes on in the world around one.

Reading only things that don't pose any intellectual challenge.

Kindness

Direct-scored items

Being kind to people, even if they do things contrary to one's beliefs.

Helping another person feel more secure, even if one doesn't like him.

Helping another achieve his own goals, even if it might interfere with your own.

Turning the other cheek, and forgiving others when they harm you.

Being considerate of others' feelings.

Findings ways to help others less fortunate than oneself.

Being utterly selfless in all one's actions.

Having a deep love of all people, whoever they are.

Going out of one's way to help someone new feel at home.

Being concerned about the happiness of other people.

Reverse-scored items

Looking out for one's own interests first.

Ridiculing other people.

Being selfish.

Ignoring the needs of other people.

Revenging wrongs that other people have done to one.

Being unable to empathize with other people.

Hurting other people's feelings.

Making jokes at the expense of other people.

Letting each person go it alone, without offering help.

Refusing any aid to people who don't deserve it.

Social skills

Direct-scored items

Being well mannered and behaving properly in social situations.

Dressing and acting in a way that is appropriate to the occasion.

Being able to get people to cooperate with one.
Being poised, gracious, and charming under all circumstances.
Always doing the right thing at the right time.
Being informed in proper etiquette.
Being able to plan social functions smoothly.
Being popular with everyone.
Always behaving properly in public.
Being concerned about what kind of impression one makes on others.

Reverse-scored items

Being a social isolate.
Dressing sloppily.
Displaying unpleasant personal habits in public.
Interrupting others while they are talking.
Constantly making social blunders.
Talking constantly and attracting attention to oneself.
Having bad manners.
Being discourteous.
Being unable to act in a way that will please others.
Being ignorant of the rules of proper behavior.

Loyalty

Direct-scored items

Defending the honor of one's group whenever it is unfairly criticized.
Working hard to improve the prestige and status of one's groups.
Helping organize group activities.
Attending all meetings of one's groups.
Upholding the honor of one's group.
Supporting all activities of one's organizations.
Doing more than one's share of the group task.
Performing unpleasant tasks, if these are required by one's group.
Remembering one's group loyalties at all times.
Taking an active part in all group affairs.

Reverse-scored items

Betraying one's group to outsiders.
Letting other people do all the work for the group, and not getting
   involved oneself.
Letting people get away with unfair criticism of one's group.
Being unconcerned with what other people think about one's group.
Being uncooperative.
Failing to support group functions.

Paying little attention to what the members of one's group think.
Criticizing one's own group in public.
Getting by with as little involvement in organizations as possible.
Not taking one's group memberships seriously.

Academic achievement (Grades)

Direct-scored items

Studying hard to get good grades in school.
Working hard to achieve academic honors.
Trying hard to understand difficult lectures and textbooks.
Striving to get the top grade-point average in the group.
Studying constantly in order to become a well educated person.
Being studious.
Getting the top grade on a test.
Treating one's studies as the most important thing in college life.
Doing well in school.
Priding oneself on good grades.

Reverse-scored items

Being content with a "gentlemanly C" grade.
Making fun of academic grinds.
Being satisfied with poor grades.
Priding oneself on being able to get by in school with little work.
Not doing well in one's coursework.
Not letting studies interfere with one's college life.
Doing one's best to avoid working hard in a course.
Being proud of poor grades.
Paying no attention to lectures and textbooks that are difficult.
Taking snap courses that don't require any work.

Physical development

Direct-scored items

Being graceful and well coordinated in physical movements.
Taking good care of one's physical self, so that one is always healthy.
Being good in some form of sport.
Developing physical strength and agility.
Developing an attractive body that others will admire.
Having a good figure or physique.
Having good muscular coordination.

Being a well developed outdoors type who enjoys physical activity.
Keeping in good physical shape.
Exercising regularly.

Reverse-scored items

Being physically weak and puny.
Being an indoor type, and avoiding outdoor activities.
Being poorly proportioned physically.
Being uninterested in sports.
Being listless and uninterested in strenuous activity.
Being awkward in bearing and walk.
Being unable to do anything that requires physical effort.
Being unskilled in any form of athletics.
Ignoring one's own physical condition.
Avoiding any form of exercise.

Status

Direct-scored items

Being respected by people who are themselves worthwhile.
Gaining recognition for one's achievements.
Being in a position to direct and mold others' lives.
Making sure that one is respected.
Doing what one is told.
Being in a position to command respect from others.
Having all the respect that one is entitled to.
Being dignified in bearing and manner.
Being looked up to by others.
Enjoying great prestige in the community.

Reverse-scored items

Acting beneath one's dignity.
Not being able to do anything better than other people.
Not being recognized for one's true worth.
Being in a subordinate position.
Having little effect on other people's actions.
Being unable to exert any influence on things around one.
Failing to develop contacts that could improve one's position.
Being content with an inferior position all one's life.
Associating with worthless people.
Not taking pride in one's achievements.

Honesty

Direct-scored items

Never cheating or having anything to do with cheating situations, even for a friend.

Always telling the truth, even though it may hurt oneself or others.

Never telling a lie, even though to do so would make the situation more comfortable.

Sticking up for the truth under all circumstances.

Always representing one's own true thoughts and feelings honestly.

Speaking one's mind truthfully, without regard for the consequences.

Testifying against friends, if need be, in order that the truth be known.

Presenting oneself completely and honestly, even if it is unnecessary to do so.

Going out of one's way to bring dishonest people to justice.

Volunteering information concerning wrongdoing, even if friends are involved.

Reverse-scored items

Helping a close friend get by a tight situation, even though one may have to stretch the truth a bit to do it.

Taking things that don't belong to one.

Telling white lies.

Deceiving others.

Using others' property without asking permission.

Telling falsehoods in order to help other people.

Helping a friend through an examination.

Using a false ID card to get into restricted places.

Stealing when necessary.

Being dishonest in harmless ways.

Religiousness

Direct-scored items

Being devout in one's religious faith.

Always living one's religion in his daily life.

Always attending religious services regularly and faithfully.

Avoiding the physical pleasures that are prohibited in the Bible.

Encouraging others to attend services and lead religious lives.

Saying one's prayers regularly.

Seeking comfort in the Bible in time of need.

Adhering to the doctrines of one's religion.
Having an inner communication with the Supreme Being.
Having faith in a Being greater than man.

Reverse-scored items

Being an atheist.
Denying the existence of God.
Paying little attention to religious matters.
Treating man, rather than God, as the measure of all things.
Abstaining from trivial religious rituals.
Not falling for religious mythology.
Taking a skeptical attitude toward religious teachings.
Seeking scientific explanations of religious miracles.
Treating the Bible only as an historical or literary work.
Regarding religions as crutches for the primitive peoples of the world.

Self-control

Direct-scored items

Practicing self-control.
Replying to anger with gentleness.
Never losing one's temper, no matter what the reason.
Not expressing anger, even when one has a reason for doing so.
Suppressing hostility.
Keeping one's feelings hidden from others.
Suppressing the urge to speak hastily in anger.
Hiding one's feelings of frustration from other people.
Keeping one's hostile feelings to himself.
Not getting upset when things go wrong.

Reverse-scored items

Losing one's temper easily.
Showing one's feelings readily.
Telling people off when they offend one.
Expressing one's anger openly and directly when provoked.
Getting upset when things don't go well.
Letting others see how one really feels.
Letting off steam when one is frustrated.
Swearing when one is angry.
Becoming so angry that other people know about it.
Letting people know when one is annoyed with them.

Creativity (Originality)

Direct-scored items

Being able to create beautiful and artistic objects.
Developing new and different ways of doing things.
Constantly developing new ways of approaching life.
Inventing gadgets for the fun of it.
Trying out new ideas.
Being original in one's thoughts and ways of looking at things.
Always looking for new roads to travel.
Doing unusual things.
Creating unusual works of art.
Being an innovator.

Reverse-scored items

Doing routine things all the time.
Not having any new ideas.
Always doing things in the same way.
Enjoying a routine, patterned life.
Doing things the same way that other people do them.
Abiding by traditional ways of doing things.
Repeating the ideas of others, without any innovation.
Working according to a set schedule that doesn't vary from day to day.
Painting or composing or writing in a traditional style.
Keeping one's life from changing very much.

Independence

Direct-scored items

Being a freethinking person, who doesn't care what others think of his opinions.
Being outspoken and frank in expressing one's likes and dislikes.
Being independent.
Standing up for what one thinks right, regardless of what others think.
Going one's own way as he pleases.
Being a non-conformist.
Being different from other people.
Encouraging other people to act as they please.
Thinking and acting freely, without social restraints.
Living one's own life, independent of others.

Reverse-scored items

Conforming to the requirements of any situation and doing what is expected of one.

Going along with the crowd.

Acting in such a way as to gain the approval of others.

Keeping one's opinions to himself when they differ from the group's.

Being careful not to express an idea that might be contrary to what other people believe.

Always basing one's behavior on the recognition that he is dependent on other people.

Acting so as to fit in with other people's way of doing things.

Always checking on whether or not one's intended actions would be acceptable to other people.

Never acting so as to violate social conventions.

Suppressing one's desire to be unique and different.

TABLE A-2

HOMOGENEITIES OF REVISED VALUE SCALES AND
CORRELATIONS WITH ORIGINAL SCALES

Value	*Homogeneity* H.R.[a]	r_{tt}[b]	*Correlation with Original Scale*
Intellectualism	.20	.82	.66
Kindness	.22	.85	.76
Social skills	.25	.87	.76
Loyalty	.28	.89	.79
Academic achievement	.19	.82	.75
Physical development	.29	.89	.81
Status	.20	.83	.67
Honesty	.17	.80	.75
Religiousness	.29	.88	.81
Self-control	.24	.85	.78
Creativity	.22	.84	.62
Independence	.19	.82	.74

[a]Homogeneity Ratio (**Scott**, 1960a), which equals the mean of all inter-item correlations, each weighted by the geometric mean of the item variances.

[b]Cronbach's (1961) coefficient *alpha* for estimating scale reliability.

CORRELATIONS WITH RATED BEHAVIORS

There is evidently some tendency toward correspondence between a person's scores on the revised value scales and his overt

TABLE A-3
INTERCORRELATIONS AMONG REVISED VALUE SCALES
($n = 254$)

	Indep.	Intell.	Creat.	Acad.	Hon.	Relig.	Self-cont.	Kind.	Loy.	Soc. sk.	Status	Phys.
Independence	(.82)											
Intellectualism	.18	(.82)										
Creativity	.54	.48	(.84)									
Academic achievement	.01	.47	.26	(.82)								
Honesty	−.04	.25	.10	.52	(.80)							
Religiousness	−.19	.21	.03	.35	.39	(.88)						
Self-control	−.08	.29	.14	.33	.32	.29	(.85)					
Kindness	−.12	.40	.18	.43	.47	.41	.42	(.85)				
Loyalty	−.10	.36	.19	.51	.45	.41	.38	.48	(.89)			
Social skills	−.30	.41	.10	.49	.40	.36	.42	.40	.65	(.87)		
Status	.19	.46	.46	.39	.22	.24	.25	.12	.42	.54	(.83)	
Physical development	−.05	.32	.27	.42	.21	.25	.29	.16	.42	.59	.50	(.89)

behavior, as judged by others. This is what one would expect from the considerations and results presented elsewhere in this volume (see pp. 36–38).Judgments of behavoir were obtained in connection with some General Psychology laboratories at the University of Colorado. As part of his laboratory work in test validation, each student obtained, from two of his friends, a ranking of the degree to which each of the twelve value descriptions (p. 24) applied to himself. The two friends' rankings were added, and the sum was correlated with scores the students had obtained on a pilot version of the revised values instrument, which had been administered two months earlier. One hundred sixty-two of the final 240 items appeared in this pilot instrument, and each of the revised scales was represented by a number of the final items, ranging from 7 (status scale) to all 20 (kindness and religiousness scales). Thus, one may reasonably use these results to estimate those which would be obtained if the entire scales were correlated with independent ratings of subjects' behaviors.

TABLE A-4

CORRELATIONS BETWEEN
PROFESSED VALUES AND BEHAVIORS
AS JUDGED BY FRIENDS
($n = 259$)

Value	r
Intellectualism	−.07
Kindness	.32***
Social skills	.33***
Loyalty	.27***
Academic achievement	.11*
Physical development	.14*
Status	.04
Honesty	.23***
Religiousness	.52***
Self-control	.12*
Creativity	.17**
Independence	.27***

* $\alpha < .05$.
** $\alpha < .01$.
***$\alpha < .001$.

From Table A-4 it may be seen that, for ten of the twelve values, there is a significant correlation between subjects' scores and the way their friends judge them. The two exceptions to this general trend occur for the values of intellectualism and status. Either these two values are not well manifest in overt behavior or else the raters judged them by cues different from those referred to in the scale items. By contrast, the correlation between judged religiousness and score on the religious value was .52 (95% confidence interval between .43 and .60), which indicates a considerable degree of consensus in the culture concerning the meaning and behavioral manifestations of this value.

MEASURE OF GUILT OVER VALUE VIOLATION

The following items deal with various situations that might arise in everyday life. We are interested in how *you* would feel in such situations. Indicate how you would feel by selecting one of the following statements, and writing its number in the space beside each item:

1. Would not bother me at all.
2. Would bother me a bit, but I would soon forget it.
3. I would try to forget it, but it would bother me whenever I thought about it.
4. Would bother me a lot.

_____To be unable to read any books or magazines for several weeks.

_____To be unable to see friends for several weeks.

_____To be unable to get along with people I'd like to.

_____To have to turn in a friend for doing something wrong.

_____To get a poor grade in a course.

_____To have to give up all forms of physical exercise.

_____Not having others respect me for what I'm worth.

_____To say or do something dishonest to get by a tight situation.

_____To miss going to church several weeks in a row.

_____To have a terrific temper tantrum.

_____To have to do routine work day in and day out, and never get a chance to be original.

_____To have to go along with the crowd and do what they do.

SOCIOMETRIC INSTRUMENTS

Instructions

1. On the following pages are listed the names of all members [or all actives, or all pledges, depending on the organization — see Chapter 4, p. 120] of the organization. Also on each page is a description of some characteristic. In the space beside each person's name, write a *number from 1 to* 7, rating the person on that characteristic. For example, you might be asked to rate people on their athletic ability. If a person were outstanding in athletic ability (one of the few top people in the house), you would write 1. If he were very good, but not tops, you would write 2. And so on, down to 7, for a person who is very low in athletic ability (at the bottom of the house).

2. Keep the following scale in mind when you are rating these people. It tells what the different numbers should mean.

   1. Outstanding — one of the few top people in the house
   2. Very high — but not quite tops
   3. Quite high — better than average
   4. About average for the house
   5. Somewhat below average
   6. Rather low — but not at the bottom
   7. Very low — in the bottom group of the house

3. *Try not to omit* anyone from the rating. If you are not sure how to rate a person on a particular characteristic, make the best guess you can. If you don't know the person at all, leave the space blank.

Rating characteristics [appeared on succeeding pages, together with membership lists, arranged alphabetically]:

   Studiousness — "How seriously they take their school work"
   House Activities — "Their contribution to house activities"
   Social Skills — "Their ability to get along with other people"
   Friendship — "How much you like them"

VARIANCE COMPONENTS OF
INTERPERSONAL RATING MATRICES

An interpersonal rating matrix consists of the numerical ratings given by every member of a group to every other member on some designated attribute. (See Table D-1.) Sociometric choices can be represented in this form by using the number 1 to represent choosing and the number 0 to represent a failure of choosing. A more sensitive instrument would provide a range of numbers to indicate degree of liking.

TABLE D-1
INTERPERSONAL RATING MATRIX

Subject (S)	Object (O)					Bias (M_s)
	1	2	3	4	5	
1		2	2	5	3	3.0
2	1		2	4	3	2.5
3	5	1		5	3	3.5
4	5	4	3		4	4.0
5	3	2	1	1		1.8
Status (M_o)	3.5	2.3	2.0	3.8	3.3	

Traditionally, matrices of this type have been analyzed to determine the status of the several individuals on the designated attribute — such as popularity status derived from friendship ratings — and to identify sub-groups (cliques) of individuals involved in mutual choices. It is possible also to analyze such a matrix in total, so as to yield information about group characteristics, without regard for the particular individuals involved.

One group property that may be of interest is *status differentiation* — or the degree to which members differ from one another on the rated attribute. A member's *status* can be represented as the mean rating received from his colleagues. The amount of observed variability among statuses can be compared with some a priori standard, such as the variability of a normal distribution, a rectangular distribution, or a two-point distribution at the extremes of the rating scale. Alternatively, the observed variability among standings may be compared with the amount of variability that would be expected if the ratings actually given by group members were randomly distributed among all of them.

The latter basis of comparison — observed variability among the entire set of ratings — provides the basis for the index to be presented here. To the extent that mean ratings received by members differ widely in relation to the total variability of all ratings, the group as a whole is characterized by a high degree of status differentiation on the particular attribute. This approach to defining status differentiation is identical with that which would be used to assess the reliability of several sets of ratings by the analysis-of-variance technique (McNemar, 1955, pp. 290–294). The intra-class correlation (Haggard, 1958) is used to represent the degree of inter-rater agreement, or in other words, the degree of consensus concerning statuses of the objects rated.

The degree of status differentiation depends on the variability among mean ratings *received by* group members. The interpersonal rating matrix can also be analyzed to determine the degree of inter-member difference in mean ratings *given to* others. Analogously, the results of such an analysis can be interpreted as representing the degree of inter-rater *bias differentiation* — or the degree to which members differ in leniency or severity of their average ratings. (This *bias* component is frequently eliminated by the form in which ratings are elicited—for instance, subjects may be required to "pick 3 friends" or to "rank-order all members" on the attribute, thus equating both means and variances among the raters. Needless to say, if the bias component is eliminated by the rating instructions, it cannot subsequently be treated as an object of analysis.)

Status differentiation and bias differentiation are determined symmetrically; the one depends on differences among column means, the other on differences among row means, in relation to the total variability within the matrix. Each source of variance limits the other: There cannot be maximum status differentiation in a group if the members differ in bias.

Both of these sources of variance in an interpersonal rating matrix may be limited to some extent by a tendency for some pairs of members to reciprocate ratings. This consideration leads to an analysis of a third component of variance, called *mutuality*. Algebraically, this depends on the degree of variability among means of mutual pairs, in relation to the total variability in the matrix—in other words, on the degree to which every pair of members rates one another similarly, in comparison with the total similarity of all ratings combined.

Mutuality of ratings can take either of two forms. It may be either consonant with, or discrepant from, the mean ratings given and received by the two members of a pair. Consonant mutualities would be found if member *A* tended to rate every colleague high on an attribute, and was himself rated high by others, in relation to the average for the matrix. Discrepant mutualities occur if *A* rates *B* higher (or lower) than he rates other members, and *B*'s rating of *A* is similarly out of line with other ratings received by *A*. Such a circumstance gives evidence of cliquishness within the group, for *A*'s and *B*'s impressions of one another are not shared by the rest of the members.

The kind of mutuality which conforms to group consensus may be termed *status-bias concordance*. It is measured by the intra class correlation over all members between mean ratings given to others and mean ratings received from them. Clique-based reciprocal ratings may be referred to as *differential mutuality*. The amount of differential mutuality in the entire matrix may be measured by the average covariance between members' ratings given to others and received from these same others — when the scores are measured in σ-units of discrepancy from the mean ratings given or received.

ALGEBRAIC DEFINITIONS OF COMPONENTS

The sum of squares (SS) associated with status differentiation may be defined as:

$$SS_{status} = (n-1) \sum_{o=1}^{n} (M_o - M)^2,$$

where n is the number of group members ($n-1$ is used as the multiplier, under the assumption that each member is rated by $n-1$ other persons, excluding himself);
M_o is the mean rating received by the oth person (object); and
M is the grand mean of the matrix.

A computing formula may be derived from the above:

$$(1) \qquad SS_{status} = \frac{n \sum\limits_{o=1}^{n} \left(\sum\limits_{s=1}^{n-1} X_{so} \right)^2 - \left(\sum\limits_{s=1}^{n} \sum\limits_{o=1}^{n-1} X_{so} \right)^2}{n(n-1)},$$

where the first term in the numerator indicates that the ratings *received* by each person (object) are added together, the sum of these squared and added over all objects, and the total sum is multiplied by n, the number of objects. The second term in the numerator is simply the square of the sum of all ratings in the matrix. (See below for computational example.)

The sum of squares associated with bias differentiation is defined as:

$$SS_{bias} = (n-1) \sum\limits_{s=1}^{n} (M_s - M)^2,$$

where M_s is the mean rating given by the sth person (subject).

An analogous computing formula may be derived:

$$(2) \qquad SS_{bias} = \frac{n \sum\limits_{s=1}^{n} \left(\sum\limits_{o=1}^{n-1} X_{so} \right)^2 - \left(\sum\limits_{s=1}^{n} \sum\limits_{o=1}^{n-1} X_{so} \right)^2}{n(n-1)}.$$

In calculating the first term of the numerator, the ratings *given* by each person (subject) are added together, the sum squared and added over all subjects, and the total sum multiplied by n. The second term in the numerator is identical with the corresponding term in formula (1).

The total sum of squares associated with mutuality of ratings is defined as:

$$SS_{tot\ mut} = 2 \sum\limits_{p=1}^{n(n-1)/2} (M_p - M)^2,$$

where M_p is the mean of the pth pair of ratings — the rating that S gives to O and the rating that O returns to S.

The computational formula derives to:

$$(3)\ SS_{tot\ mut} =$$
$$\frac{n(n-1) \left[\sum\limits_{s=1}^{n} \sum\limits_{o \neq s}^{n} X_{so}\ X_{os} + \sum\limits_{s=1}^{n} \sum\limits_{o=1}^{n-1} X_{so}^2 \right] - 2 \left(\sum\limits_{s=1}^{n} \sum\limits_{o=1}^{n-1} X_{so} \right)^2}{2n(n-1)},$$

where the first term enclosed within brackets in the numerator indicates that each subject's (S's) rating of each object (O) is multiplied by that O's rating of S, and the products are added together, first over O's for a given S, then over all Ss. This computation utilizes each score in the matrix twice — once as a rating *given* by S to O, and again as a rating *received* by O from S. The second term within brackets is simply the sum of squares of all scores in the matrix. The last term in the numerator is the same as those in formulas (1) and (2), this time multiplied by 2.

The deviation of a mutual pair mean from the grand mean may be subdivided into two parts: (1) the deviation of the pair mean from the mean ratings given and received by each of the members and (2) the deviation of the member's mean rating given and received from the total matrix mean. Part (2) represents the degree of correspondence between the member's bias and status, while part (1) represents the degree to which the member departs from his general bias in rating a particular colleague in the same manner that that colleague's rating of the member departs from the member's status (mean rating received).

Correspondingly, $SS_{tot\ mut}$ may be divided into two components, which ultimately become:

$$SS_{tot\ mut} = SS_{diff\ mut} + SS_{status\text{-}bias\ concordance}$$

$$(4) = \frac{2(n-1)\left[\sum_{s=1}^{n}\sum_{o\neq s}^{n} X_{so} X_{os} + \sum_{s=1}^{n}\sum_{o=1}^{n-1} X_{so}^2\right] - \sum_{s=1}^{n}\left(\sum_{o=1}^{n-1} X_{so}\right)^2}{4(n-1)}$$

$$- \frac{\sum_{o=1}^{n}\left(\sum_{s=1}^{n-1} X_{so}\right)^2 + 2\sum_{s=o=1}^{n}\left(\sum_{o=1}^{n-1} X_{so}\right)\left(\sum_{s=1}^{n-1} X_{so}\right)}{4(n-1)}$$

$$+ \frac{2n\sum_{s=o=1}^{n}\left(\sum_{o=1}^{n-1} X_{so}\right)\left(\sum_{s=1}^{n-1} X_{so}\right) + n\sum_{s=1}^{n}\left(\sum_{o=1}^{n-1} X_{so}\right)^2}{4n(n-1)}$$

$$+ \frac{n\sum_{o=1}^{n}\left(\sum_{s=1}^{n-1} X_{so}\right)^2 - 4\left(\sum_{s=1}^{n}\sum_{o=1}^{n-1} X_{so}\right)^2}{4n(n-1)}$$

The first component (representing differential mutuality) includes the sum of products of all mutual pairs (each taken twice), the sum of all squared ratings, the sum of squared row sums, the sum of squared column sums, and (twice) the sum of products of corresponding row and column sums. The second component (representing status-bias concordance) includes three of these same terms and also (4 times) the squared sum of all ratings. All of these terms —

which are also used in formulas (1) and (2) — may be obtained from simultaneous accumulations on an automatic desk calculator (see illustration below).

INDICES OF STATUS, BIAS, AND MUTUALITY

An appropriate index of status differentiation is provided by the intra-class correlation coefficient, which represents the amount of variance between column means (due to status differences) in relation to the total variance:[1]

$$
(5) \qquad \rho_{status} = \frac{(n-2) \, SS_{status} - SS_{within \, cols}}{(n-2) \, SS_{total}}.
$$

The sum of squares within columns is defined according to usual analysis-of-variance procedures as:

$$
SS_{within \, cols} = \sum_{o=1}^{n} \sum_{s=1}^{n-1} (X_{so} - M_o)^2,
$$

where M_o is the mean rating *received* by a particular object. This may be calculated from the formula:

$$
SS_{within \, cols} = \frac{(n-1) \sum_{s=1}^{n-1} \sum_{o=1}^{n} X_{so}^2 - \sum_{o=1}^{n} \left(\sum_{s=1}^{n-1} X_{so} \right)^2}{n-1},
$$

or, more conveniently, as the difference between the total sum of squares and SS_{status}.

$$
SS_{within \, cols} = SS_{total} - SS_{status}, \text{ where}
$$

$$
SS_{total} = \sum_{s=1}^{n} \sum_{o=1}^{n-1} (X_{so} - M)^2, \quad \text{calculated as:}
$$

$$
(6) \qquad SS_{total} \frac{n(n-1) \sum_{s=1}^{n} \sum_{o=1}^{n-1} X_{so}^2 - \left(\sum_{s=1}^{n} \sum_{o=1}^{n-1} X_{so} \right)^2}{n(n-1)}.
$$

[1] The indices presented here are intended as descriptive statistics, rather than estimates of population parameters. Hence the formula for ρ, the intra-class correlation, differs somewhat from that presented by Haggard (1958).

A direct computing formula for ρ_{status} may be derived:

(7) $\rho_{status} =$

$$\frac{n(n-1) \sum\limits_{o=1}^{n} \left(\sum\limits_{s=1}^{n-1} X_{so} \right)^2 - n(n-1) \sum\limits_{s=1}^{n} \sum\limits_{o=1}^{n-1} X_{so}^2 - (n-2) \left(\sum\limits_{s=1}^{n} \sum\limits_{o=1}^{n-1} X_{so} \right)^2}{n(n-1)(n-2) \sum\limits_{s=1}^{n} \sum\limits_{o=1}^{n-1} X_{so}^2 - (n-2) \left(\sum\limits_{s=1}^{n} \sum\limits_{o=1}^{n-1} X_{so} \right)^2}$$

A comparable index of bias differentiation — that is, of variability among raters' biases — is provided by an intra-class correlation co-efficient relating the between-rows variance to the total variance:

(8) $$\rho_{bias} = \frac{(n-2)\, SS_{bias} - SS_{within\ rows}}{(n-2)\, SS_{total}}.$$

The sums of squares within rows is defined as:

$$SS_{within\ rows} = \sum\limits_{s=1}^{n} \sum\limits_{o=1}^{n-1} (X_{so} - M_s)^2,$$

where M_s is the mean rating given by a particular subject. This may be calculated from the formula:

$$SS_{within\ rows} = \frac{(n-1) \sum\limits_{s=1}^{n} \sum\limits_{o=1}^{n-1} X_{so}^2 - \sum\limits_{s=1}^{n} \left(\sum\limits_{o=1}^{n-1} X_{so} \right)^2}{n-1},$$

or as the difference between the total sum of squares and SS_{bias}.

$$SS_{within\ rows} = SS_{total} - SS_{bias}$$

A direct computing formula for ρ_{bias} is:

(9) $\rho_{bias} =$

$$\frac{n(n-1) \sum\limits_{s=1}^{n} \left(\sum\limits_{o=1}^{n-1} X_{so} \right)^2 - n(n-1) \sum\limits_{s=1}^{n} \sum\limits_{o=1}^{n-1} X_{so}^2 - (n-2)\left(\sum\limits_{s=1}^{n} \sum\limits_{o=1}^{n-1} X_{so} \right)^2}{n(n-1)(n-2) \sum\limits_{s=1}^{n} \sum\limits_{o=1}^{n-1} X_{so}^2 - (n-2) \left(\sum\limits_{s=1}^{n} \sum\limits_{o=1}^{n-1} X_{so} \right)^2}$$

An index of total mutuality is provided by the intra-class correlation relating $SS_{tot\ mut}$ to SS_{total}:

(10) $$\rho_{tot\ mut} = \frac{SS_{tot\ mut} - SS_{non\text{-}mut}}{SS_{total}},$$

where $SS_{tot\ mut}$ is defined as in formula (3),

SS_{total} is defined as in formula (6),

and $SS_{non\text{-}mut}$ is derived from the differences within pairs of mutual ratings:

$$SS_{non-mut} = \sum_{p=1}^{n(n-1)/2} \left[(X_{so} - M_p)^2 + (X_{os} - M_p)^2 \right].$$

This may be calculated as:

$$SS_{non-mut} = \frac{\sum_{s=1}^{n} \sum_{o=1}^{n-1} X_{so}^2 - \sum_{s=1}^{n} \sum_{o \neq s}^{n} X_{so} X_{os}}{2},$$

or as

$$SS_{non-mut} = SS_{total} - SS_{tot\ mut}.$$

(See formula (3) and accompanying description for definitions of terms.)

A calculating form for $\rho_{tot\ mut}$ may be derived from the foregoing:

$$(11) \quad \rho_{tot\ mut} = \frac{n(n-1) \sum_{s=1}^{n} \sum_{o \neq s}^{n} X_{so} X_{os} - \left(\sum_{s=1}^{n} \sum_{o=1}^{n-1} X_{so} \right)^2}{n(n-1) \sum_{s=1}^{n} \sum_{o=1}^{n-1} X_{so}^2 \left(\sum_{s=1}^{n} \sum_{o=1}^{n-1} X_{so} \right)^2}.$$

An index of status-bias concordance is provided by an intra-class correlation relating the covariance of row mean and column mean associated with each person to the total variance among row and column means:

$$(12) \quad \rho_{status \times bias} = \frac{SS_{status-bias\ concordance} - SS_{non-concordance}}{SS_{row\ and\ col\ means}}.$$

$$SS_{status-bias\ concordance} = (n-1) \sum_{s=o=1}^{n} (M_{so} - M)^2,$$

where M_{so} is the mean of the row (ratings given) and column (ratings received) for a particular subject. This derives to:

$$SS_{status-bias\ concordance} = \frac{2n \sum_{s=o=1}^{n} \left(\sum_{o=1}^{n-1} X_{so} \right) \left(\sum_{s=1}^{n-1} X_{so} \right)}{4n(n-1)}$$

$$+ \frac{n \sum_{s=1}^{n} \left(\sum_{o=1}^{n-1} X_{so} \right)^2 + n \sum_{o=1}^{n} \left(\sum_{s=1}^{n-1} X_{so} \right)^2 - 4 \left(\sum_{c=1}^{n} \sum_{o=1}^{n-1} X_{so} \right)^2}{4n(n-1)}$$

which is identical to the second pair of terms in formula (4).

$$SS_{non-concordance} = \frac{n-1}{2} \sum_{s=1}^{n} \left[(M_s - M_{so})^2 + (M_o - M_{so})^2 \right].$$

The terms within brackets are the squared discrepancies between mean ratings given (M_s) or received (M_o) by a single subject and the

270

combined mean (M_{so}) of ratings given and received by that same subject. This derives to:

$$SS_{non\text{-}concordance} =$$

$$\frac{\left(\sum\limits_{s=1}^{n} \sum\limits_{o=1}^{n-1} X_{so} \right)^2 + \sum\limits_{o=1}^{n} \left(\sum\limits_{s=1}^{n-1} X_{so} \right)^2 - 2 \sum\limits_{s=o=1}^{n} \left(\sum\limits_{o=1}^{n-1} X_{so} \right)\left(\sum\limits_{s=1}^{n-1} X_{so} \right)}{4(n-1)}.$$

$$SS_{row\ and\ col\ means} = \frac{n-1}{2} \sum\limits_{s=o=1}^{n} \left[(M_s - M)^2 + (M_o - M)^2 \right],$$

where

M_s is the mean rating given by a particular subject,
M_o is the mean rating received by a particular subject, and
M is the total matrix mean.

This derives to:

$$SS_{row\ and\ col\ means} =$$

$$\frac{n \sum\limits_{s=1}^{n} \left(\sum\limits_{o=1}^{n-1} X_{so} \right)^2 + n \sum\limits_{o=1}^{n} \left(\sum\limits_{s=1}^{n-1} X_{so} \right)^2 - 2 \left(\sum\limits_{s=1}^{n} \sum\limits_{o=1}^{n-1} X_{so} \right)^2}{2n(n-1)},$$

which is also equal to $SS_{status\text{-}bias\ concordance} + SS_{non\text{-}concordance}$.

A simplified calculating form for $\rho_{status \times bias}$, derived from the above, is:

(13) $\rho_{status \times bias} =$

$$\frac{2n \sum\limits_{s=o=1}^{n} \left(\sum\limits_{o=1}^{n-1} X_{so} \right)\left(\sum\limits_{s=1}^{n-1} X_{so} \right) - 2 \left(\sum\limits_{s=1}^{n} \sum\limits_{o=1}^{n-1} X_{so} \right)^2}{n \sum\limits_{s=1}^{n} \left(\sum\limits_{o=1}^{n-1} X_{so} \right)^2 + n \sum\limits_{o=1}^{n} \left(\sum\limits_{s=1}^{n-1} X_{so} \right)^2 - \left(\sum\limits_{s=1}^{n} \sum\limits_{o=1}^{n-1} X_{so} \right)^2}.$$

As an index of differential mutuality, one might use the intra-class correlation derived from the sum of squares for differential mutuality:

$$\rho_{diff\ mut} = \frac{SS_{diff\ mut} - SS_{non\text{-}mut}}{SS_{diff\ mut} + SS_{non\text{-}mut}}, \text{ which derives to:}$$

(14) $\rho_{diff\ mut} =$

$$\frac{4(n-1) \sum\limits_{s=1}^{n} \sum\limits_{o \neq s}^{n} X_{so} X_{os} - \sum\limits_{s=1}^{n} \left(\sum\limits_{o=1}^{n-1} X_{so} \right)^2 - \sum\limits_{o=1}^{n} \left(\sum\limits_{s=1}^{n-1} X_{so} \right)^2 - 2 \sum\limits_{s=o=1}^{n} \left(\sum\limits_{o=1}^{n-1} X_{so} \right)\left(\sum\limits_{s=1}^{n-1} X_{so} \right)}{4(n-1) \sum\limits_{s=1}^{n} \sum\limits_{o=1}^{n-1} X_{so}^2 - \sum\limits_{s=1}^{n} \left(\sum\limits_{o=1}^{n-1} X_{so} \right)^2 - \sum\limits_{o=1}^{n} \left(\sum\limits_{s=1}^{n-1} X_{so} \right)^2 - 2 \sum\limits_{s=o=1}^{n} \left(\sum\limits_{o=1}^{n-1} X_{so} \right)\left(\sum\limits_{s=1}^{n-1} X_{so} \right)}.$$

This intra-class correlation is sensitive to differences between corresponding row and column means. To the extent that these differ — that is, to the extent that subjects receive different mean ratings than they give — $\rho_{diff\ mut}$ will be reduced. Since these differences in mean ratings given and received have already been represented in $\rho_{status \times bias}$, it is desirable to construct an index of differential mutuality which ignores them. We wish to represent the degree of *relative* agreement between ratings given and received by each subject, after allowance has been made for differences between bias and status. This may be accomplished by means of the average product-moment correlation between ratings given and ratings received. A product-moment r is simply an intra-class ρ computed on sets of scores that have been standardized separately to their own means and σs. Standardizing each row separately gives:

$$z_{so} = \frac{X_{so} - M_s}{\sigma_s}, \text{ where}$$

M_s is the mean rating given by a particular subject, and σ_s is the standard deviation of that subject's ratings.

Under these conditions,

$$\sum_{o=1}^{n-1} z_{so} = 0, \text{ and } \sum_{o=1}^{n-1} z_{so}^2 = n-1, \text{ for a given subject.}$$

Similarly, standardizing within columns, so that

$$z_{so} = \frac{X_{so} - M_o}{\sigma_o}, \text{ gives}$$

$$\sum_{s=1}^{n-1} z_{so} = 0, \text{ and } \sum_{s=1}^{n-1} z_{so}^2 = n-1, \text{ for a given object.}$$

Formula (14) then becomes:

$$r'_{diff\ mut} = \frac{4(n-1) \sum_{s=1}^{n} \sum_{o \neq s}^{n} \left(\frac{X_{so} - M_s}{\sigma_s}\right)\left(\frac{X_{os} - M_o}{\sigma_o}\right)}{4n(n-1)^2}, \text{ which derives to:}$$

(15) $r'_{diff\ mut} =$

$$\frac{1}{n} \sum_{s=1}^{n} \frac{(n-1) \sum_{o \neq s}^{n} X_{so} X_{os} - \left(\sum_{o=1}^{n-1} X_{so} \right)\left(\sum_{o=1}^{n-1} X_{os} \right)}{\sqrt{\left[(n-1) \sum_{o=1}^{n-1} X_{so}^2 - \left(\sum_{o=1}^{n-1} X_{so} \right)^2 \right]\left[(n-1) \sum_{o=1}^{n-1} X_{os}^2 - \left(\sum_{o=1}^{n-1} X_{os} \right)^2 \right]}}$$

This is the average product-moment correlation between ratings given and ratings received by each person. It represents the degree to which members whom person A rates higher than average (for him) reciprocate with ratings that are higher than the average received by A, and correspondingly for lower than average ratings given and received.

The computation of $r'_{diff\ mut}$ by formula (15) is somewhat tedious, for it requires separate products of standard deviations for each corresponding row and column. A slightly different index of differential mutuality, which is logically defensible and leads to a simpler computing procedure, is

$$r_{diff\ mut} = \frac{\sum\limits_{s=1}^{n} \sigma_s \sigma_o r_s}{\sum\limits_{s=1}^{n} \sigma_o \sigma_s} =$$

(16)

$$\frac{(n-1) \sum\limits_{s=1}^{n} \sum\limits_{o \neq s}^{n} X_{so} X_{os} - \sum\limits_{s=o=1}^{n} \left(\sum\limits_{o=1}^{n-1} X_{so} \right)\left(\sum\limits_{o=1}^{n-1} X_{so} \right)}{\sum\limits_{s=1}^{n} \sqrt{\left[(n-1) \sum\limits_{o=1}^{n-1} X_{so}^2 - \left(\sum\limits_{o=1}^{n-1} X_{so} \right)^2 \right]\left[(n-1) \sum\limits_{o=1}^{n-1} X_{os}^2 - \left(\sum\limits_{o=1}^{n-1} X_{os} \right)^2 \right]}}$$

That is, $r_{diff\ mut}$ is a weighted average correlation between ratings given and ratings received, in which the correlation for each person is weighted by the geometric mean of the variances of ratings given and ratings received. Those subjects and objects with the higher dispersions are weighted more heavily in the average.

A final simplification is achieved if an approximation is substituted for the denominator of formula (16):

(17) $r_{diff\ mut} =$

$$\frac{(n-1) \sum\limits_{s=1}^{n} \sum\limits_{o \ne s}^{n} X_{so} X_{os} - \sum\limits_{s=o=1}^{n} \left(\sum\limits_{o=1}^{n-1} X_{so} \right) \left(\sum\limits_{s=1}^{n-1} X_{so} \right)}{\sqrt{\left[(n-1) \sum\limits_{s=1}^{n} \sum\limits_{o=1}^{n-1} X_{so}^2 - \sum\limits_{s=1}^{n} \left(\sum\limits_{o=1}^{n-1} X_{so} \right)^2 \right] \left[(n-1) \sum\limits_{s=1}^{n} \sum\limits_{o=1}^{n-1} X_{so}^2 - \sum\limits_{o=1}^{n-1} \left(\sum\limits_{s=1}^{n-1} X_{so} \right)^2 \right]}}$$

Formula (17) will provide a very close approximation to (16) when the variances of ratings given by the several subjects are not too different, and when the variances of ratings received are also not too different. To the extent that there are wide differences among subjects in variances of ratings given or of ratings received, $r_{diff\ mut}$ will be underestimated by formula (17).

COMPUTATIONAL EXAMPLE

The principal indices presented here are:

(5) $\rho_{status} = \dfrac{(n-2)\ SS_{status} - SS_{within\ cols}}{(n-2)\ SS_{total}}$

(7) $= \dfrac{n(n-1) \sum\limits_{o} (\sum\limits_{s} X_{so})^2 - n(n-1) \sum\limits_{s} \sum\limits_{o} X_{so}^2 - (n-2)(\sum\limits_{s} \sum\limits_{o} X_{so})^2}{n(n-1)\ (n-2) \sum\limits_{s} \sum\limits_{o} X_{so}^2 - (n-2)\ (\sum\limits_{s} \sum\limits_{o} X_{so})^2}$

(8) $\rho_{bias} = \dfrac{(n-2)\ SS_{bias} - SS_{within\ rows}}{(n-2)\ SS_{total}}$

(9) $= \dfrac{n(n-1) \sum\limits_{s} (\sum\limits_{o} X_{so})^2 - n(n-1) \sum\limits_{s} \sum\limits_{o} X_{so}^2 - (n-2)(\sum\limits_{s} \sum\limits_{o} X_{so})^2}{n(n-1)\ (n-2) \sum\limits_{s} \sum\limits_{o} X_{so}^2 - (n-2)\ (\sum\limits_{s} \sum\limits_{o} X_{so})^2} .$

(10) $\rho_{tot\ mut} = \dfrac{SS_{tot\ mut} - SS_{non\text{-}mut}}{SS_{total}}$

(11) $= \dfrac{n(n-1) \sum\limits_{s} \sum\limits_{o} X_{so} X_{os} - (\sum\limits_{s} \sum\limits_{o} X_{so})^2}{n(n-1) \sum\limits_{s} \sum\limits_{o} X_{so}^2 (-(\sum\limits_{s} \sum\limits_{o} X_{so})^2}$

(12) $\rho_{status \times bias} = \dfrac{SS_{status\text{-}bias\ concordance} - SS_{non\text{-}concordance}}{SS_{row\ and\ column\ means}}$

(13) $= \dfrac{2n \sum\limits_{s=o} (\sum\limits_{o} X_{so})(\sum\limits_{s} X_{so}) - 2\ (\sum\limits_{s} \sum\limits_{o} X_{so})^2}{n \sum\limits_{s} (\sum\limits_{o} X_{so})^2 + n \sum\limits_{o} (\sum\limits_{s} X_{so})^2 - 2\ (\sum\limits_{s} \sum\limits_{o} X_{so})^2}$

274

(17) $r_{diff\ mut} =$

$$\frac{(n-1) \sum\limits_{s} \sum\limits_{o} X_{so}\ X_{os} - \sum\limits_{s=o} (\sum\limits_{o} X_{so})\ (\sum\limits_{s} X_{so})}{\sqrt{[(n-1) \sum\limits_{s} \sum\limits_{o} X_{so}^2 - \sum\limits_{s} (\sum\limits_{o} X_{so})^2][(n-1) \sum\limits_{s} \sum\limits_{o} X_{so}^2 - \sum\limits_{o} (\sum\limits_{s} X_{so})^2]}}$$

$$= \frac{4\,SS_{diff\ mut} - SS_{within\ rows} - SS_{within\ cols}}{2\,\sqrt{(SS_{within\ rows})\,(SS_{within\ cols})}}$$

The components needed for these several indices are:

$\sum\limits_{s} \sum\limits_{o} X_{so}X_{os}$ (twice the sum of the products of reciprocated scores);

$\sum\limits_{s} \sum\limits_{o} X_{so}^2$ (the sum of all squared scores);

$(\sum\limits_{s} \sum\limits_{o} X_{so})^2$ (the square of the sum of all scores);

$\sum\limits_{s} (\sum\limits_{o} X_{so})^2$ (the sum of the squares of row totals);

$\sum\limits_{o} (\sum\limits_{s} X_{so})^2$ (the sum of squares of column totals);

$\sum\limits_{s=o} (\sum\limits_{o} X_{so})\ (\sum\limits_{s} X_{so})$ (the sum of products of corresponding row and column totals).

All of these components can be computed in a series of accumulating operations on an automatic desk calculator. Table D-2 illustrates the steps.

1. Calculate the components of the correlation between column 1 and row 1. These are $\sum X_{s1}$, $\sum\limits_{s} X_{s1}^2$, $\sum\limits_{o} X_{1o}$, $\sum\limits_{o} X_{1o}^2$, and $\sum\limits_{o} X_{1o}X_{o1}$, which can be cumulated simultaneously. (In the example, they are 14, 60, 12, 42, and 46, respectively.)

2. Repeat step 1 for every column-row pair.

3. Calculate the components of the correlation between the row sums and the corresponding column sums. These are $\sum\limits_{s}(\sum\limits_{o} X_{so})$, $\sum\limits_{s}(\sum\limits_{o} X_{so})^2$, $\sum\limits_{o}(\sum\limits_{s} X_{so})$, $\sum\limits_{o}(\sum\limits_{s} X_{so})^2$, and $\sum\limits_{s=o}(\sum\limits_{o} X_{so})\ (\sum\limits_{s} X_{so})$, which can all be cumulated simultaneously. The first and third sums should be equal; this serves as a check on calculations up to this point. The remaining three sums are entered below the table. (In this example they are 745, 735, and 701.)

4. Accumulate the totals over all subjects of $\sum X_{so}^2$ and $\sum\limits_{o} X_{so}X_{os}$. The first of these should be identical with the sum over all objects of $\sum\limits_{s} X_{so}^2$.

5. Using these components, calculate the indices according to the formulas provided.

TABLE D-2
ILLUSTRATIVE CALCULATION

Subject	Object					$\sum X_{so}$ o	$\sum X^2_{so}$ o	$\sum X_{so} X_{os}$ o
	1	2	3	4	5			
1		2	2	5	3	12	42	46
2	1		2	4	3	10	30	26
3	5	1		5	3	14	60	30
4	5	4	3		4	16	66	60
5	3	2	1	1		7	15	22
$\sum X_{so}$ s	14	9	8	15	13	59		
$\sum X^2_{so}$ s	60	25	18	67	43		213	

$$\sum_{o}(\sum_{s} X_{so})^2 = 735 \qquad\qquad \sum_{s}\sum_{o} X^2_{so} = \sum_{o}\sum_{s} X^2_{so} = 213$$

$$\sum_{s}(\sum_{o} X_{so})^2 = 745 \qquad\qquad \sum_{s}\sum_{o} X_{so} X_{os} = 184$$

$$\sum_{s=o}(\sum_{o} X_{so})(\sum_{s} X_{so}) = 701 \qquad\qquad (\sum_{s}\sum_{o} X_{so})^2 = 3481$$

(7) $\quad \rho_{status} = \dfrac{5(4)(735) - 5(4)(213) - 3(3481)}{5(4)(3)(213) - 3(3481)} = .00$

(9) $\quad \rho_{bias} = \dfrac{5(4)(745) - 5(4)(213) - 3(3481)}{5(4)(3)(213) - 3(3481)} = .08$

(11) $\quad \rho_{tot\ mut} = \dfrac{5(4)(184) - 3481}{5(4)(213) - 3481} = .26$

(13) $\quad \rho_{status \times bias} = \dfrac{2(5)(701) - 2(3481)}{5(745) - 5(735) - 2(3481)} = .11$

(17) $\quad r_{diff\ mut} = \dfrac{4(184) - 701}{\sqrt{[4(213) - 745]\ [4(213) - 735]}} = .31$

INDEX OF ATTRACTION
TO THE ORGANIZATION

1. How important is membership in this organization to you?
   _____Not important at all; I'd rather not be in it.
   _____Not very important; I could do without it all right.
   _____Somewhat important; I'm rather glad to be in it.
   __*__Quite important; the organization means a lot to me.
   __*__Extremely important; right now it's the most important group in my life.

2. If you moved to another university, would you join the same organization immediately, or would you wait to see what it was like first?
   __*__Join immediately.
   _____Wait and see what it was like.

3. If your girl friend (or boy friend) were to visit you from New York on the night of initiation, what would you do?
   _____Skip the initiation, and not give it another thought.
   _____Try to get excused from initiation, but go out with my date anyway if they wouldn't excuse me.
   __*__Come to the initiation if they wouldn't excuse me.
   __*__Come to the initiation without asking to be excused.

4. Which would you prefer to do, hold an office in this organization or an office in a campus-wide group, such as ASUC?
   __*__This organization.
   _____Campus-wide group.

* In scoring, all items were dichotomized empirically as close to a median split as possible; the starred alternatives were scored 1, unstarred alternatives 0.

5. Do you intend to keep active in the organization as an alumnus?
   __*__ Yes, definitely.
   __*__ Can't tell yet, but probably yes.
   __*__ Uncertain.
   _____ Can't tell yet, but probably not.
   _____ Definitely not.

6. If your organization were to take top honors in a campus activity, how would you feel?
   _____ Nothing in particular.
   _____ Somewhat proud.
   __*__ Exceedingly proud.
   __*__ "Out of this world."

7. If your organization were to lose a hard-fought contest with other campus groups, how would you feel?
   _____ Nothing in particular.
   _____ Somewhat disappointed.
   __*__ Greatly disappointed.
   __*__ "We was robbed."

REFERENCES

Adler, F. The value concept in sociology. *Amer. sociol. Rev.*, 1956, 62, 272-279.

Adorno, T. W., Frenkel-Brunswik, Else, Levinson, D. J., & Sanford, R. N. *The authoritarian personality.* New York: Harper, 1950.

Allport, G. W., Vernon, P. E., & Lindzey, G. *A study of values.* (Rev. ed.) Boston: Houghton Mifflin, 1951.

Back, K. W. Influence through social communication. *J. abnorm. soc. Psychol.*, 1951, 46, 9-23.

Bandura, A., & Walters, R. H. *Social learning and personality development.* New York: Holt, Rinehart, & Winston, 1963.

Bay, C. A social theory of intellectual development. In R. N. Sanford (Ed.), *The American college.* New York: Wiley, 1962. Pp. 972-1005.

Beilin, H. The prediction of adjustment over a four year interval. *J. clin. Psychol.*, 1957, 13, 270-274.

Beilin, H. The effects of social (occupational) role and age upon the criteria of mental health. *J. soc. Psychol.*, 1958, 48, 247-256.

Brown, D. R. Personality, college environment, and academic productivity. In R. N. Sanford (Ed.), *The American college.* New York: Wiley, 1962. Pp. 536-562.

Bushnell, J. H. Student culture at Vassar. In R. N. Sanford (Ed.), *The American college.* New York: Wiley, 1962. Pp. 489-514.

Byrne, D. Interpersonal attraction and attitude similarity. *J. abnorm. soc. Psychol.*, 1961, 62, 713-715.

Campbell, D. T. Common fate, similarity, and other indices of the status of aggregates of persons as social entities. *Behav. Sci.*, 1958, 3, 14-25.

Campbell, D. T., & Fiske, D. W. Convergent and discriminant validation by the multitrait-multimethod matrix. *Psychol. Bull.*, 1959, 56, 81-105.

Catton, W. R. A theory of value. *Amer. sociol. Rev.*, 1959, 24, 311-317.

Cronbach, L. J. Coefficient *alpha* and the internal structure of tests. *Psychometrika*, 1951, 16, 297-334.

Dukes, W. F. Psychological studies of values. *Psychol. Bull.*, 1955, 52, 24-50.

Etzioni, A. *A comparative analysis of complex organizations.* New York: The Free Press of Glencoe (Macmillan), 1961.

Faguy-Coté, Elizabeth. Academic achievement of sorority and non-sorority students at the University of Colorado. Unpublished master's thesis, Univer. of Colorado, 1960.

Fiedler, F. E. The maintenance of adjustive interpersonal relations in small groups. (University of Illinois, mimeographed), 1963.

Fillenbaum, S. Own position in relation to estimates of average standing and desirability for more and less self-comparable objects. *J. Pers.*, 1961, 29, 195-204.

Fisher, R. A. *Statistical methods for research workers.* (8th ed., rev.) Edinburgh: Oliver & Boyd, 1941.

Freud, S. *The ego and the id.* (Eng. trans.) London: Hogarth, 1935.

Goffman, E. *Asylums: essays on the social situation of mental patients and other inmates.* Garden City, N. Y.: Anchor Books, 1961.

Gulliksen, H. *Theory of mental tests.* New York: Wiley, 1950.

Haggard, E. A. *Intraclass correlation and the analysis of variance.* New York: Dryden, 1958.

Hartshorne, H., & May, M. A. *Studies in the nature of character: Vol. 1, Studies in deceit.* New York: Macmillan, 1928.

Heider, F. Attitudes and cognitive organization. *J. Psychol.*, 1946, 21, 107-112.

Hill, W. F. Learning theory and the acquisition of values. *Psychol. Rev.*, 1960, 67, 317-331.

Hughes, E. C., Becker, H. S., & Geer, Blanche. Student culture and academic effort. In R. N. Sanford (Ed.), *The American college.* New York: Wiley, 1962. Pp. 515-530.

Hull, C. H. Moral values, behaviorism, and the world crisis. *Trans. N. Y. Acad. Sci.*, 1945, 7, 80-84.

Izard, C. E. Personality similarity and friendship. *J. abnorm. soc. Psychol.*, 1960, 61, 47-51.

Izard, C. E. Personality similarity and friendship: a follow-up study. *J. abnorm. soc. Psychol.*, 1963, 66, 598-600.

Jacob, P. E. *Changing values in college.* New York: Harper, 1957.

Johnson, R. C. A study of children's moral judgments. *Child Develpm.*, 1962, 33, 327-354.

Kluckhohn, C. Values and value orientations in the theory of action. In T. Parsons & E. A. Shils (Eds.), *Toward a general theory of action.* Cambridge: Harvard Univer. Press. 1951. Pp. 388-433.

Kluckhohn, Florence R. Dominant and variant value orientations. In C. Kluckhohn, H. A. Murray, & D. M. Schneider (Eds.), *Personality in nature, society, and culture*. New York: Knopf, 1954. Pp. 342-357.

Kohlberg, L. Moral development and identification. *Yearb. Nat. Soc. Stud. Educ.*, 1963, 62, 277-332.

Lundberg, G. A. Human values: a research program. *Proc. Pac. sociol. Soc.*, 1950, 18, 103.

McDougall, W. *An introduction to social psychology*. Boston: Luce, 1909.

McNemar, Q. *Psychological statistics*. (2nd ed.) New York: Wiley, 1955.

Miller, N. E., & Dollard, J. *Social learning and imitation*. New Haven: Yale Univer. Press, 1941.

Newcomb, T. M. *Personality and social change*. New York: Dryden, 1943.

Newcomb, T. M. *The acquaintance process*. New York: Holt-Dryden, 1961.

Parsons, T. *The social system*. Glencoe, Ill.: Free Press, 1951.

Peck, R. F., & Havighurst, R. J. *The psychology of character development*. New York: Wiley, 1960.

Piaget, J. *The moral judgment of the child*. New York: Harcourt, Brace, 1932.

Riesman, D. *The lonely crowd: a study of the changing American character*. New Haven: Yale Univer. Press, 1950.

Sanford, R. N. (Ed.) *The American college*. New York: Wiley, 1962.

Schachter, S., Ellertson, N., McBride, Dorothy, & Gregory, Doris. An experimental study of cohesiveness and productivity. *Hum. Relat.*, 1951, 4, 229-238.

Scott, W. A. Attitude change through reward of verbal behavior. *J. abnorm. soc. Psychol.*, 1957, 55, 72-75.

Scott, W. A. Empirical assessment of values and ideologies. *Amer. sociol. Rev.*, 1959, 24, 299-310. (a)

Scott, W. A. Cognitive consistency, response reinforcement, and attitude change. *Sociometry*, 1959, 22, 219-229. (b)

Scott, W. A. Attitude acquisition by response reinforcement: replication and extension. *Sociometry*, 1959, 22, 328-335. (c)

Scott, W. A. Measures of test homogeneity. *Educ. psychol. Measmt*, 1960, 20, 751-758.

Scott, W. A. Social desirability and individual conceptions of the desirable. *J. abnorm. soc. Psychol.*, 1963, 67, 574-585.

Scott, W. A., & Wertheimer, M. *Introduction to psychological research*. New York: Wiley, 1962.

Spranger, E. *Types of men*. (Eng. trans.) Halle (Saale): Niemeyer, 1928.

Staats, Carolyn K., Staats, A. W., & Heard, W. G. Attitude development and ratio of reinforcement. *Sociometry*, 1960, 23, 338-350.

Stern, G. G. Environments for learning. In R. N. Sanford (Ed.), *The American college*. New York: Wiley, 1962. Pp. 690-730.

Summerskill, J. Dropouts from college. In R. N. Sanford (Ed.), *The American college*. New York: Wiley, 1962. Pp. 627-657.

Sumner, W. G. *Folkways*. New York: Ginn, 1906.

Vernon, P. E., & Allport, G. W. A test for personal values. *J. abnorm. soc. Psychol.*, 1931, 26, 231-248.

Webster, H., Freedman, M., & Heist, P. Personality changes in college students. In R. N. Sanford (Ed.), *The American college*. New York: Wiley, 1962. Pp. 811-846.

Williams, R. M. *American society: a sociological interpretation*. New York: Knopf, 1951.

INDEX

PRINTED IN U.S.A.